IMAGE COMICS PRESENTS

VOLUME 1

CREATED BY
TODD McFARLANE and **ROBERT KIRKMAN**

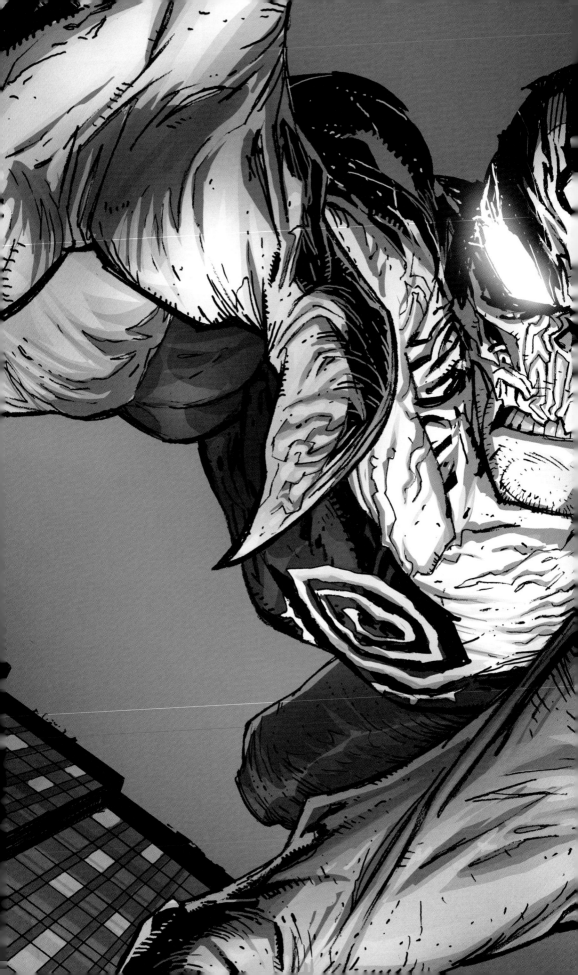

ROBERT KIRKMAN Co-creator/Writer

Layouts **GREG CAPULLO**

RYAN OTTLEY Pencils

Co-creator/Inks **TODD McFARLANE**

Color **FCO PLASCENCIA**

Lettering **RICHARD STARKINGS**

Cover Artists **TODD McFARLANE**
RYAN OTTLEY

JEN CASSIDY Managing Editor

BEN TIMMRECK Art Direction
JERRY POTEET

ERIC STEPHENSON Publisher for Image Comics

Haunt Volume 1. March 2010. First Printing. Published by IMAGE COMICS, 2134 Allston Way, Second Floor, Berkeley, CA 94704. Haunt, its logo and its symbol are registered trademarks © 2010 Todd McFarlane. All other related characters are TM and © 2010 Todd McFarlane. All rights reserved. The characters, events and stories in this publication are entirely fictional. With exception of artwork used for review purposes, none of the contents of this publication may be reprinted without the permission of Todd McFarlane. Printed by Transcontinental in CANADA.

image

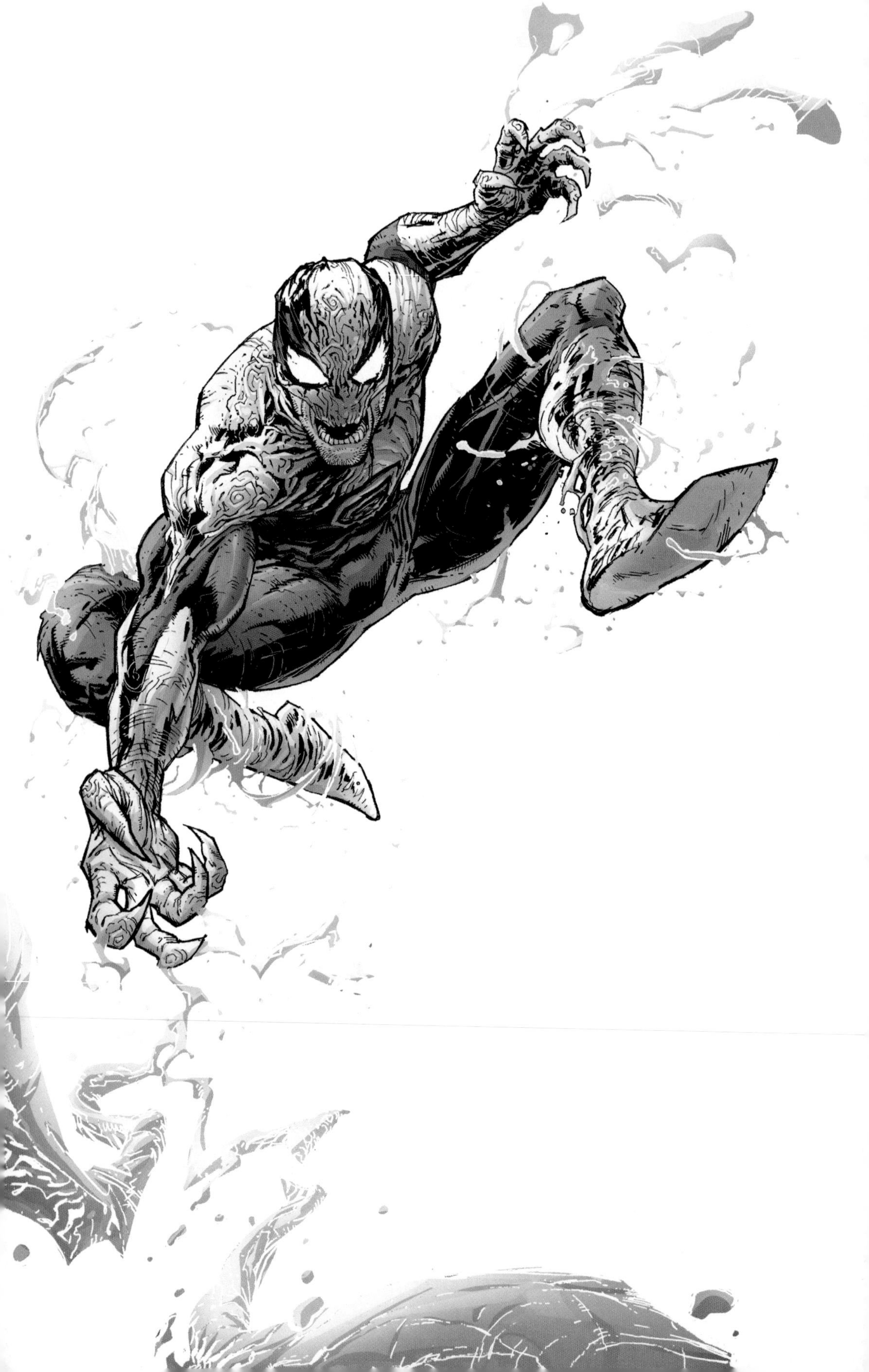

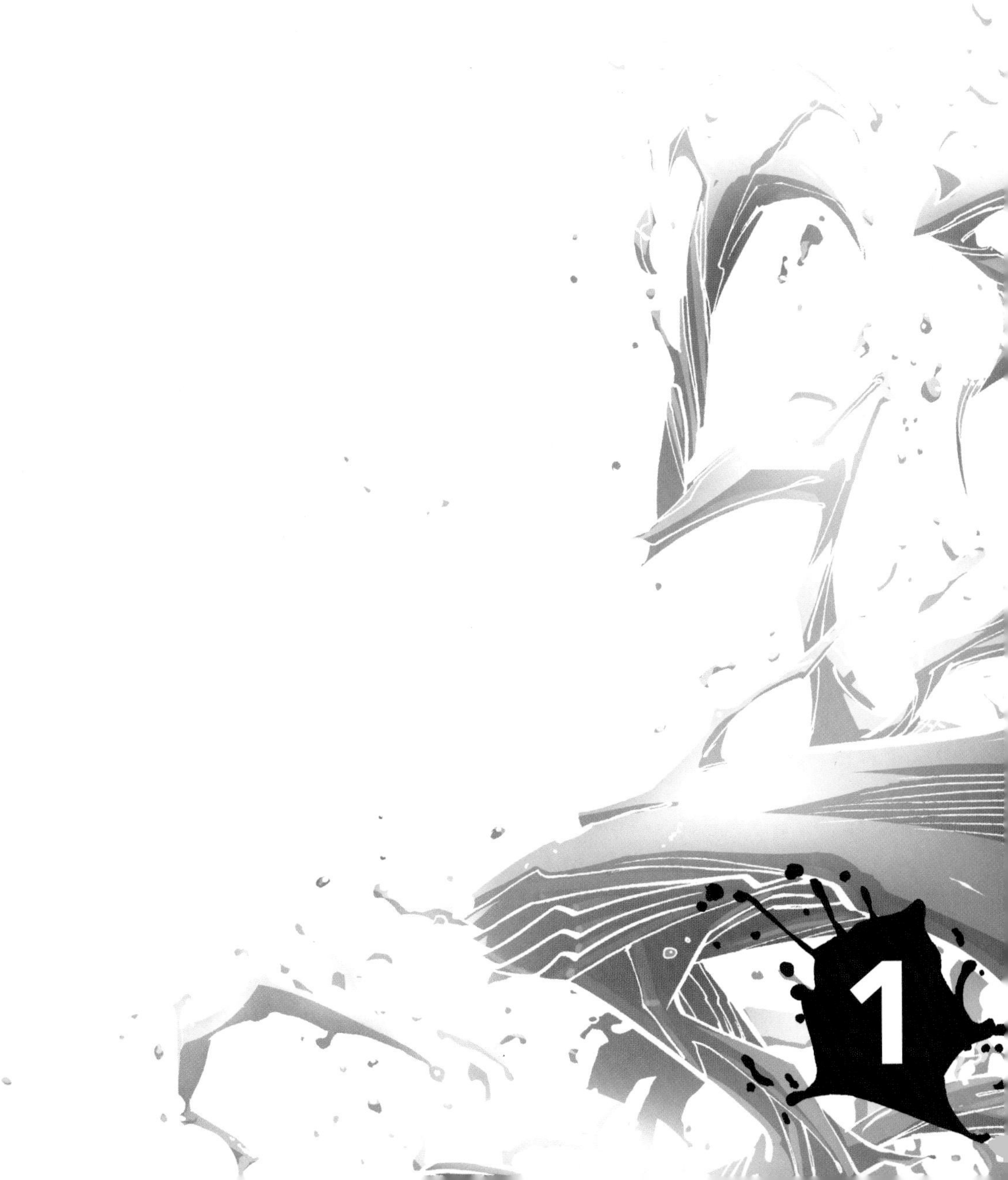
1

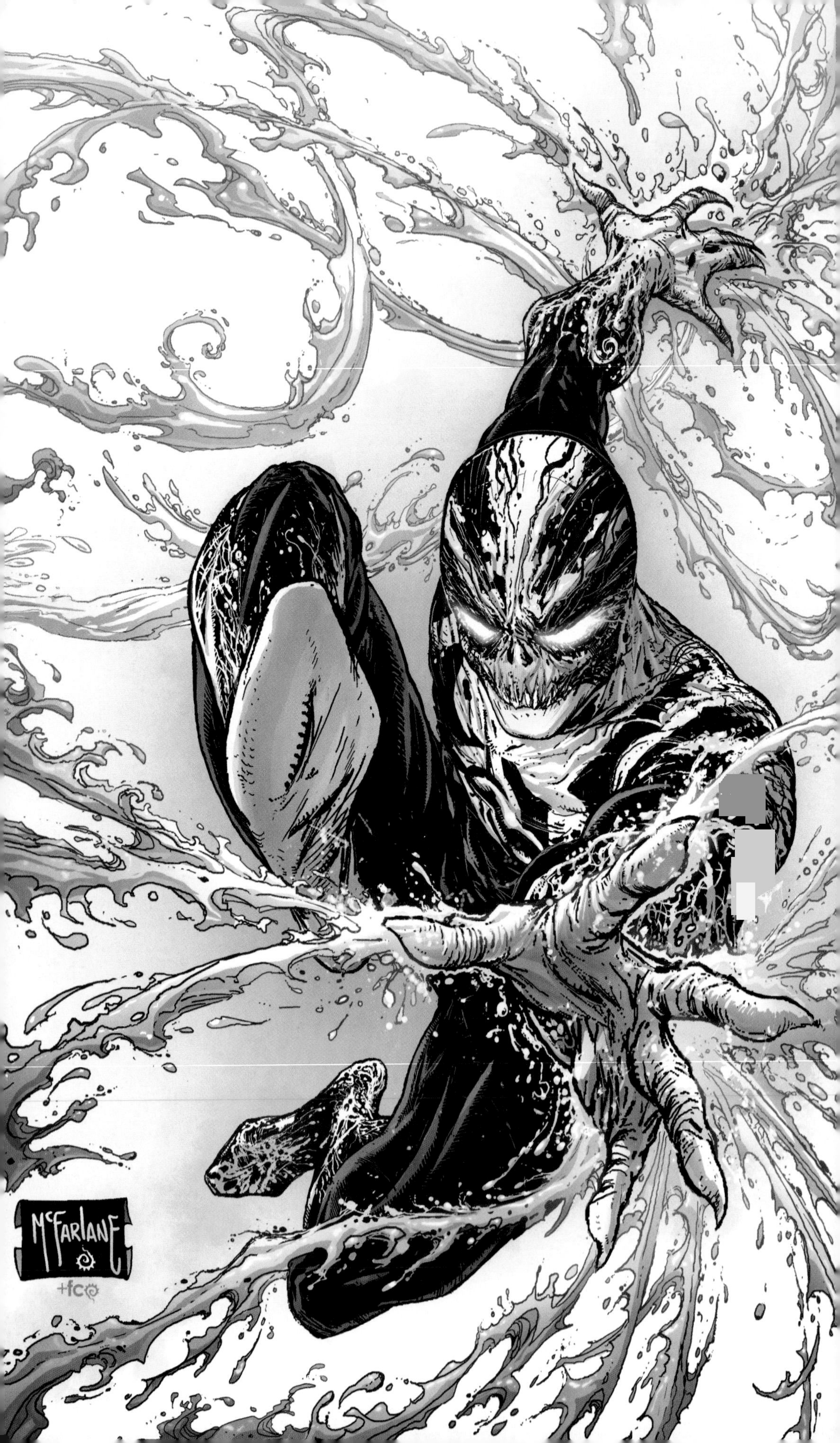
McFARLANE

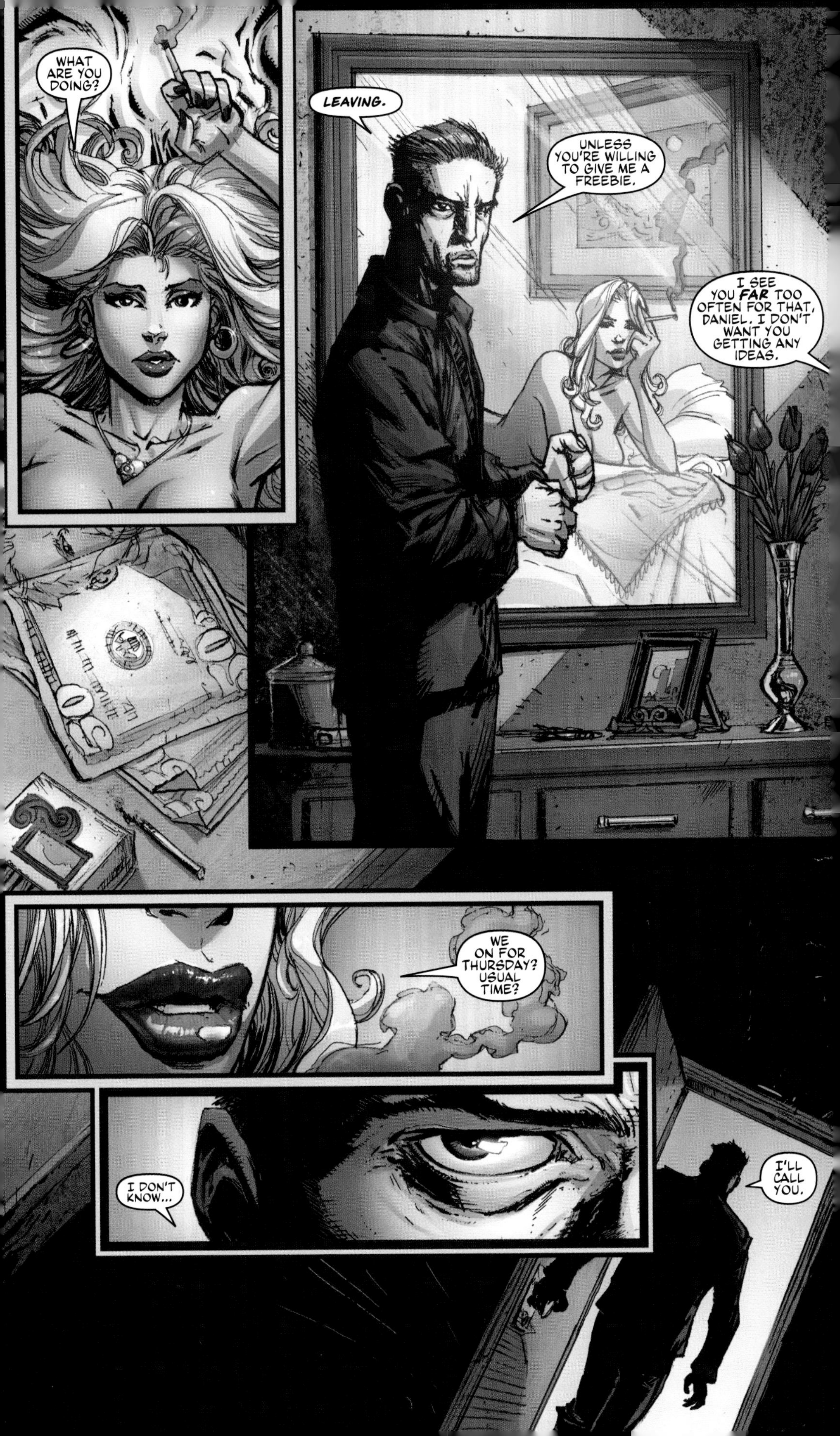
WHAT ARE YOU DOING?
LEAVING.
UNLESS YOU'RE WILLING TO GIVE ME A FREEBIE.
I SEE YOU FAR TOO OFTEN FOR THAT, DANIEL. I DON'T WANT YOU GETTING ANY IDEAS.
WE ON FOR THURSDAY? USUAL TIME?
I DON'T KNOW...
I'LL CALL YOU.

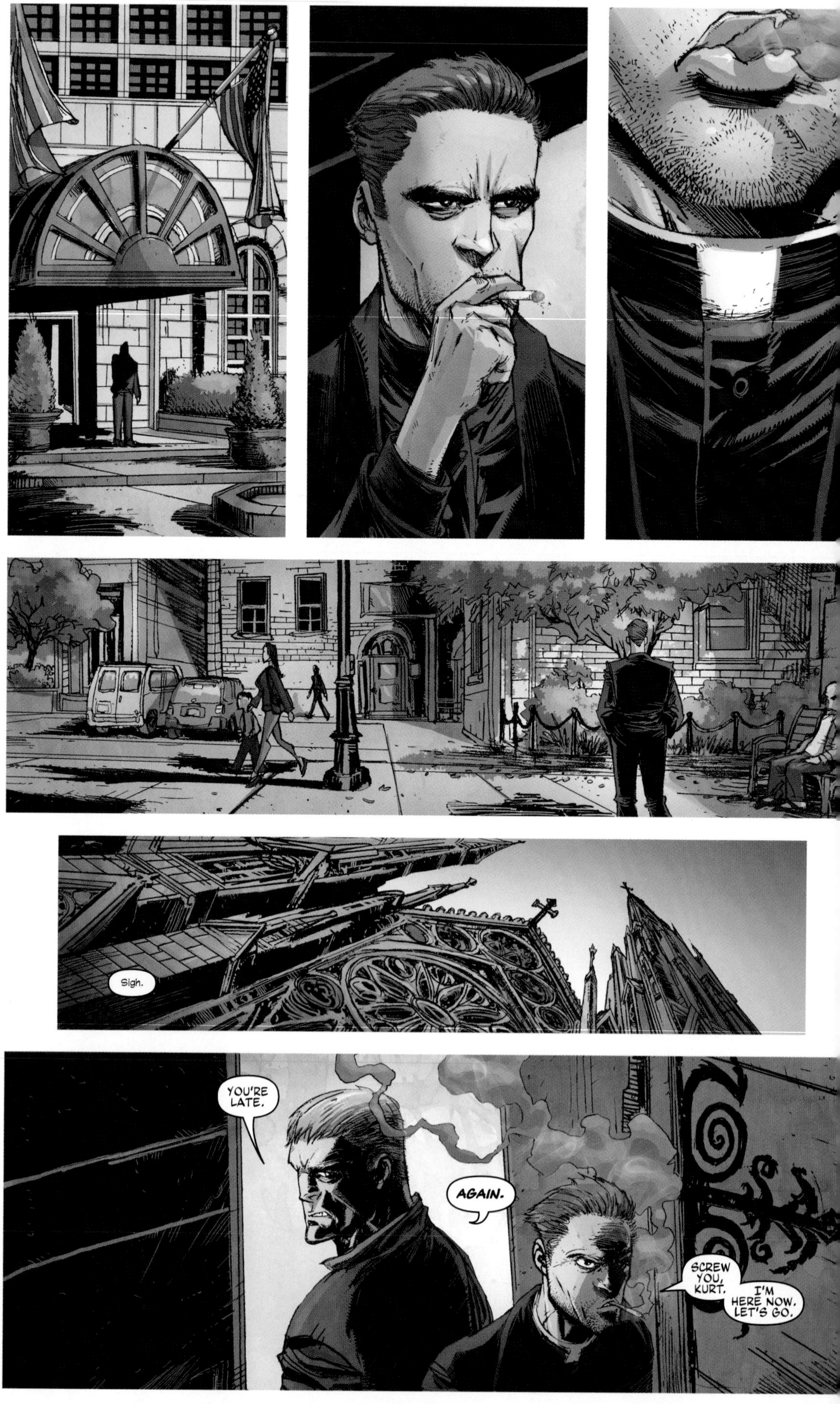
Sigh.
YOU'RE LATE.
AGAIN.
SCREW YOU, KURT.
I'M HERE NOW. LET'S GO.

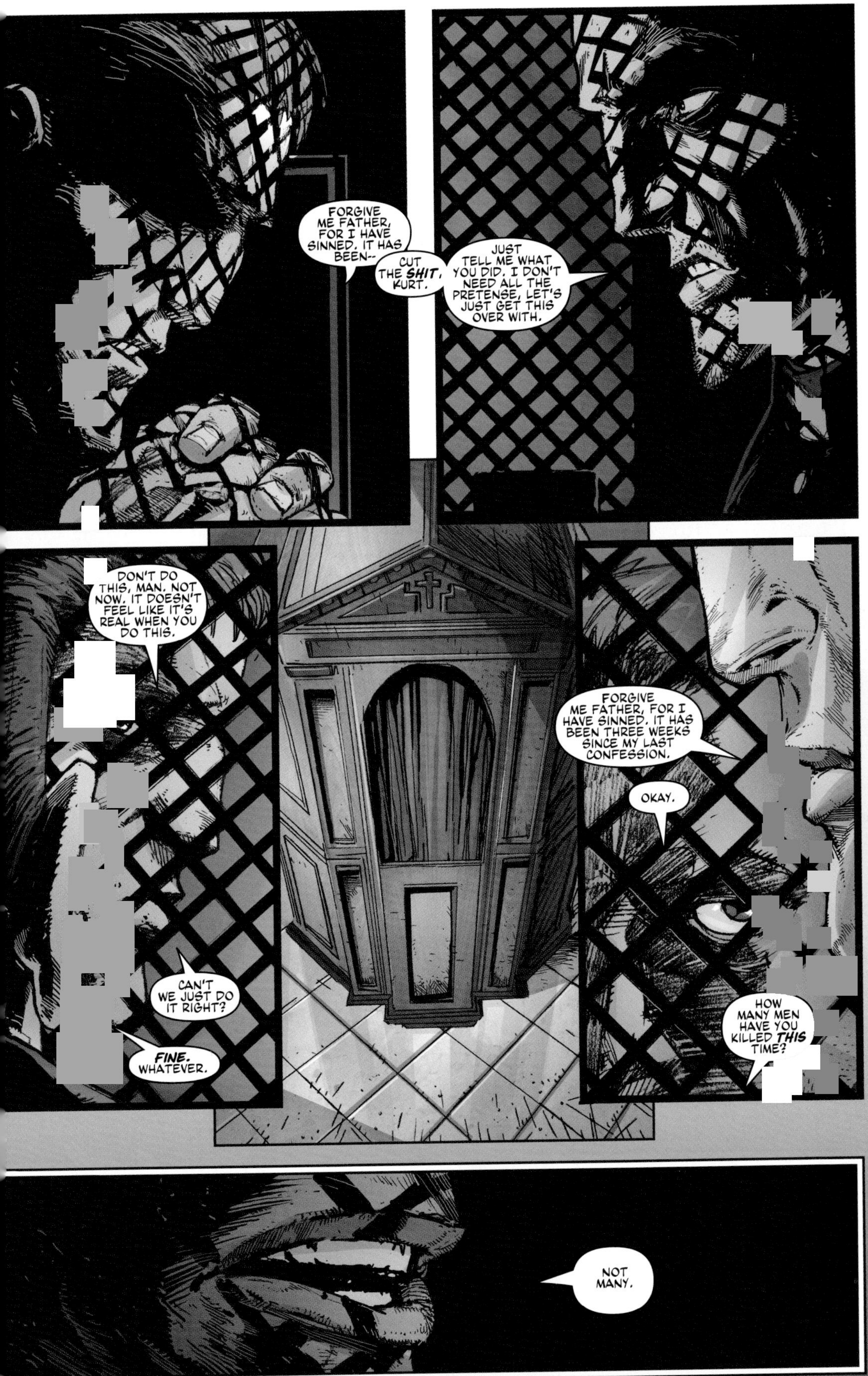
FORGIVE ME FATHER, FOR I HAVE SINNED. IT HAS BEEN--
CUT THE SHIT, KURT.
JUST TELL ME WHAT YOU DID. I DON'T NEED ALL THE PRETENSE, LET'S JUST GET THIS OVER WITH.
DON'T DO THIS, MAN. NOT NOW. IT DOESN'T FEEL LIKE IT'S REAL WHEN YOU DO THIS.
CAN'T WE JUST DO IT RIGHT?
FINE. WHATEVER.
FORGIVE ME FATHER, FOR I HAVE SINNED. IT HAS BEEN THREE WEEKS SINCE MY LAST CONFESSION.
OKAY.
HOW MANY MEN HAVE YOU KILLED THIS TIME?
NOT MANY.

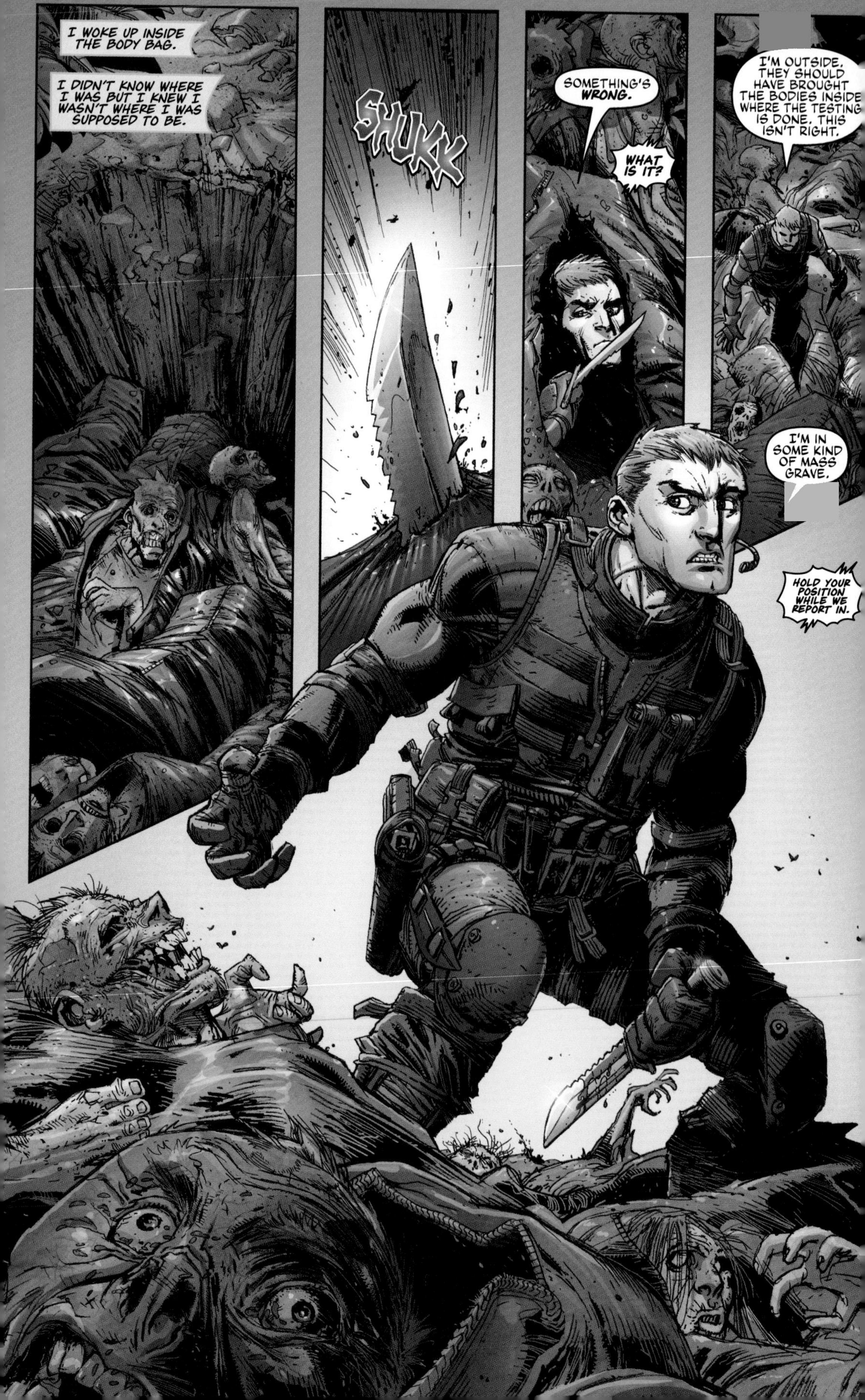
I WOKE UP INSIDE THE BODY BAG.
I DIDN'T KNOW WHERE I WAS BUT I KNEW I WASN'T WHERE I WAS SUPPOSED TO BE.
SHUKK
SOMETHING'S WRONG.
WHAT IS IT?
I'M OUTSIDE. THEY SHOULD HAVE BROUGHT THE BODIES INSIDE WHERE THE TESTING IS DONE. THIS ISN'T RIGHT.
I'M IN SOME KIND OF MASS GRAVE.
HOLD YOUR POSITION WHILE WE REPORT IN.

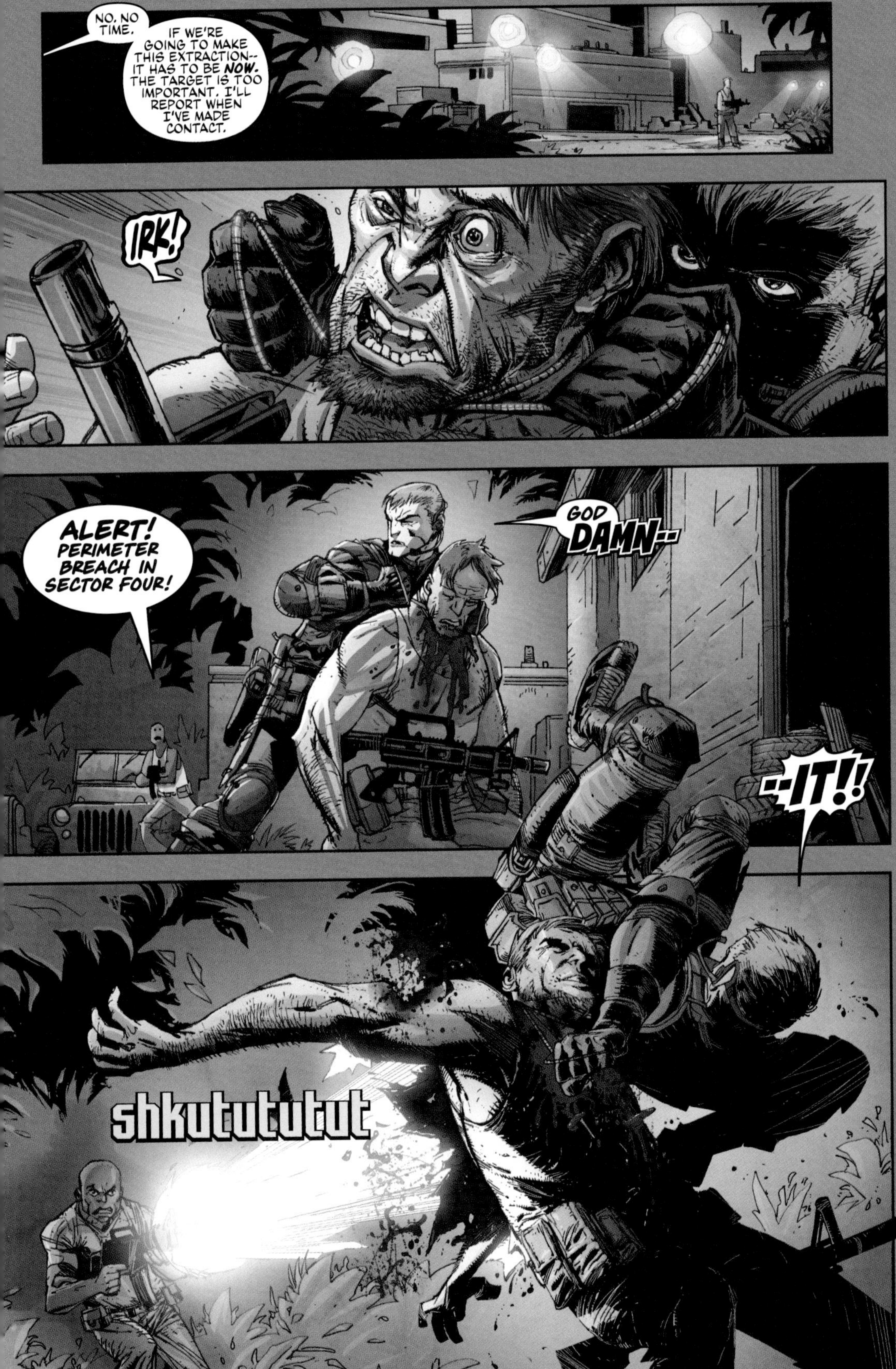
NO. NO TIME.
IF WE'RE GOING TO MAKE THIS EXTRACTION-- IT HAS TO BE NOW. THE TARGET IS TOO IMPORTANT. I'LL REPORT WHEN I'VE MADE CONTACT.
IRK!
ALERT! PERIMETER BREACH IN SECTOR FOUR!
GOD DAMN--
--IT!!
shkutututut

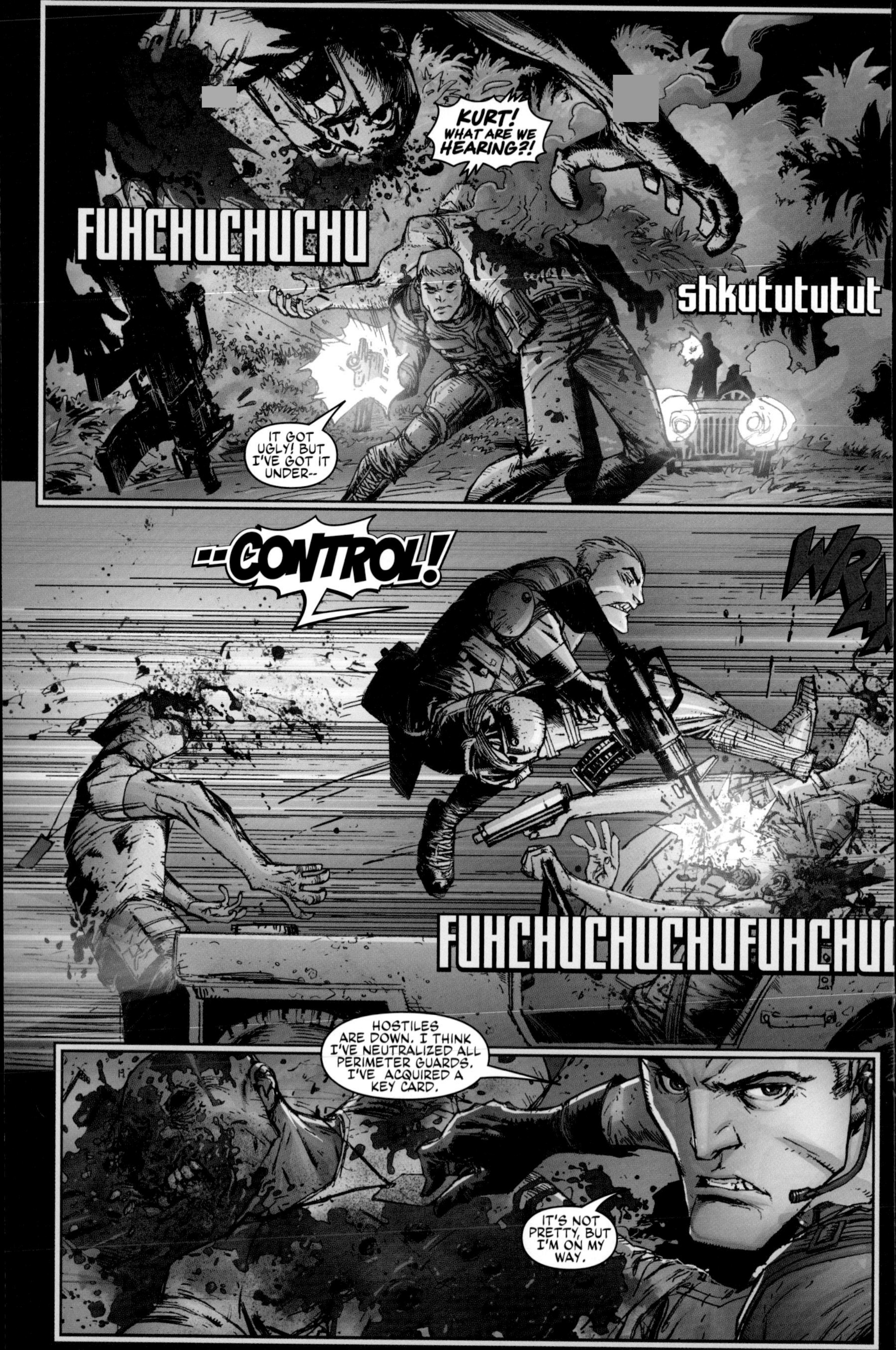

KURT! WHAT ARE WE HEARING?!
FUHCHUCHUCHU
shkututututut
IT GOT UGLY! BUT I'VE GOT IT UNDER--
--CONTROL!
FUHCHUCHUCHUFUHCHU
HOSTILES ARE DOWN. I THINK I'VE NEUTRALIZED ALL PERIMETER GUARDS. I'VE ACQUIRED A KEY CARD.
IT'S NOT PRETTY, BUT I'M ON MY WAY.

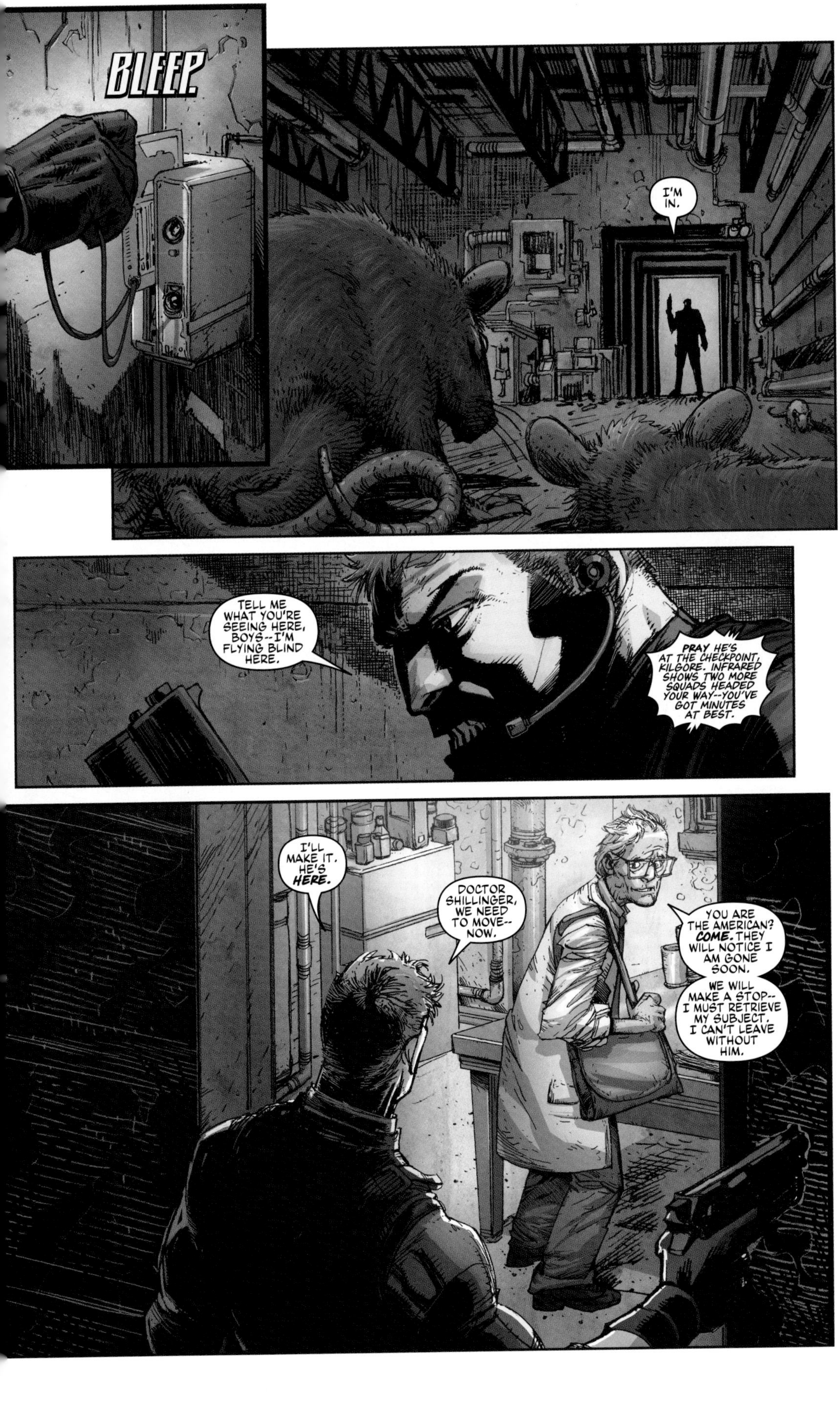
BLEEP.
I'M IN.
TELL ME WHAT YOU'RE SEEING HERE, BOYS--I'M FLYING BLIND HERE.
PRAY HE'S AT THE CHECKPOINT, KILGORE. INFRARED SHOWS TWO MORE SQUADS HEADED YOUR WAY--YOU'VE GOT MINUTES AT BEST.
I'LL MAKE IT. HE'S HERE.
DOCTOR SHILLINGER, WE NEED TO MOVE--NOW.
YOU ARE THE AMERICAN? COME. THEY WILL NOTICE I AM GONE SOON.
WE WILL MAKE A STOP--I MUST RETRIEVE MY SUBJECT. I CAN'T LEAVE WITHOUT HIM.

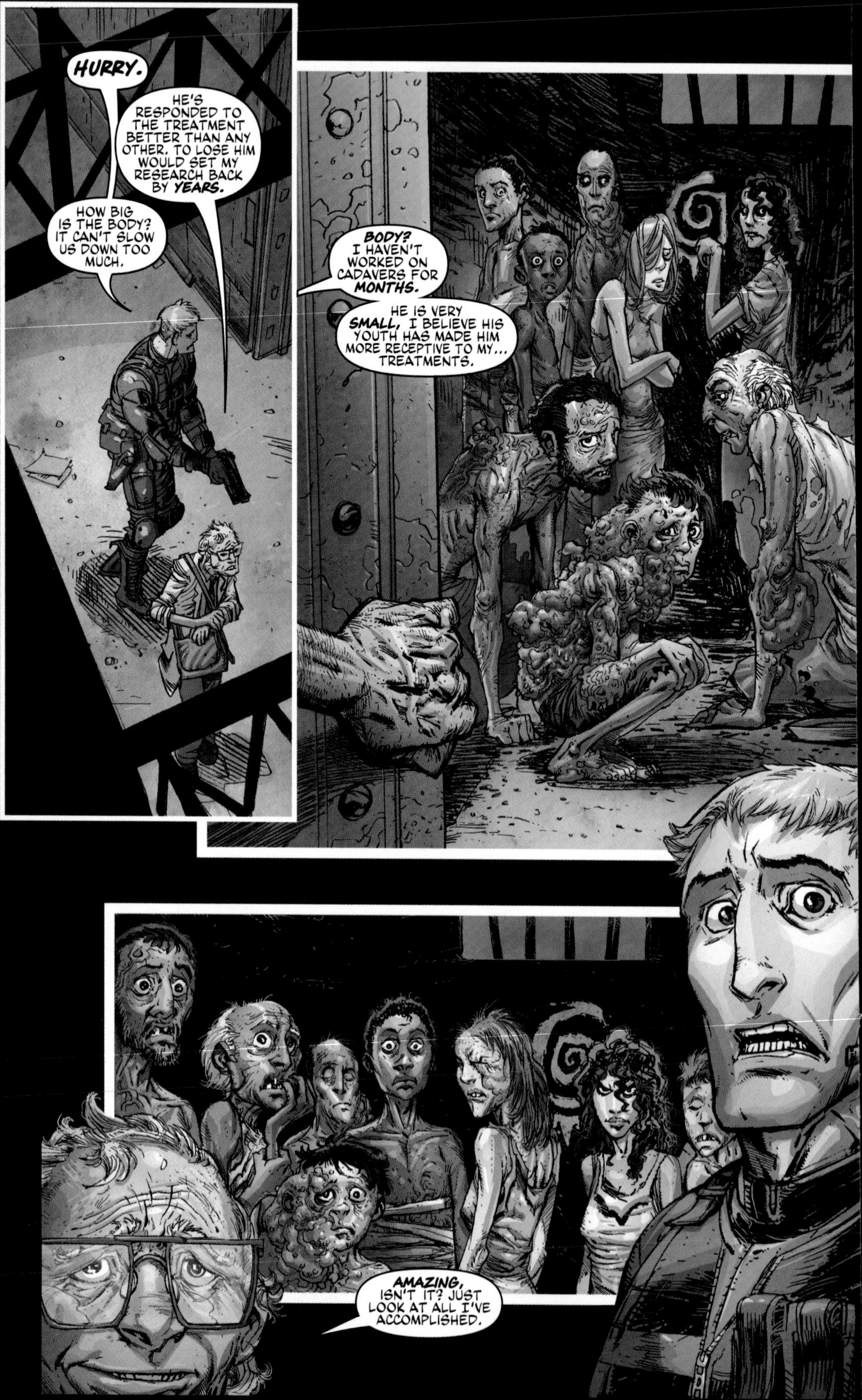
HURRY.
HE'S RESPONDED TO THE TREATMENT BETTER THAN ANY OTHER. TO LOSE HIM WOULD SET MY RESEARCH BACK BY YEARS.
HOW BIG IS THE BODY? IT CAN'T SLOW US DOWN TOO MUCH.
BODY? I HAVEN'T WORKED ON CADAVERS FOR MONTHS.
HE IS VERY SMALL, I BELIEVE HIS YOUTH HAS MADE HIM MORE RECEPTIVE TO MY... TREATMENTS.
AMAZING, ISN'T IT? JUST LOOK AT ALL I'VE ACCOMPLISHED.

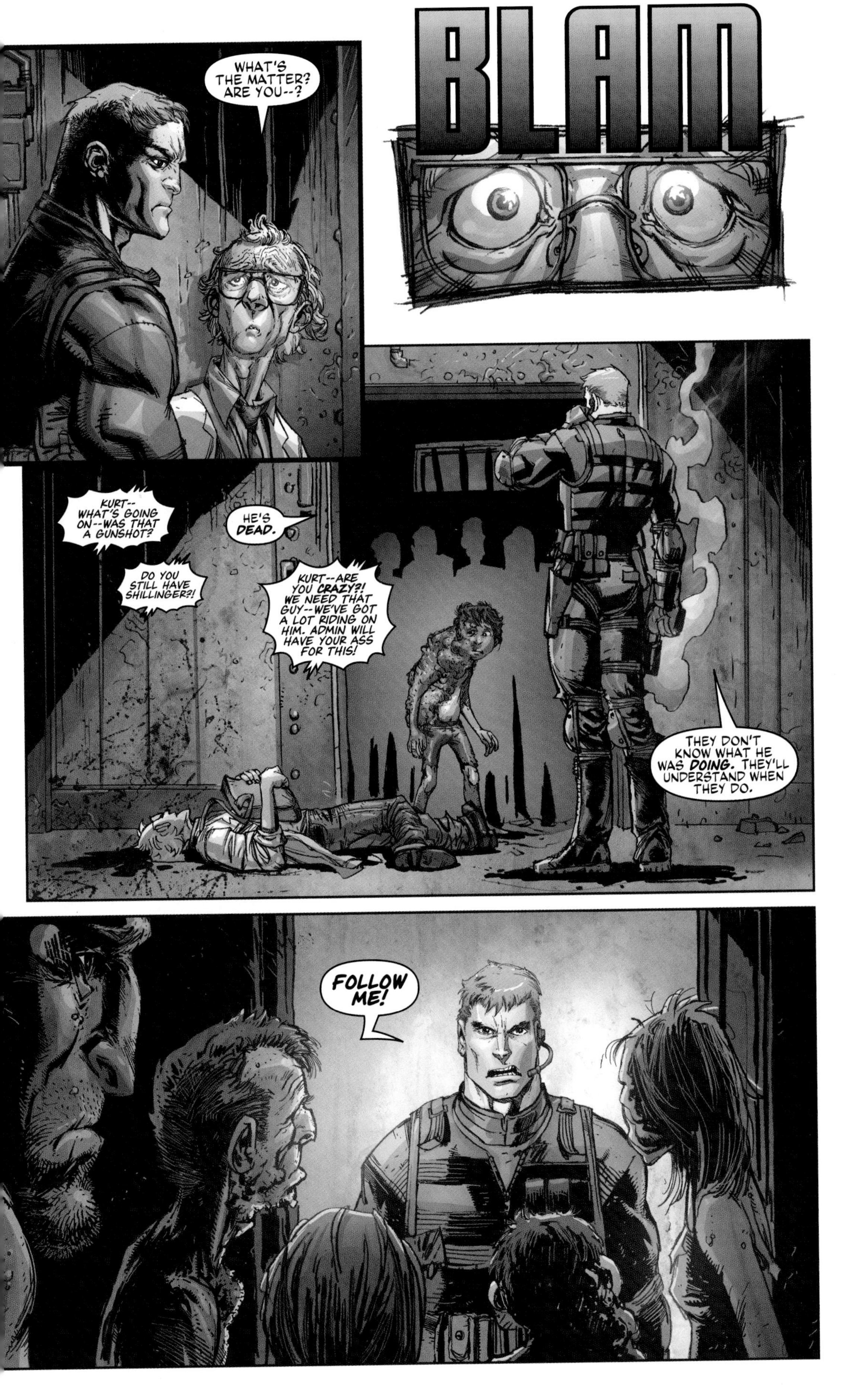

WHAT'S THE MATTER? ARE YOU--?
BLAM
KURT-- WHAT'S GOING ON--WAS THAT A GUNSHOT?
DO YOU STILL HAVE SHILLINGER?!
HE'S DEAD.
KURT--ARE YOU CRAZY?! WE NEED THAT GUY--WE'VE GOT A LOT RIDING ON HIM. ADMIN WILL HAVE YOUR ASS FOR THIS!
THEY DON'T KNOW WHAT HE WAS DOING. THEY'LL UNDERSTAND WHEN THEY DO.
FOLLOW ME!

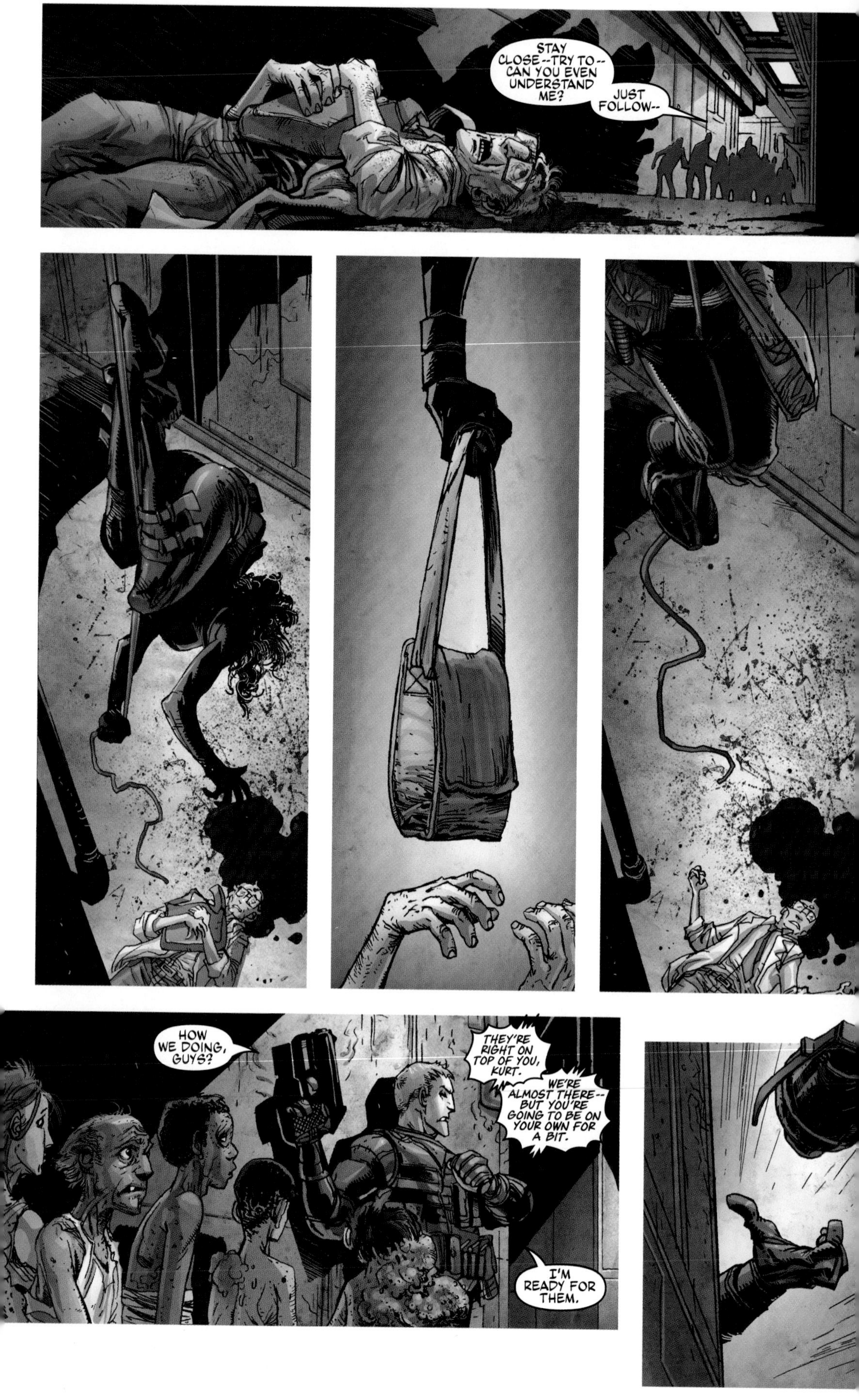
STAY CLOSE--TRY TO--CAN YOU EVEN UNDERSTAND ME?
JUST FOLLOW--
HOW WE DOING, GUYS?
THEY'RE RIGHT ON TOP OF YOU, KURT.
WE'RE ALMOST THERE--BUT YOU'RE GOING TO BE ON YOUR OWN FOR A BIT.
I'M READY FOR THEM.

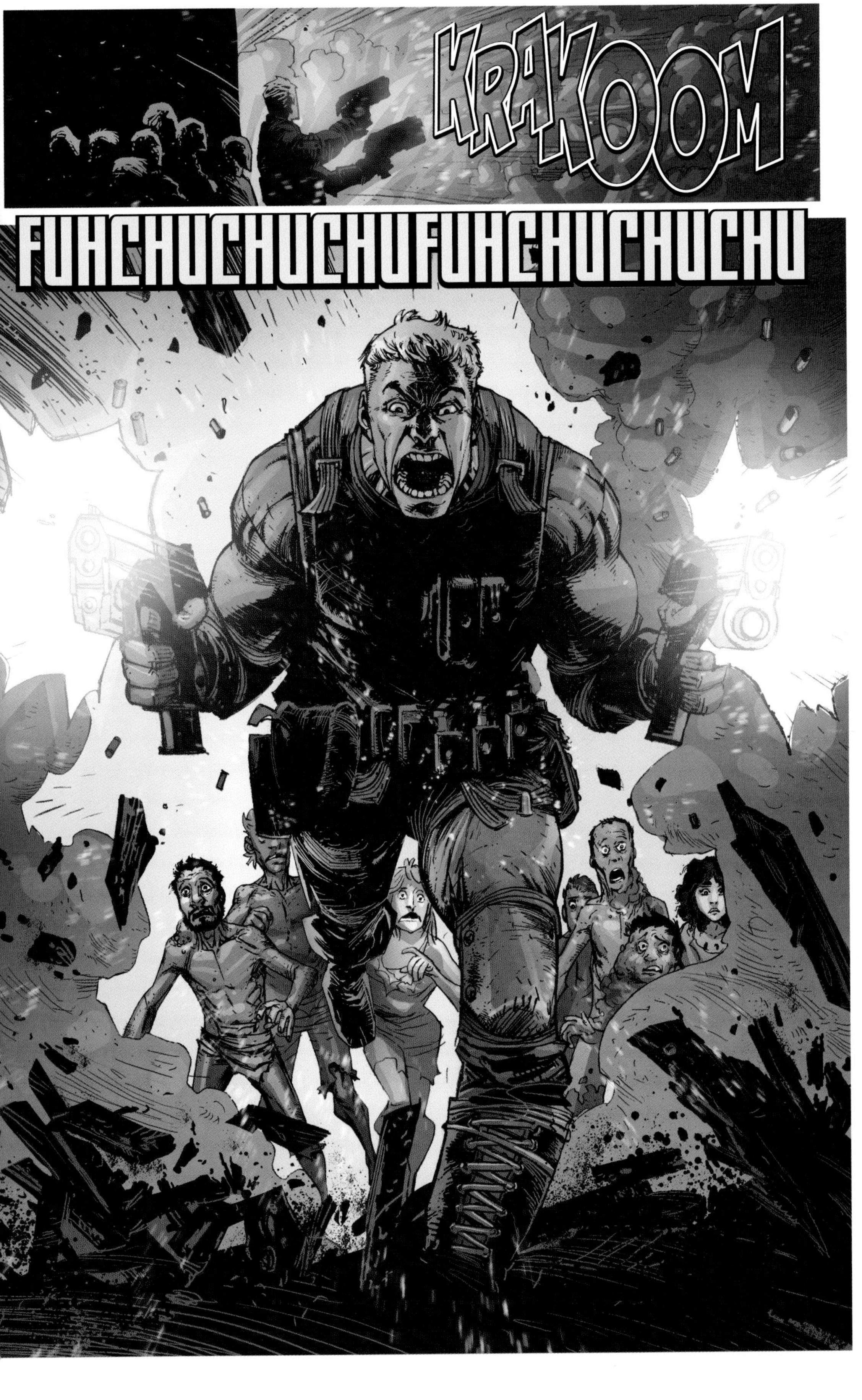
KRAKOOM
FUHCHUCHUCHUFUHCHUCHUCHU

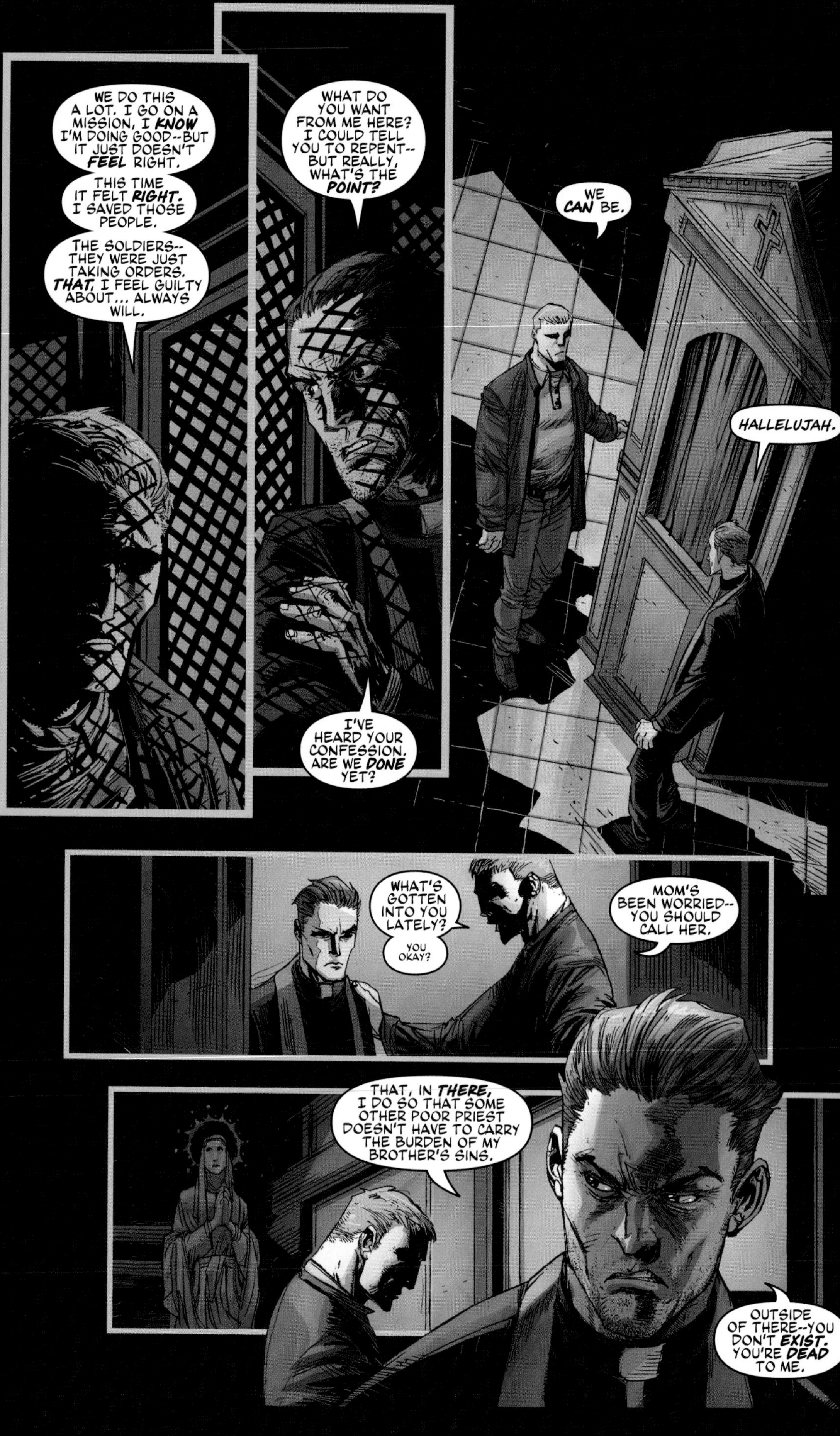
WE DO THIS A LOT. I GO ON A MISSION, I KNOW I'M DOING GOOD--BUT IT JUST DOESN'T FEEL RIGHT.
THIS TIME IT FELT RIGHT. I SAVED THOSE PEOPLE.
THE SOLDIERS--THEY WERE JUST TAKING ORDERS. THAT, I FEEL GUILTY ABOUT... ALWAYS WILL.
WHAT DO YOU WANT FROM ME HERE? I COULD TELL YOU TO REPENT--BUT REALLY, WHAT'S THE POINT?
I'VE HEARD YOUR CONFESSION. ARE WE DONE YET?
WE CAN BE.
HALLELUJAH.
WHAT'S GOTTEN INTO YOU LATELY?
YOU OKAY?
MOM'S BEEN WORRIED--YOU SHOULD CALL HER.
THAT, IN THERE, I DO SO THAT SOME OTHER POOR PRIEST DOESN'T HAVE TO CARRY THE BURDEN OF MY BROTHER'S SINS.
OUTSIDE OF THERE--YOU DON'T EXIST. YOU'RE DEAD TO ME.

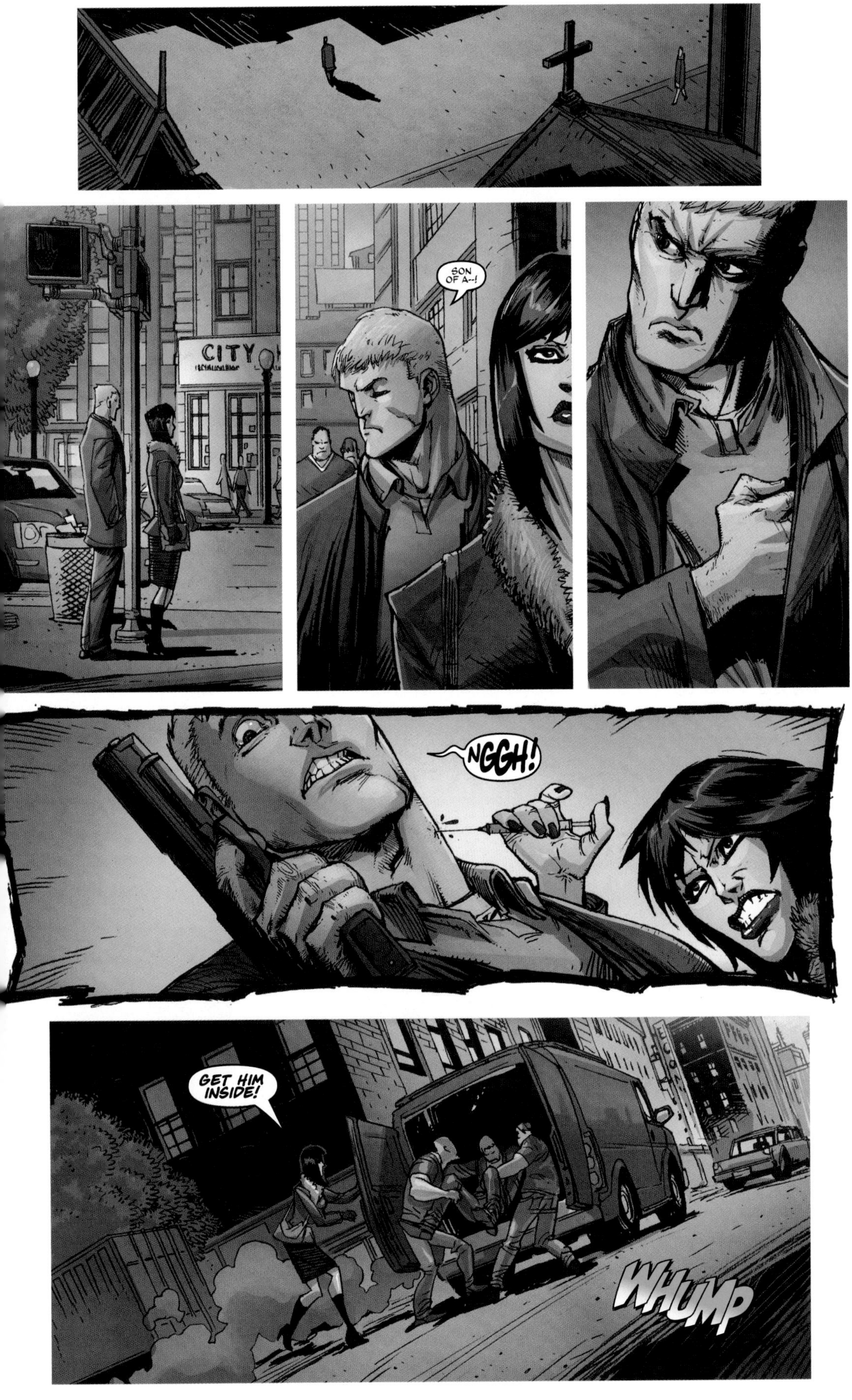
CITY
SON OF A--!
NGGH!
GET HIM INSIDE!
WHUMP

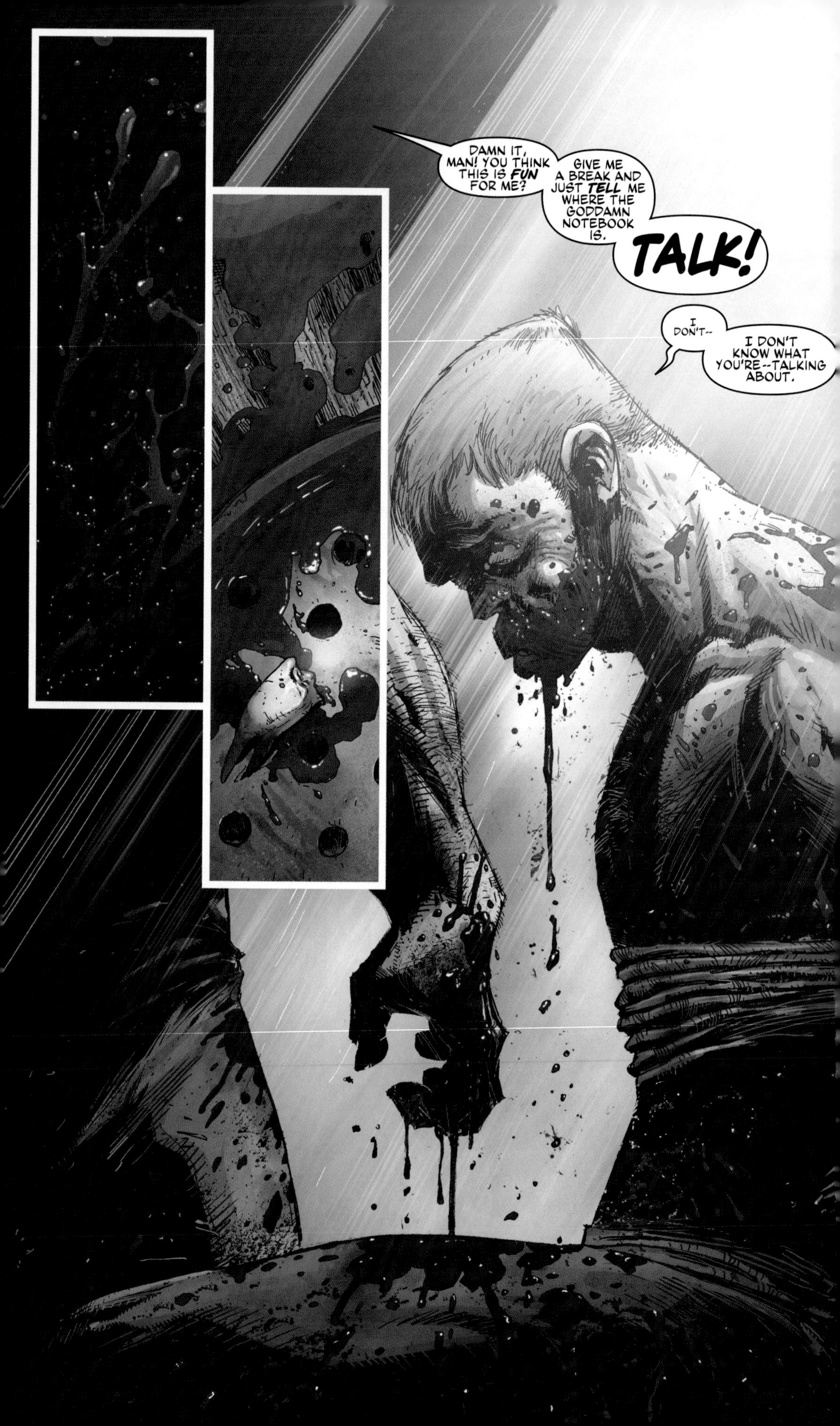
DAMN IT, MAN! YOU THINK THIS IS *FUN* FOR ME?
GIVE ME A BREAK AND JUST *TELL* ME WHERE THE GODDAMN NOTEBOOK IS.
TALK!
I DON'T--
I DON'T KNOW WHAT YOU'RE--TALKING ABOUT.

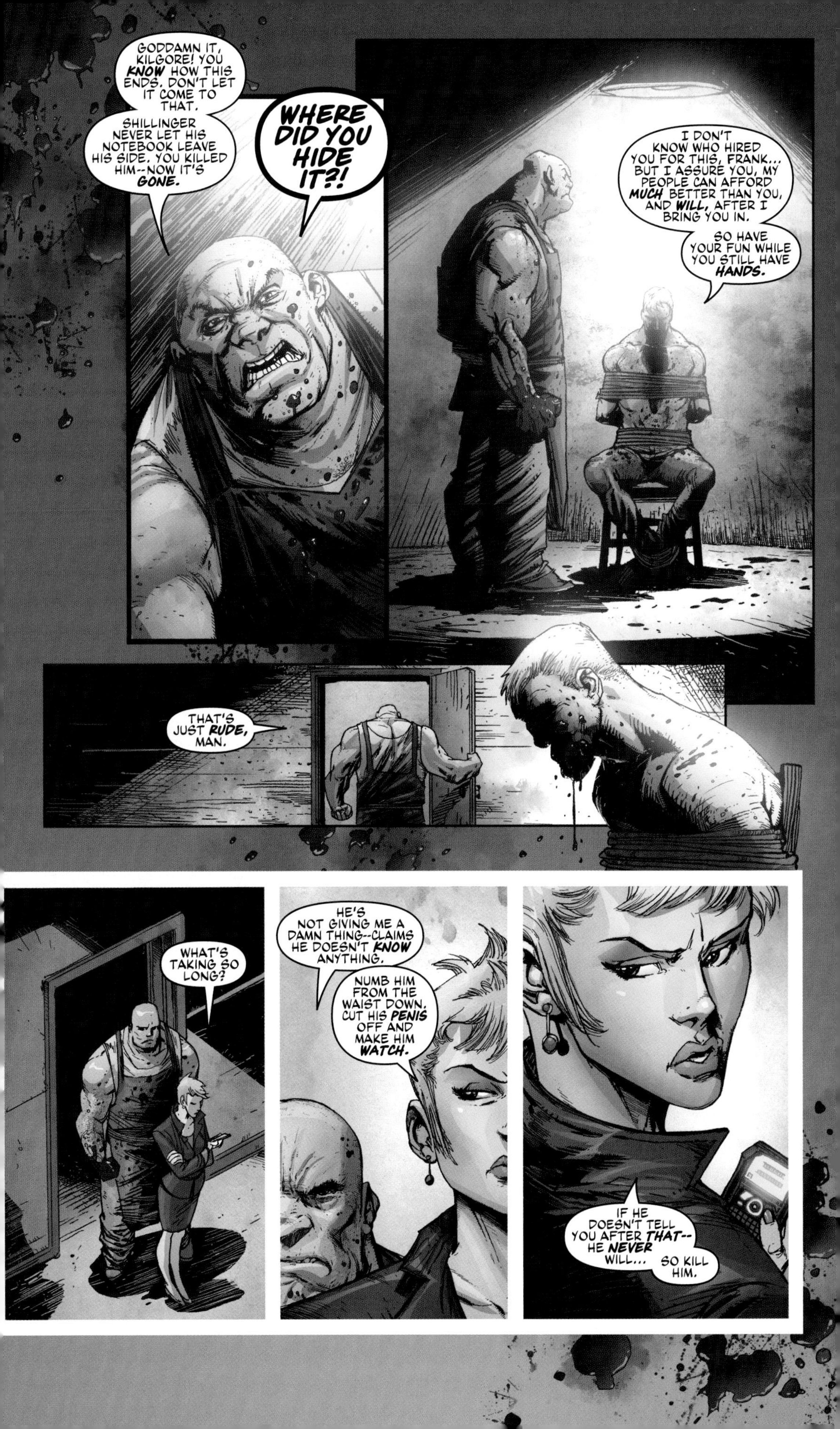
GODDAMN IT, KILGORE! YOU KNOW HOW THIS ENDS. DON'T LET IT COME TO THAT.
SHILLINGER NEVER LET HIS NOTEBOOK LEAVE HIS SIDE. YOU KILLED HIM--NOW IT'S GONE.
WHERE DID YOU HIDE IT?!
I DON'T KNOW WHO HIRED YOU FOR THIS, FRANK... BUT I ASSURE YOU, MY PEOPLE CAN AFFORD MUCH BETTER THAN YOU, AND WILL, AFTER I BRING YOU IN.
SO HAVE YOUR FUN WHILE YOU STILL HAVE HANDS.
THAT'S JUST RUDE, MAN.
WHAT'S TAKING SO LONG?
HE'S NOT GIVING ME A DAMN THING--CLAIMS HE DOESN'T KNOW ANYTHING.
NUMB HIM FROM THE WAIST DOWN. CUT HIS PENIS OFF AND MAKE HIM WATCH.
IF HE DOESN'T TELL YOU AFTER THAT--HE NEVER WILL...
SO KILL HIM.

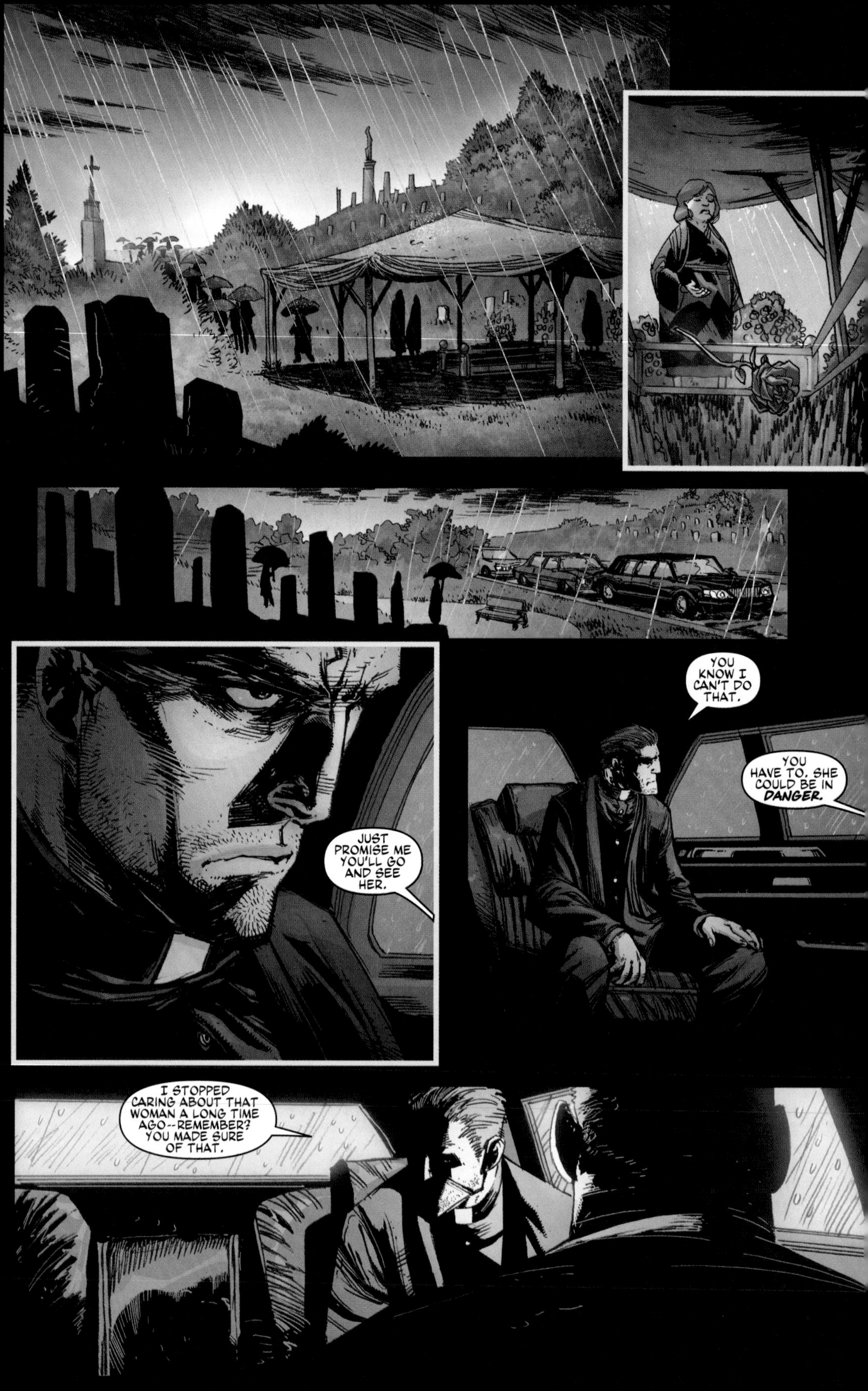
JUST PROMISE ME YOU'LL GO AND SEE HER.
YOU KNOW I CAN'T DO THAT.
YOU HAVE TO. SHE COULD BE IN DANGER.
I STOPPED CARING ABOUT THAT WOMAN A LONG TIME AGO--REMEMBER? YOU MADE SURE OF THAT.

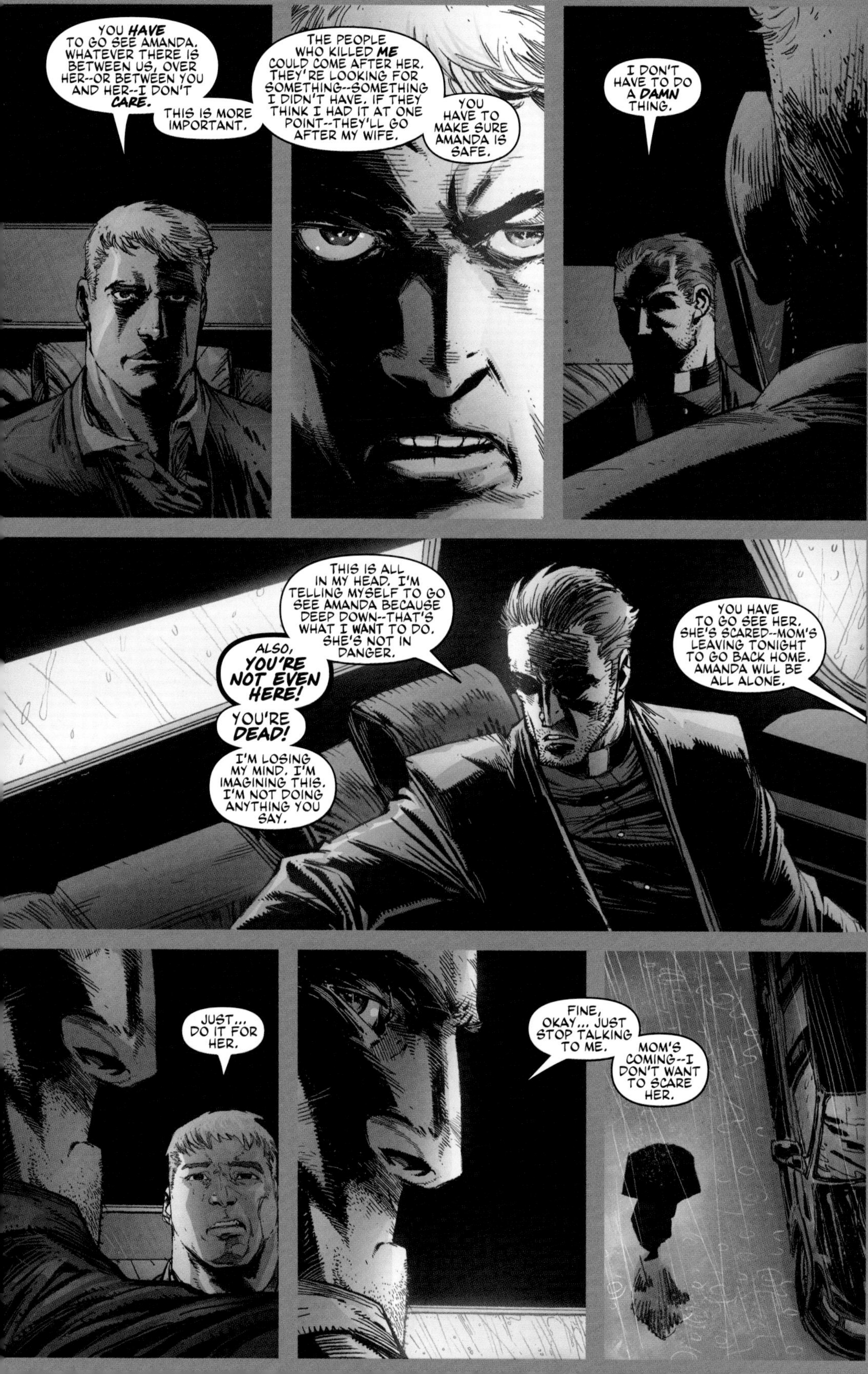

YOU HAVE TO GO SEE AMANDA. WHATEVER THERE IS BETWEEN US, OVER HER--OR BETWEEN YOU AND HER--I DON'T CARE.
THIS IS MORE IMPORTANT.
THE PEOPLE WHO KILLED ME COULD COME AFTER HER. THEY'RE LOOKING FOR SOMETHING--SOMETHING I DIDN'T HAVE. IF THEY THINK I HAD IT AT ONE POINT--THEY'LL GO AFTER MY WIFE.
YOU HAVE TO MAKE SURE AMANDA IS SAFE.
I DON'T HAVE TO DO A DAMN THING.
THIS IS ALL IN MY HEAD. I'M TELLING MYSELF TO GO SEE AMANDA BECAUSE DEEP DOWN--THAT'S WHAT I WANT TO DO. SHE'S NOT IN DANGER.
ALSO, YOU'RE NOT EVEN HERE!
YOU'RE DEAD!
I'M LOSING MY MIND. I'M IMAGINING THIS. I'M NOT DOING ANYTHING YOU SAY.
YOU HAVE TO GO SEE HER. SHE'S SCARED--MOM'S LEAVING TONIGHT TO GO BACK HOME. AMANDA WILL BE ALL ALONE.
JUST... DO IT FOR HER.
FINE, OKAY... JUST STOP TALKING TO ME.
MOM'S COMING--I DON'T WANT TO SCARE HER.

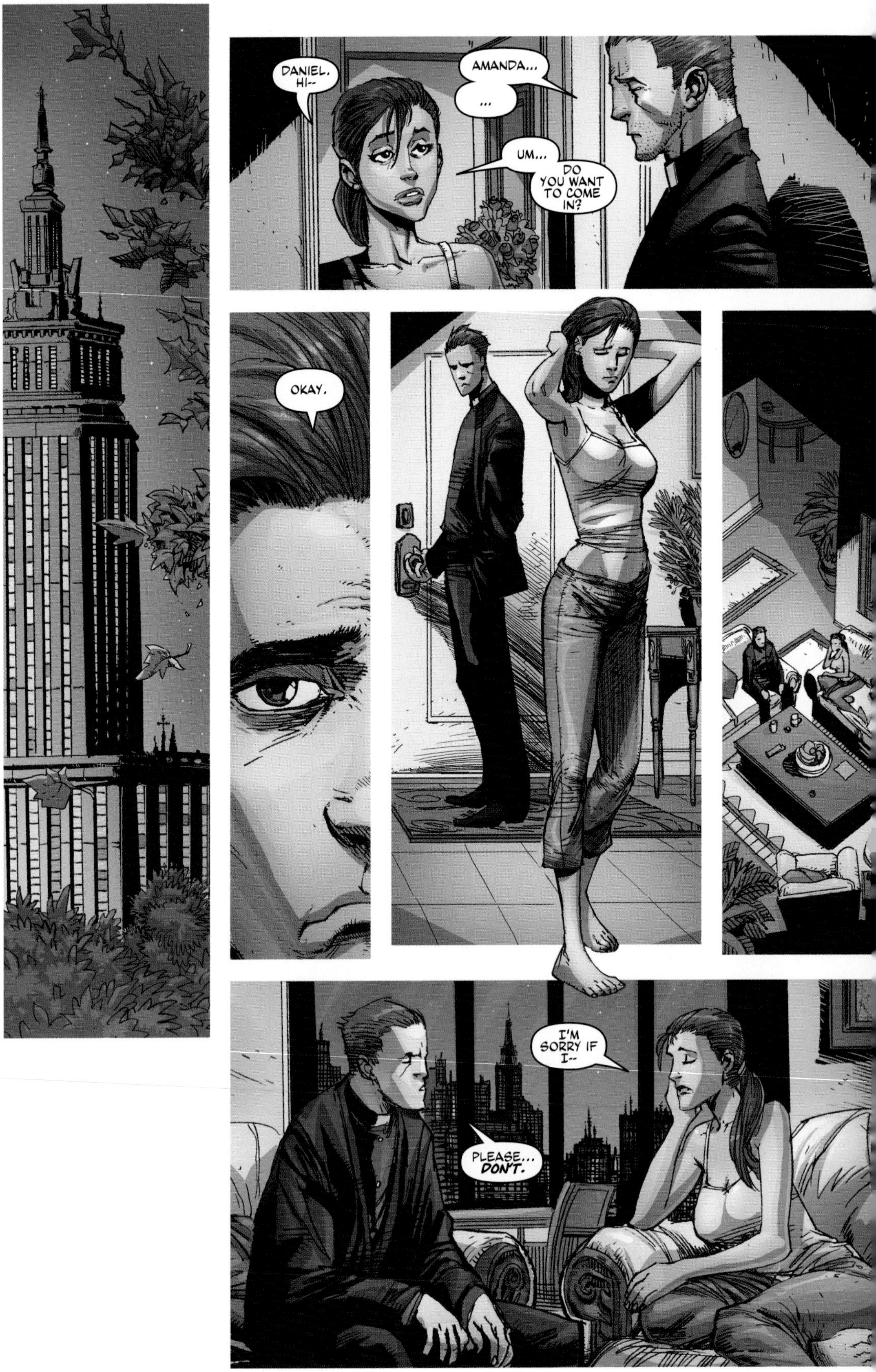
DANIEL. HI--
AMANDA...
...
UM...
DO YOU WANT TO COME IN?
OKAY.
I'M SORRY IF I--
PLEASE... **DON'T.**

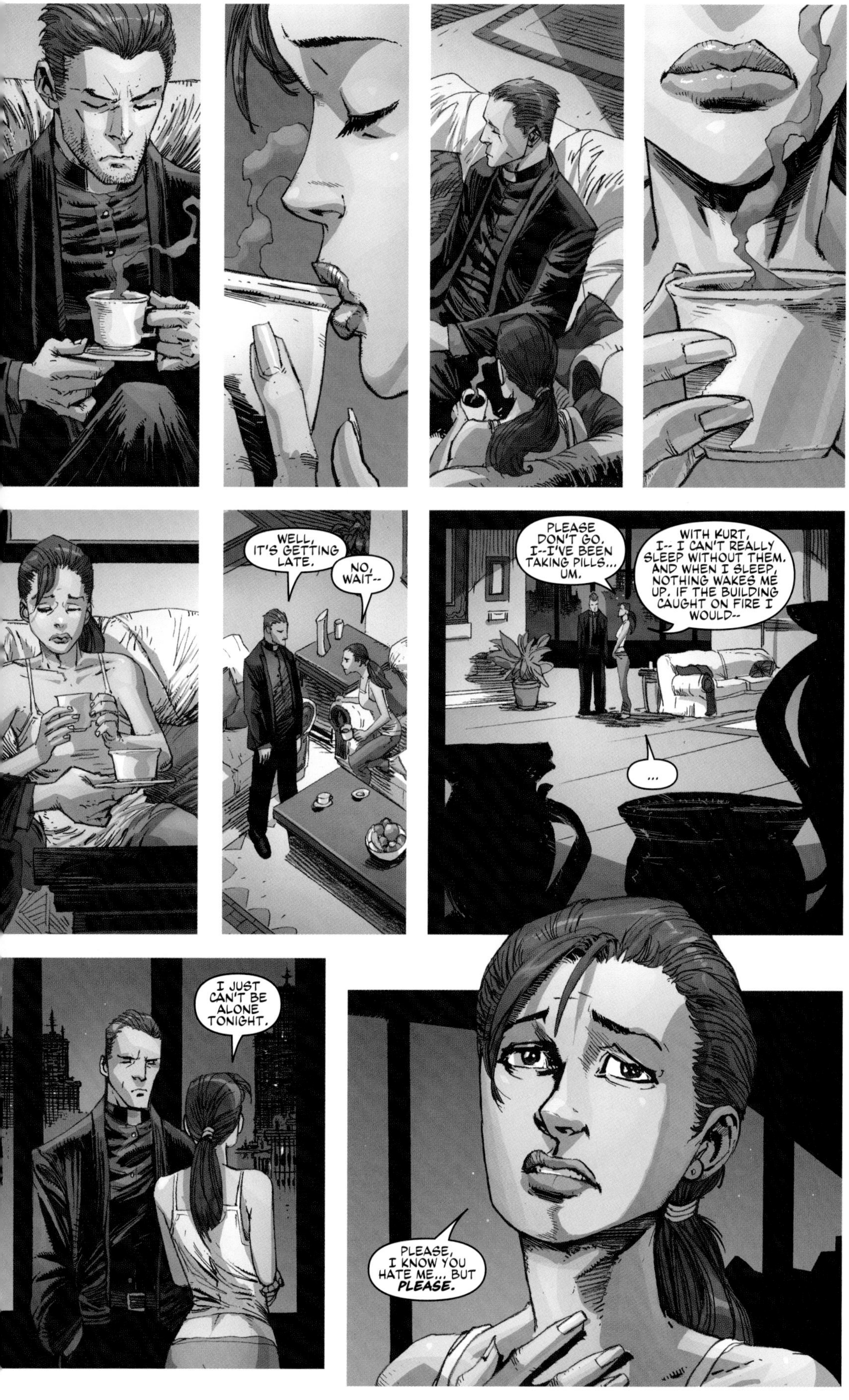
WELL, IT'S GETTING LATE.
NO, WAIT--
PLEASE DON'T GO. I--I'VE BEEN TAKING PILLS... UM.
WITH KURT, I-- I CAN'T REALLY SLEEP WITHOUT THEM. AND WHEN I SLEEP, NOTHING WAKES ME UP. IF THE BUILDING CAUGHT ON FIRE I WOULD--
...
I JUST CAN'T BE ALONE TONIGHT.
PLEASE, I KNOW YOU HATE ME... BUT **PLEASE.**

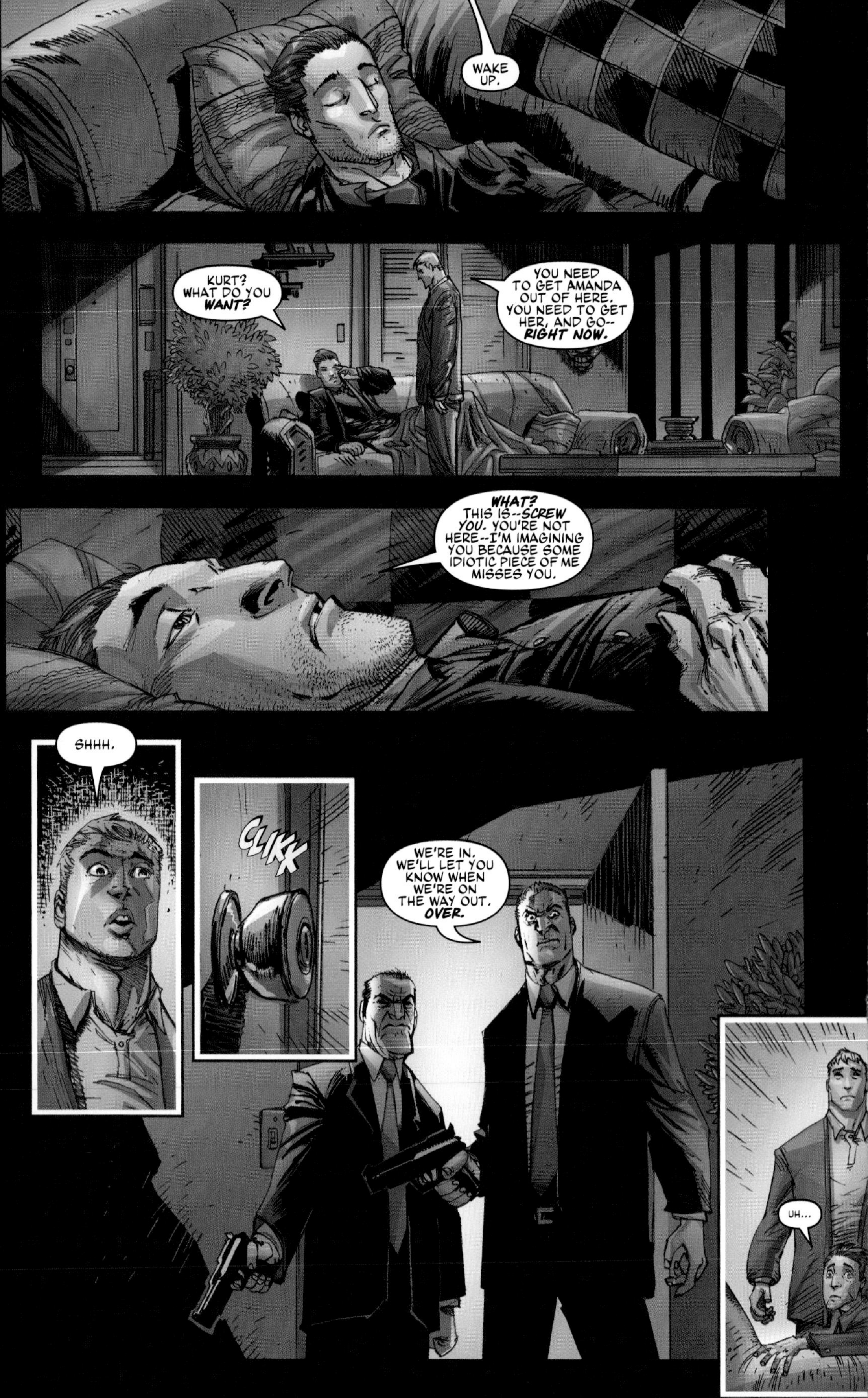
WAKE UP.
KURT? WHAT DO YOU WANT?
YOU NEED TO GET AMANDA OUT OF HERE. YOU NEED TO GET HER, AND GO-- RIGHT NOW.
WHAT? THIS IS--SCREW YOU. YOU'RE NOT HERE--I'M IMAGINING YOU BECAUSE SOME IDIOTIC PIECE OF ME MISSES YOU.
SHHH.
CLIKK
WE'RE IN. WE'LL LET YOU KNOW WHEN WE'RE ON THE WAY OUT. OVER.
UH...

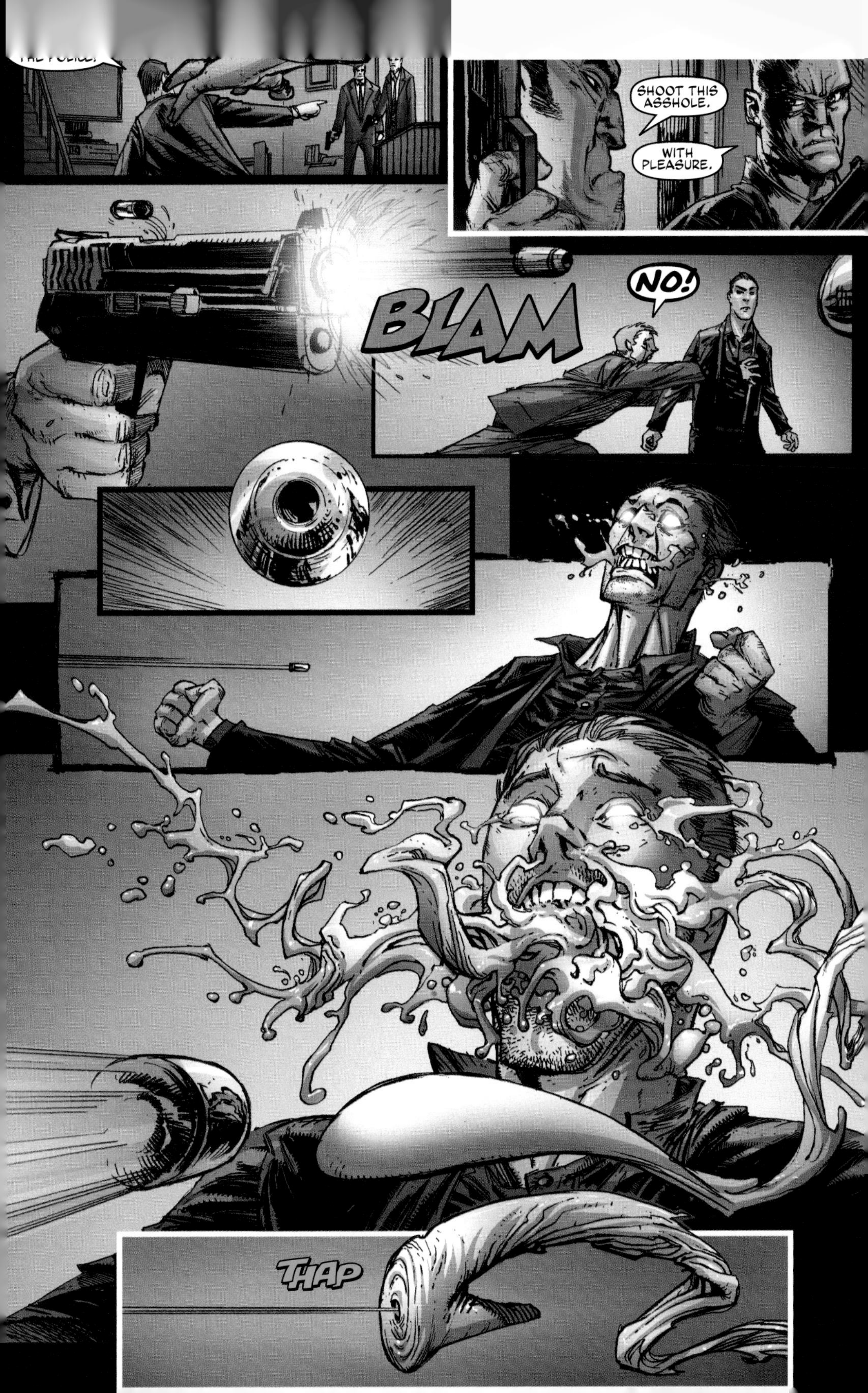
SHOOT THIS ASSHOLE.
WITH PLEASURE.
BLAM
NO!
THAP

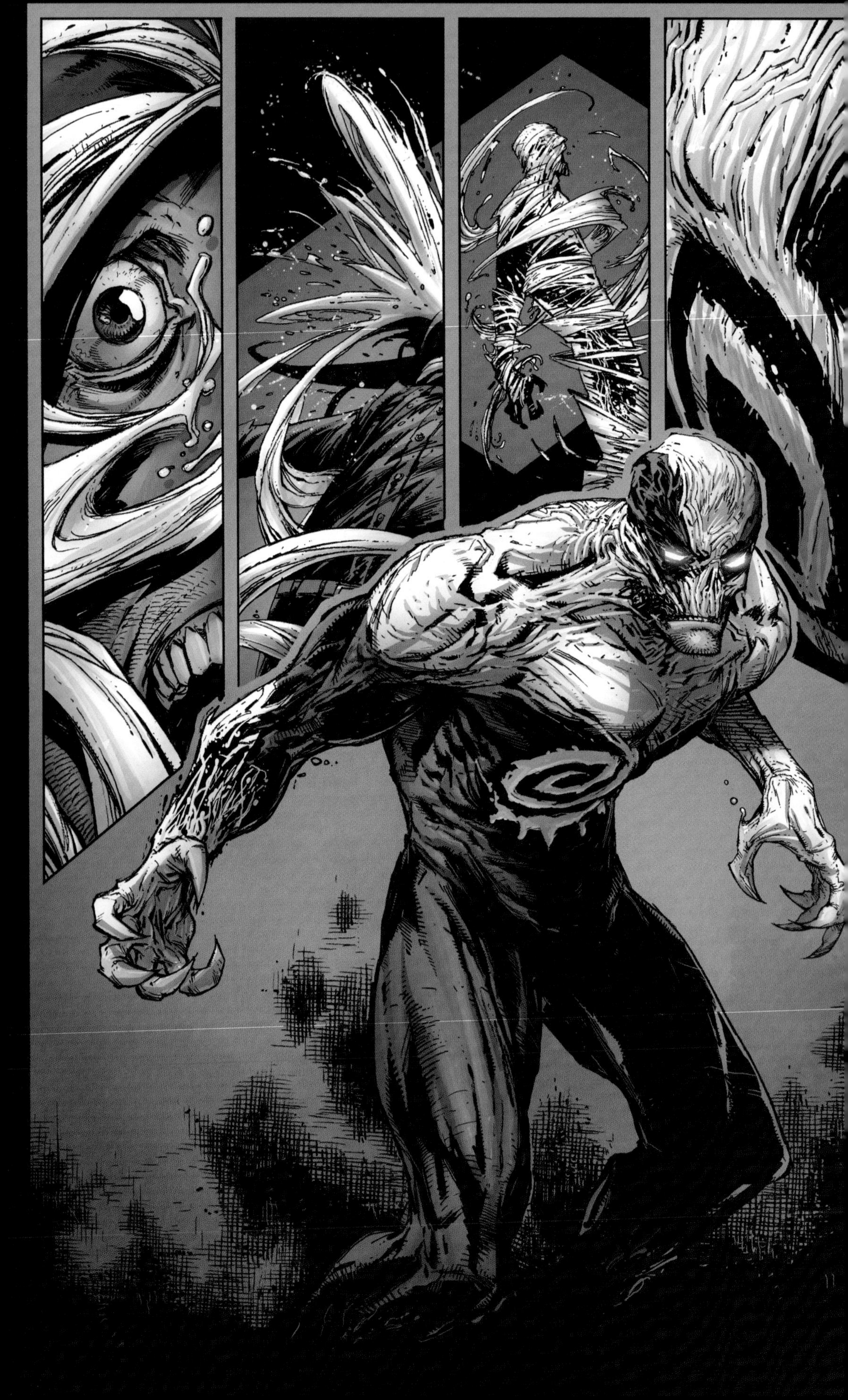

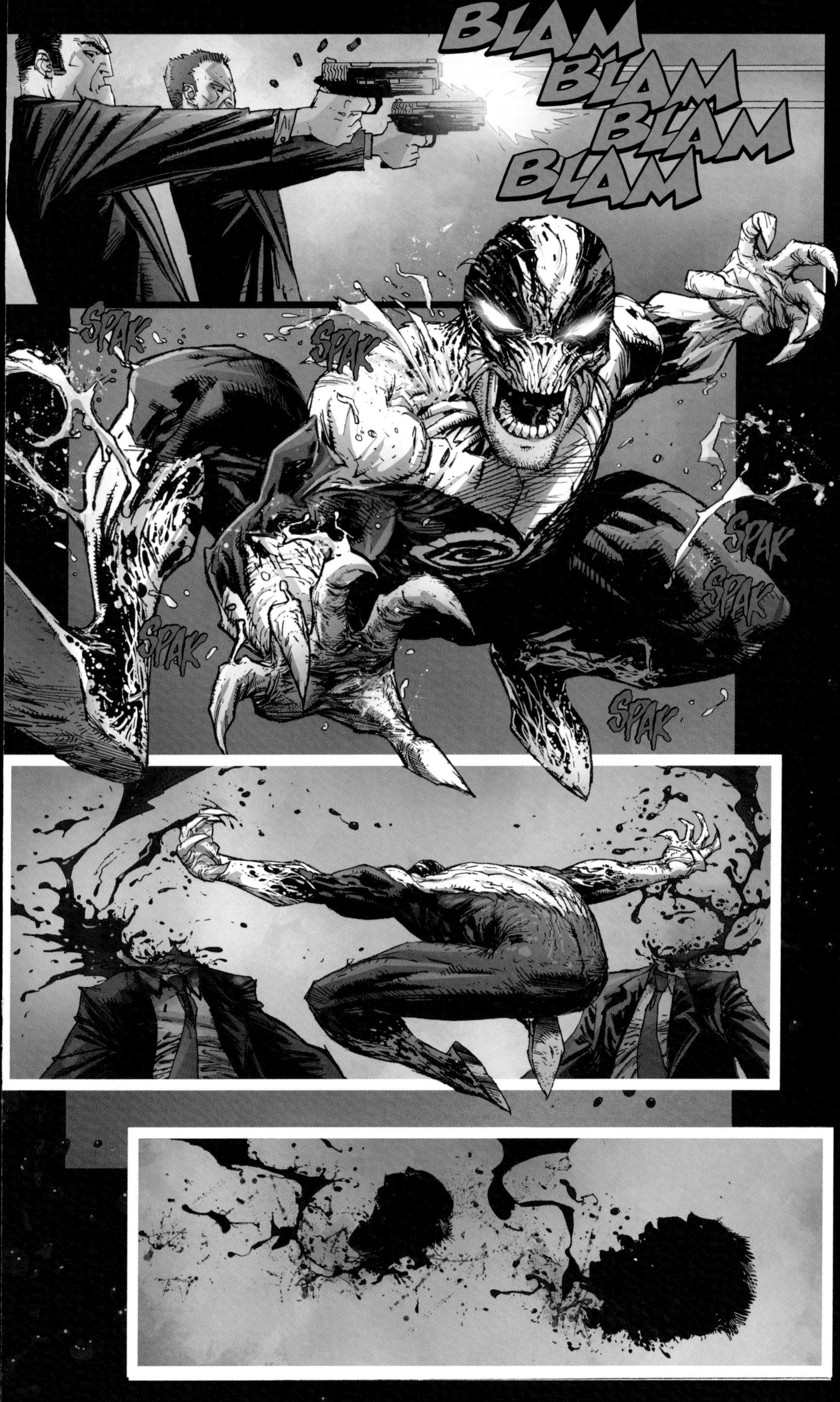
BLAM
BLAM
BLAM
BLAM
SPAK
SPAK
SPAK
SPAK
SPAK
SPAK

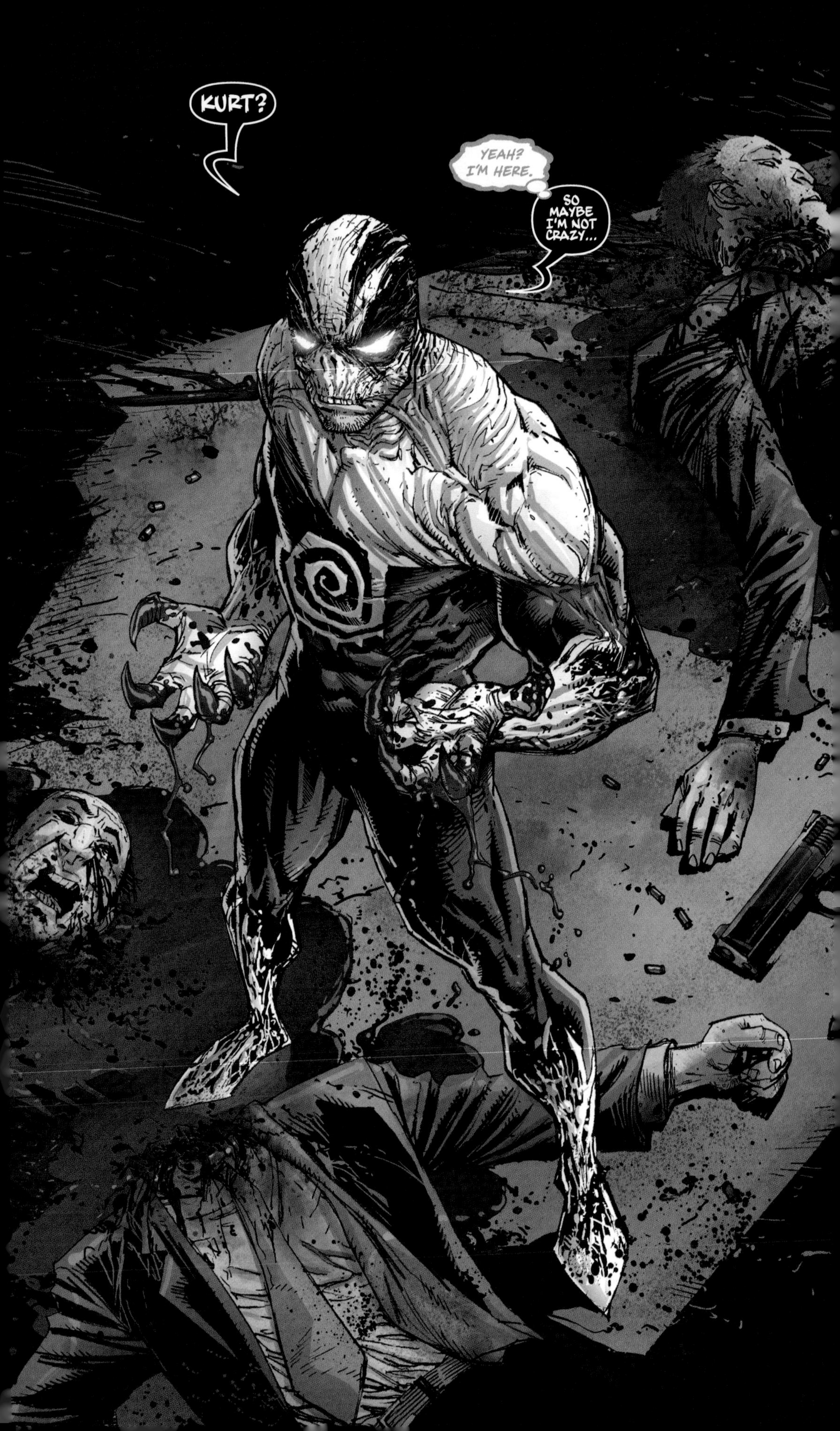
KURT?
YEAH? I'M HERE.
SO MAYBE I'M NOT CRAZY...

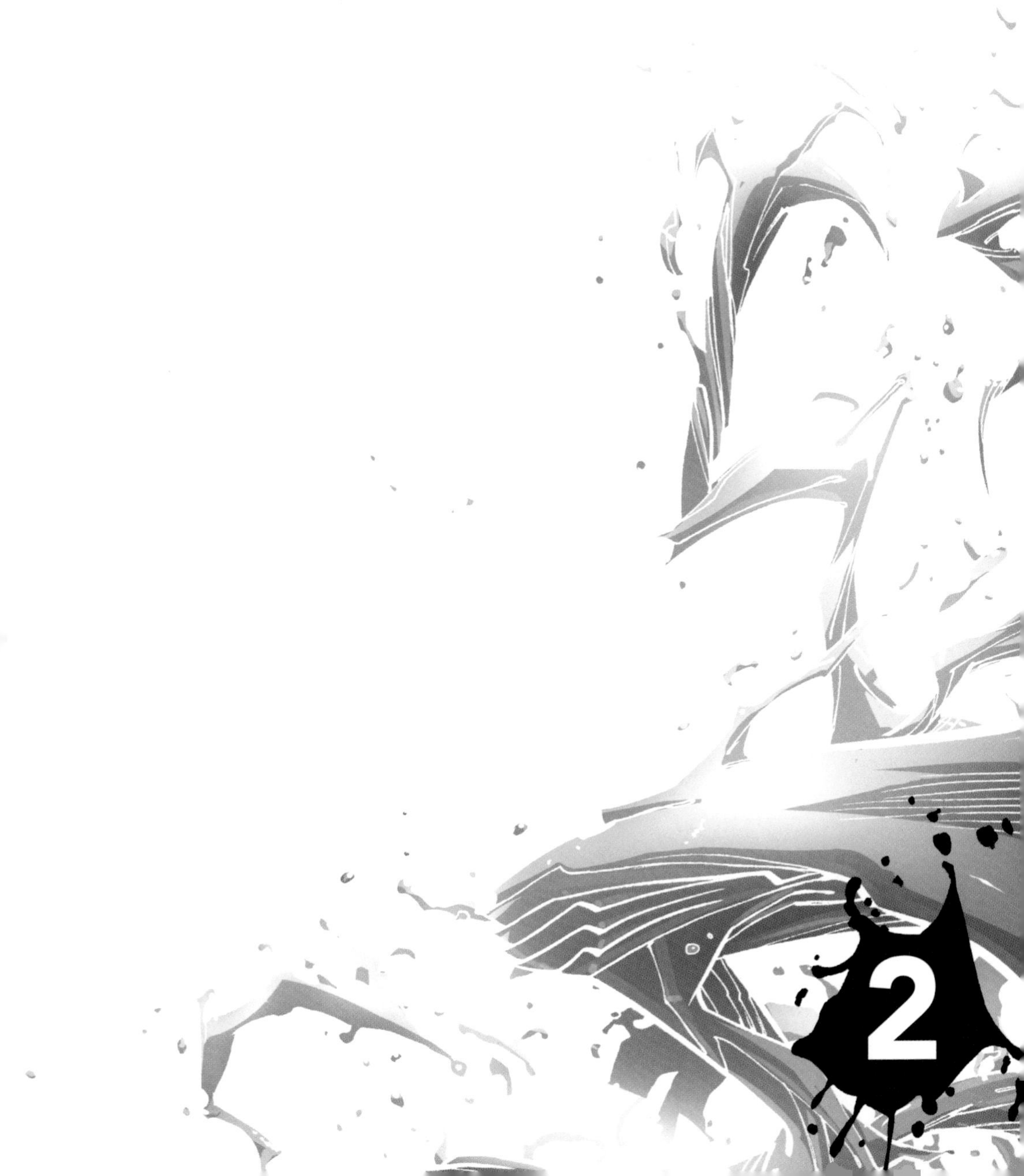
2

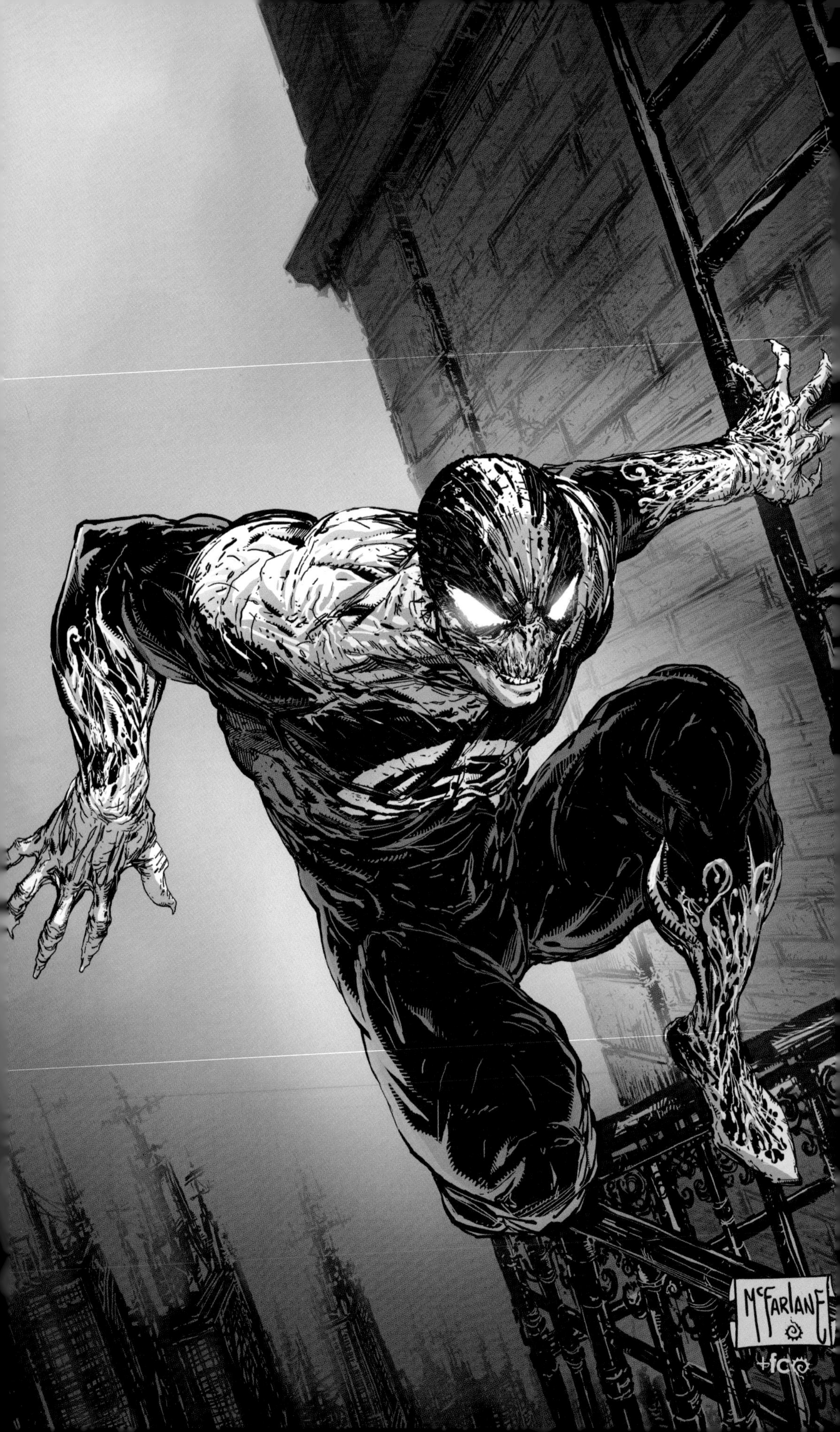
McFARLANE

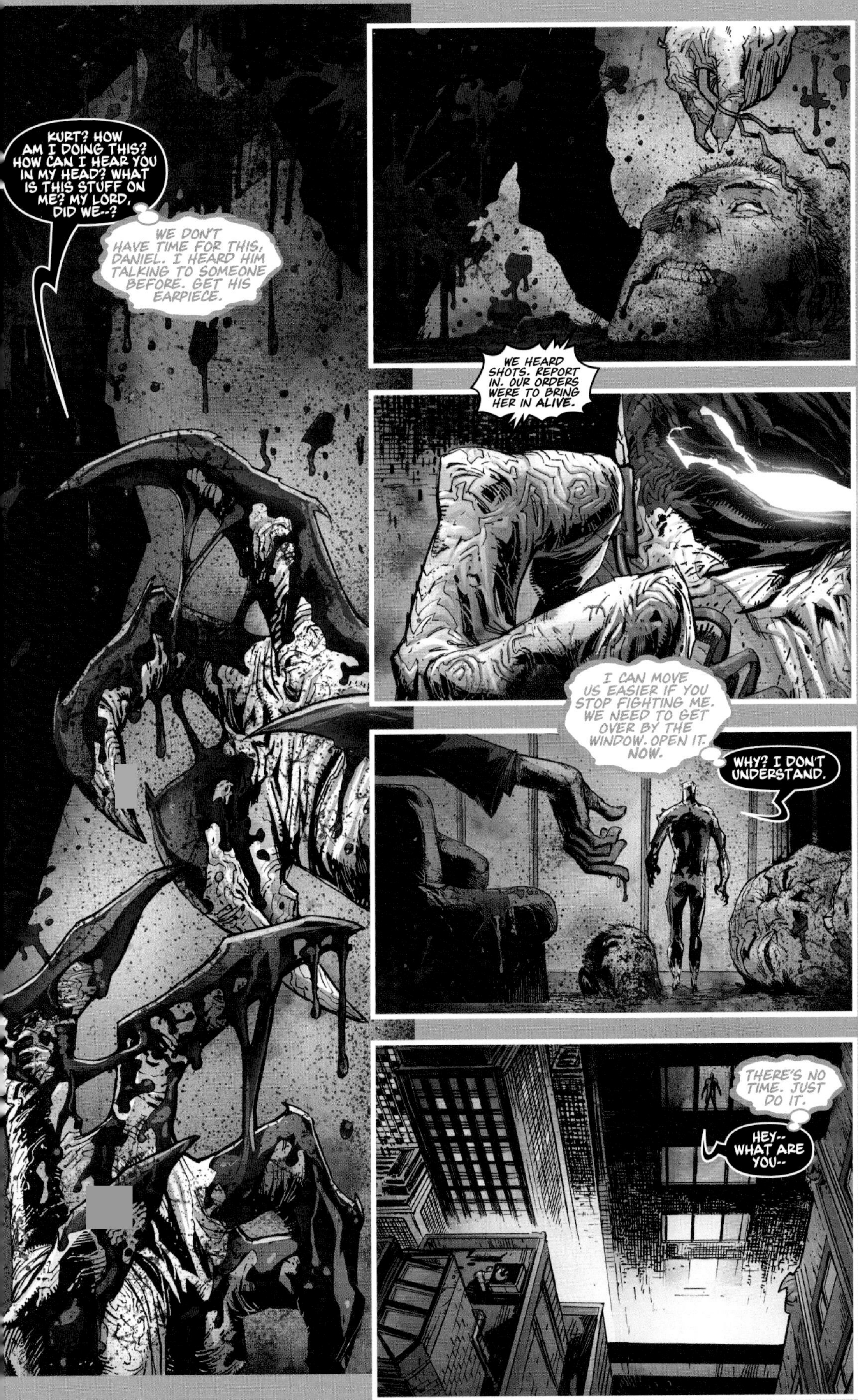
KURT? HOW AM I DOING THIS? HOW CAN I HEAR YOU IN MY HEAD? WHAT IS THIS STUFF ON ME? MY LORD, DID WE--?
WE DON'T HAVE TIME FOR THIS, DANIEL. I HEARD HIM TALKING TO SOMEONE BEFORE. GET HIS EARPIECE.
WE HEARD SHOTS. REPORT IN. OUR ORDERS WERE TO BRING HER IN ALIVE.
I CAN MOVE US EASIER IF YOU STOP FIGHTING ME. WE NEED TO GET OVER BY THE WINDOW. OPEN IT. NOW.
WHY? I DON'T UNDERSTAND.
THERE'S NO TIME. JUST DO IT.
HEY-- WHAT ARE YOU--

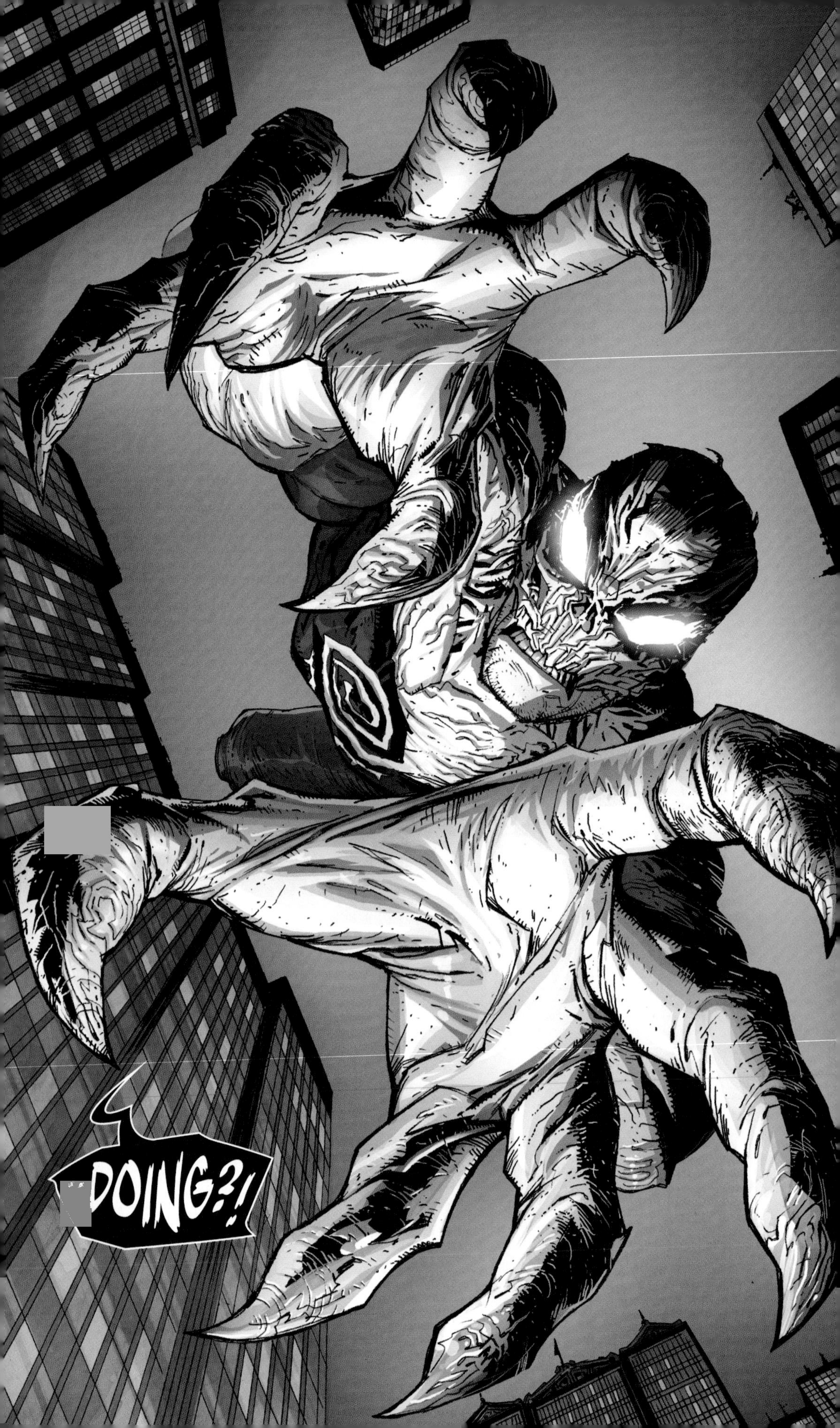
DOING?!

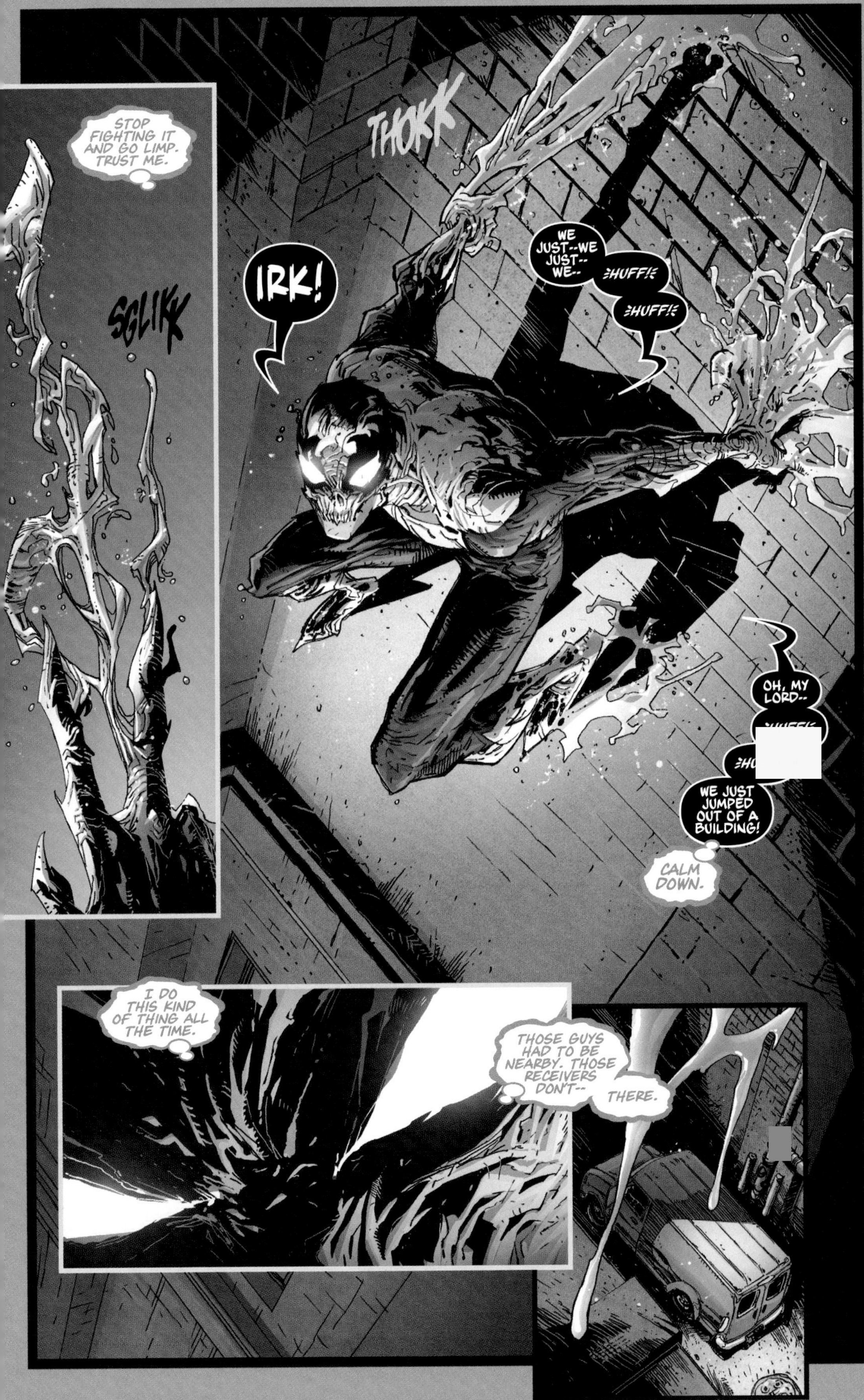
STOP FIGHTING IT AND GO LIMP. TRUST ME.
SGLIKK
THOKK
IRK!
WE JUST--WE JUST-- WE--
HUFF!
HUFF!
OH, MY LORD--
WE JUST JUMPED OUT OF A BUILDING!
CALM DOWN.
I DO THIS KIND OF THING ALL THE TIME.
THOSE GUYS HAD TO BE NEARBY. THOSE RECEIVERS DON'T--
THERE.

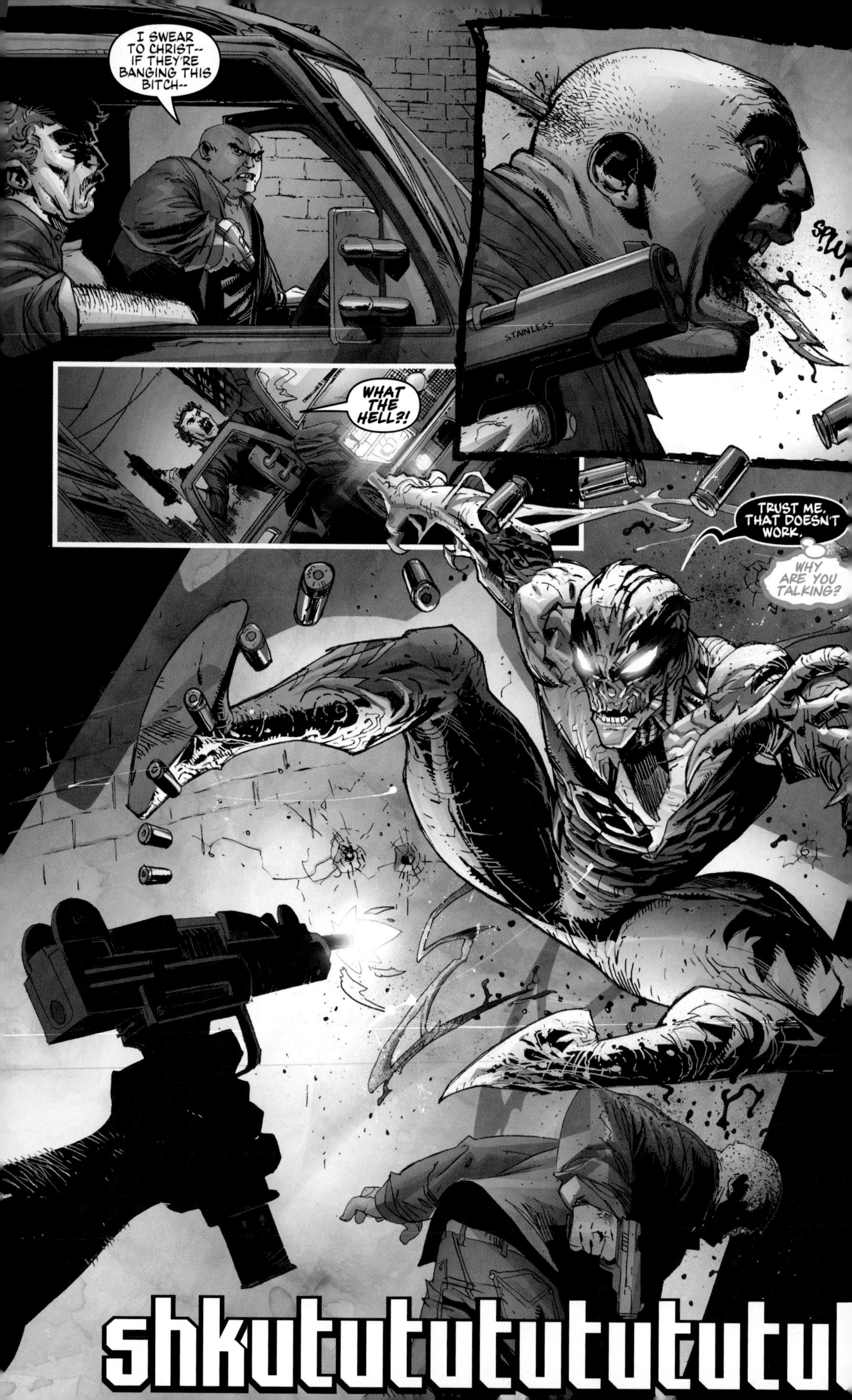

I SWEAR TO CHRIST-- IF THEY'RE BANGING THIS BITCH--
SPLUT
STAINLESS
WHAT THE HELL?!
TRUST ME. THAT DOESN'T WORK.
WHY ARE YOU TALKING?
shkututututututut

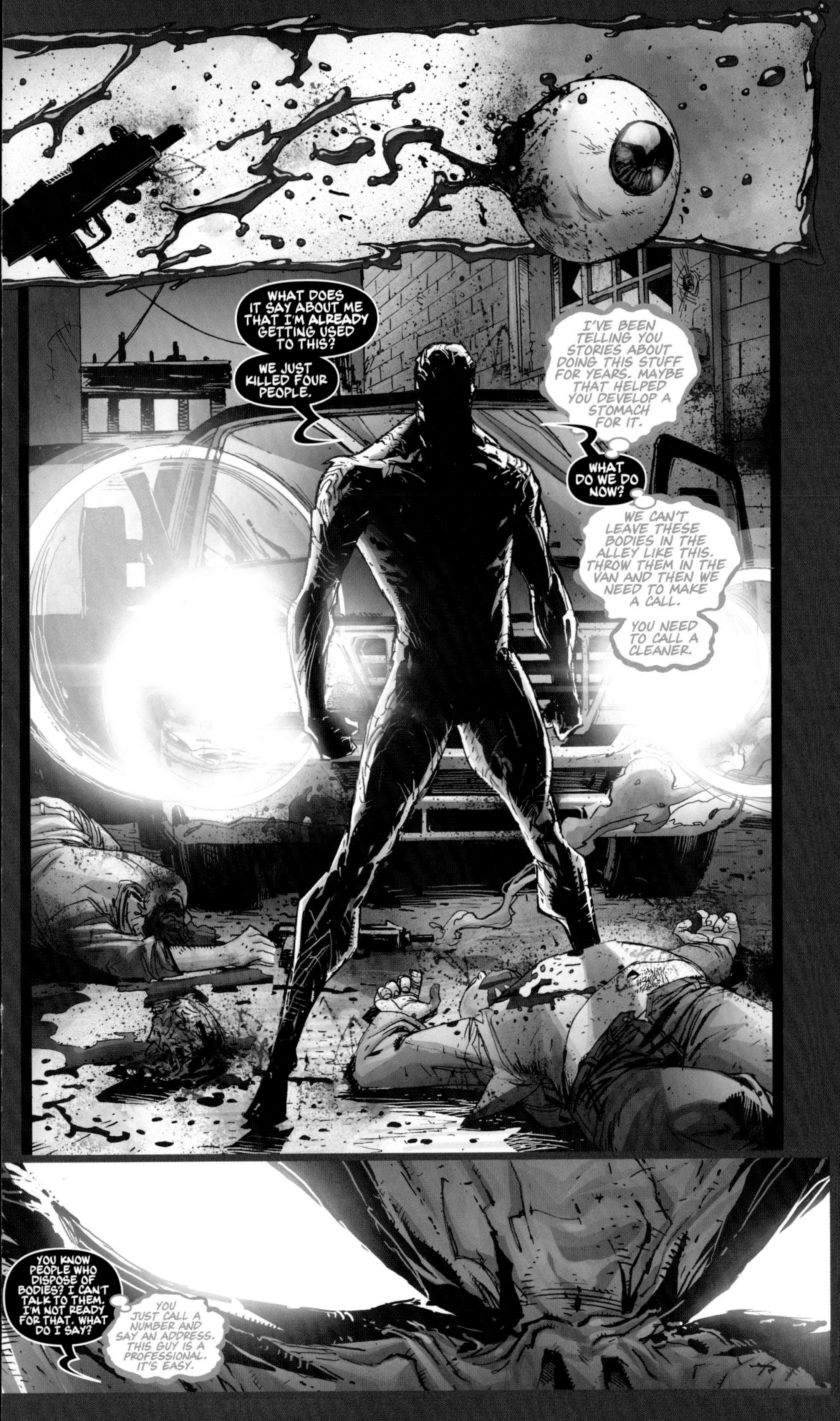
WHAT DOES IT SAY ABOUT ME THAT I'M ALREADY GETTING USED TO THIS?
WE JUST KILLED FOUR PEOPLE.
I'VE BEEN TELLING YOU STORIES ABOUT DOING THIS STUFF FOR YEARS. MAYBE THAT HELPED YOU DEVELOP A STOMACH FOR IT.
WHAT DO WE DO NOW?
WE CAN'T LEAVE THESE BODIES IN THE ALLEY LIKE THIS. THROW THEM IN THE VAN AND THEN WE NEED TO MAKE A CALL.
YOU NEED TO CALL A CLEANER.
YOU KNOW PEOPLE WHO DISPOSE OF BODIES? I CAN'T TALK TO THEM. I'M NOT READY FOR THAT. WHAT DO I SAY?
YOU JUST CALL A NUMBER AND SAY AN ADDRESS. THIS GUY IS A PROFESSIONAL. IT'S EASY.

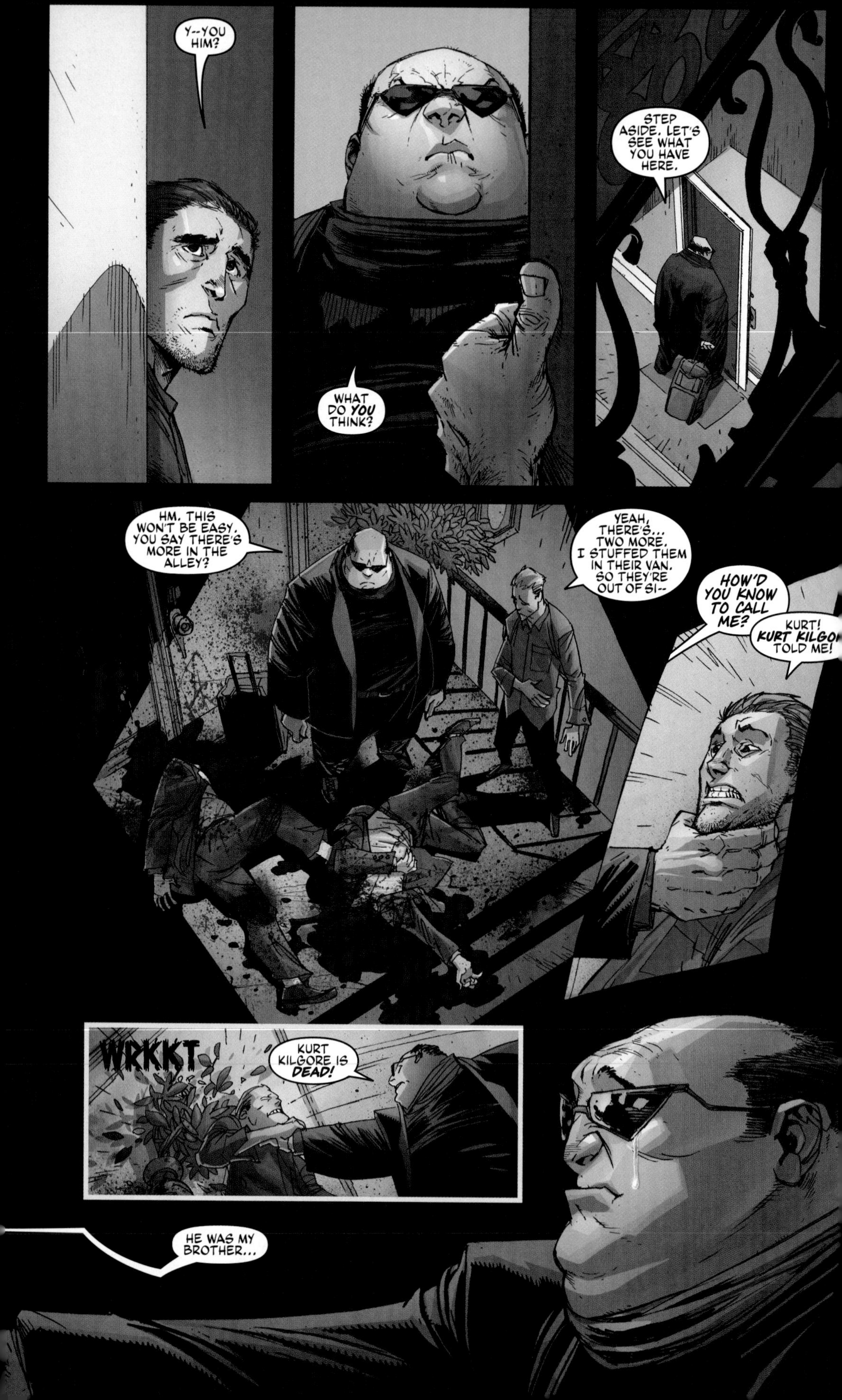

Y--YOU HIM?
WHAT DO *YOU* THINK?
STEP ASIDE. LET'S SEE WHAT YOU HAVE HERE.
HM. THIS WON'T BE EASY. YOU SAY THERE'S MORE IN THE ALLEY?
YEAH, THERE'S... TWO MORE. I STUFFED THEM IN THEIR VAN. SO THEY'RE OUT OF SI--
HOW'D YOU KNOW TO CALL ME?
KURT! *KURT KILGO* TOLD ME!
WRKKT
KURT KILGORE IS *DEAD!*
HE WAS MY BROTHER...

HE WAS--LIKE A BROTHER TO ME, TOO.

I MISS HIM SO MUCH!

I'M SO SORRY FOR YOUR LOSS. SO SORRY.

IT'S OKAY.

IT'S OKAY.

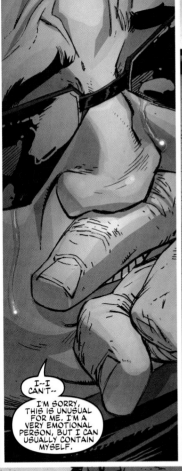

I--I CAN'T--

I'M SORRY, THIS IS UNUSUAL FOR ME. I'M A VERY EMOTIONAL PERSON, BUT I CAN USUALLY CONTAIN MYSELF.

KURT REALLY MEANT A LOT TO ME.

...

OKAY, TALK TO ME. WHAT'S OUR SITUATION?

NOT GOOD.

KURT'S WIFE IS SLEEPING IN THE BEDROOM-- SHE'S OUT COLD. SLEEPING PILLS.

BUT SHE'S GOT WORK IN THE MORNING, SO SHE'LL BE UP.

WE'VE GOT FOUR HOURS. OKAY, YOU'RE IN THE HANDS OF A PROFESSIONAL.

SHE'LL NEVER KNOW I WAS HERE.

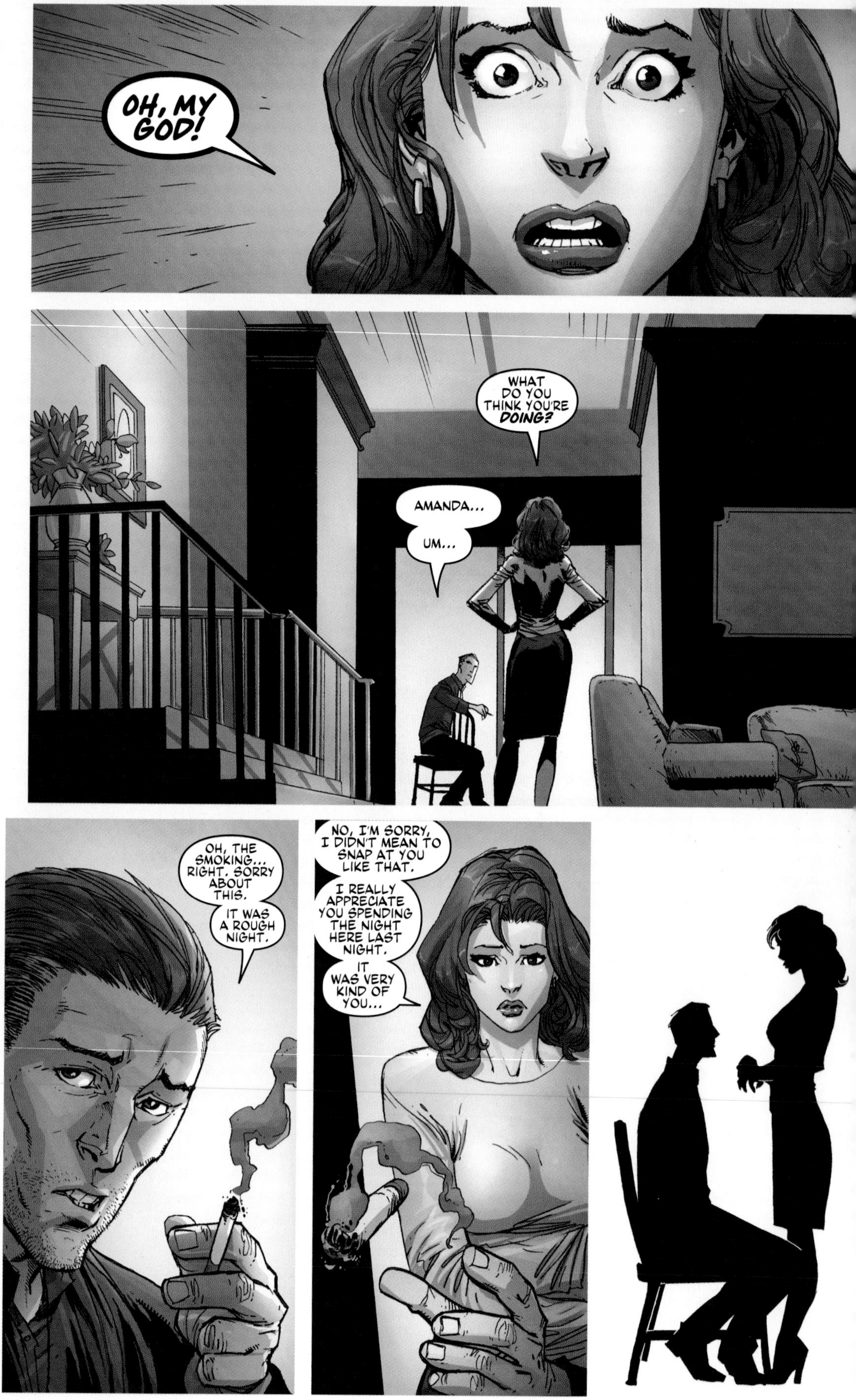
OH, MY GOD!
WHAT DO YOU THINK YOU'RE DOING?
AMANDA...
UM...
OH, THE SMOKING... RIGHT. SORRY ABOUT THIS.
IT WAS A ROUGH NIGHT.
NO, I'M SORRY, I DIDN'T MEAN TO SNAP AT YOU LIKE THAT.
I REALLY APPRECIATE YOU SPENDING THE NIGHT HERE LAST NIGHT.
IT WAS VERY KIND OF YOU...

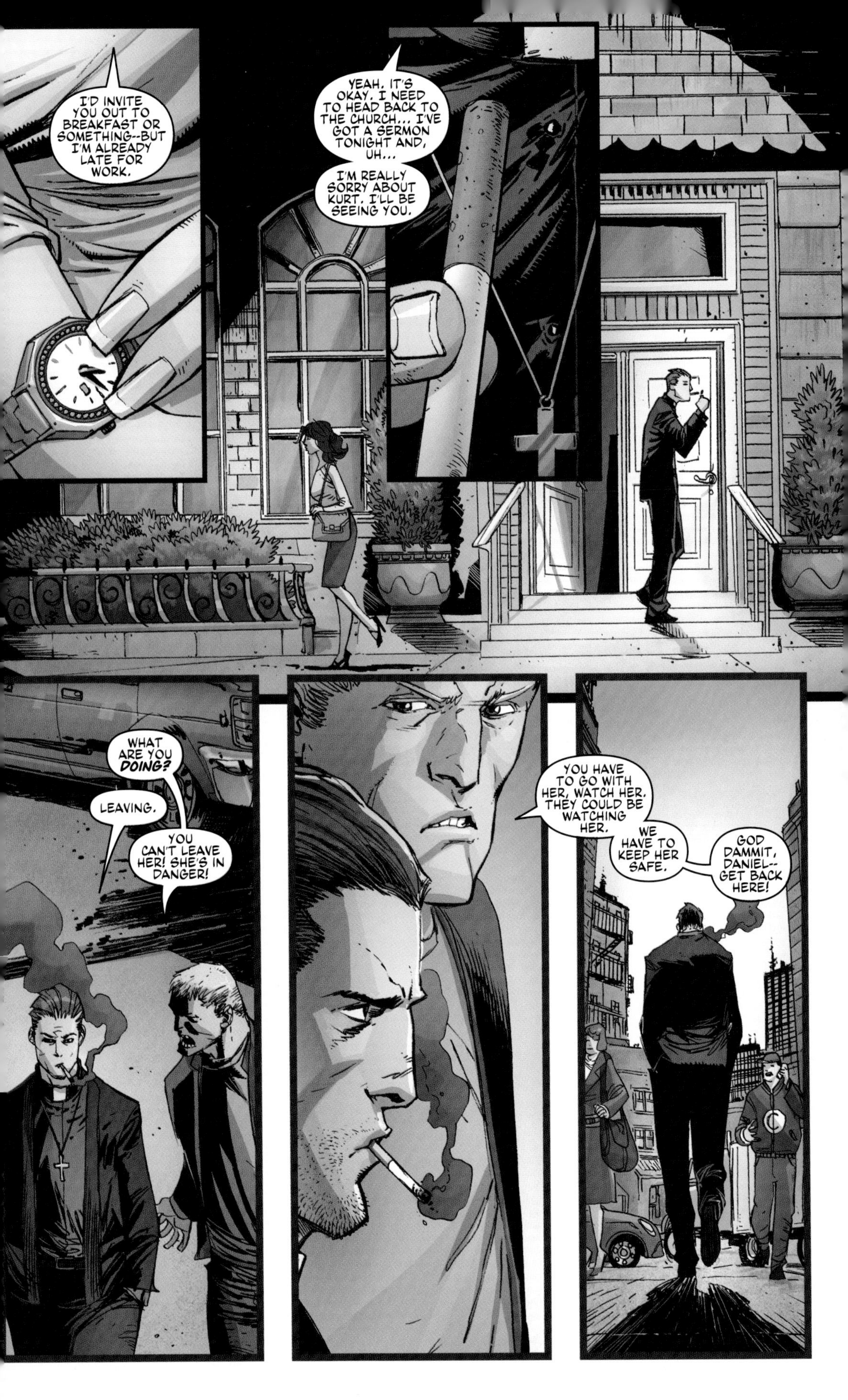
I'D INVITE YOU OUT TO BREAKFAST OR SOMETHING--BUT I'M ALREADY LATE FOR WORK.
YEAH. IT'S OKAY. I NEED TO HEAD BACK TO THE CHURCH... I'VE GOT A SERMON TONIGHT AND, UH...
I'M REALLY SORRY ABOUT KURT. I'LL BE SEEING YOU.
WHAT ARE YOU *DOING?*
LEAVING.
YOU CAN'T LEAVE HER! SHE'S IN DANGER!
YOU HAVE TO GO WITH HER, WATCH HER. THEY COULD BE WATCHING HER.
WE HAVE TO KEEP HER SAFE.
GOD DAMMIT, DANIEL-- GET BACK HERE!

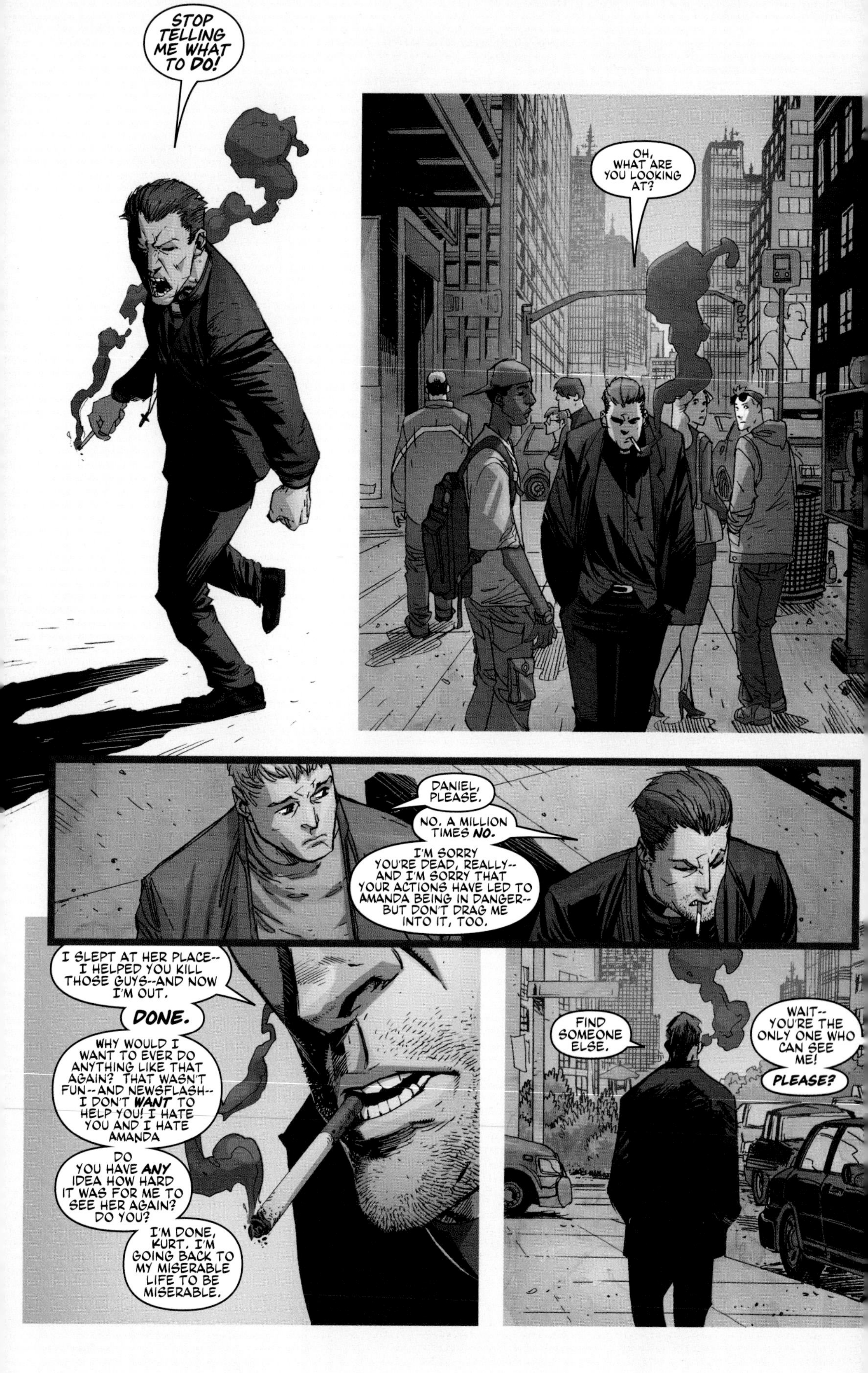
STOP TELLING ME WHAT TO DO!
OH, WHAT ARE YOU LOOKING AT?
DANIEL, PLEASE.
NO. A MILLION TIMES NO.
I'M SORRY YOU'RE DEAD, REALLY-- AND I'M SORRY THAT YOUR ACTIONS HAVE LED TO AMANDA BEING IN DANGER-- BUT DON'T DRAG ME INTO IT, TOO.
I SLEPT AT HER PLACE-- I HELPED YOU KILL THOSE GUYS--AND NOW I'M OUT.
DONE.
WHY WOULD I WANT TO EVER DO ANYTHING LIKE THAT AGAIN? THAT WASN'T FUN--AND NEWSFLASH-- I DON'T WANT TO HELP YOU! I HATE YOU AND I HATE AMANDA
DO YOU HAVE ANY IDEA HOW HARD IT WAS FOR ME TO SEE HER AGAIN? DO YOU?
I'M DONE, KURT. I'M GOING BACK TO MY MISERABLE LIFE TO BE MISERABLE.
FIND SOMEONE ELSE.
WAIT-- YOU'RE THE ONLY ONE WHO CAN SEE ME!
PLEASE?

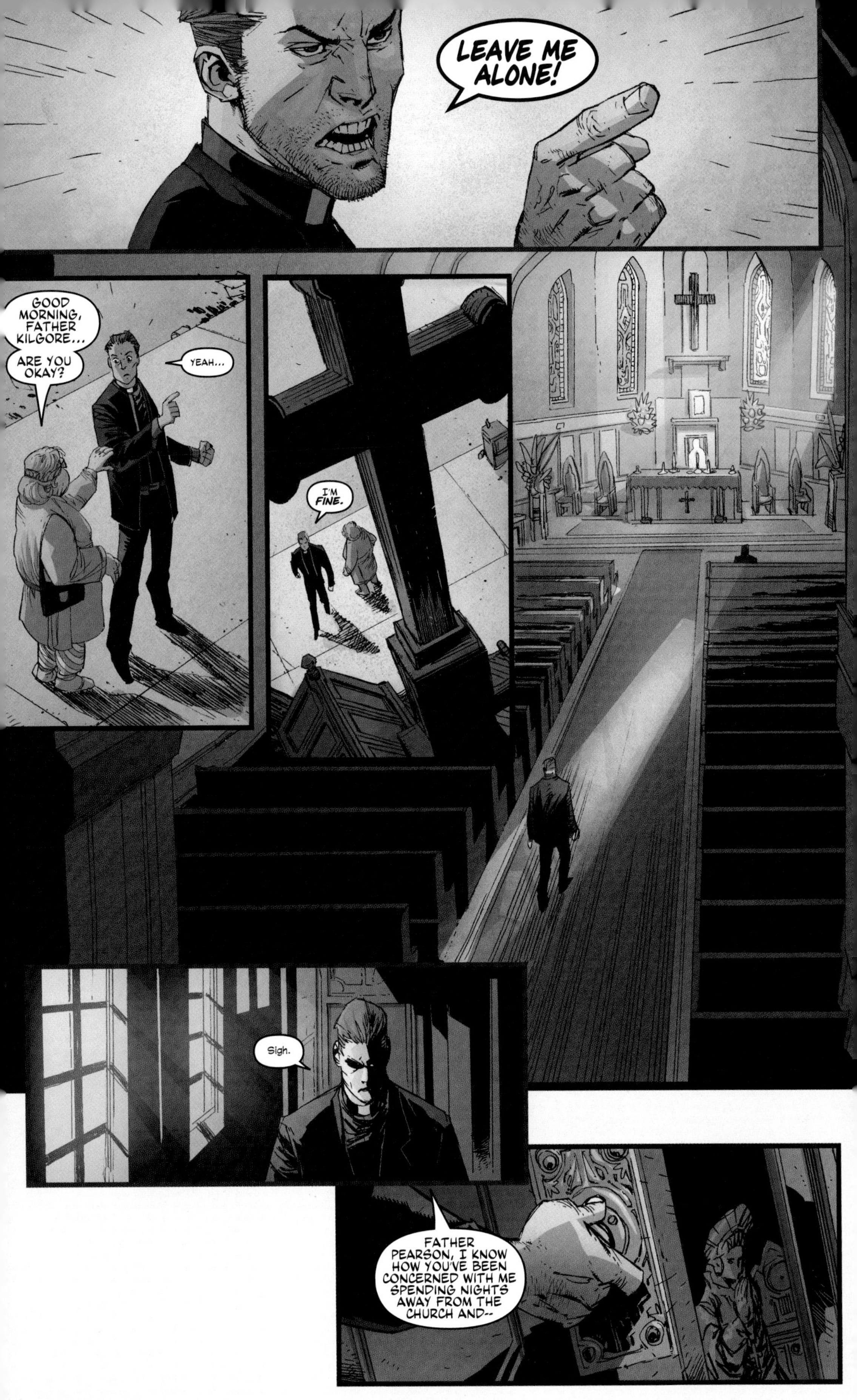
LEAVE ME ALONE!
GOOD MORNING, FATHER KILGORE...
ARE YOU OKAY?
YEAH...
I'M FINE.
Sigh.
FATHER PEARSON, I KNOW HOW YOU'VE BEEN CONCERNED WITH ME SPENDING NIGHTS AWAY FROM THE CHURCH AND--

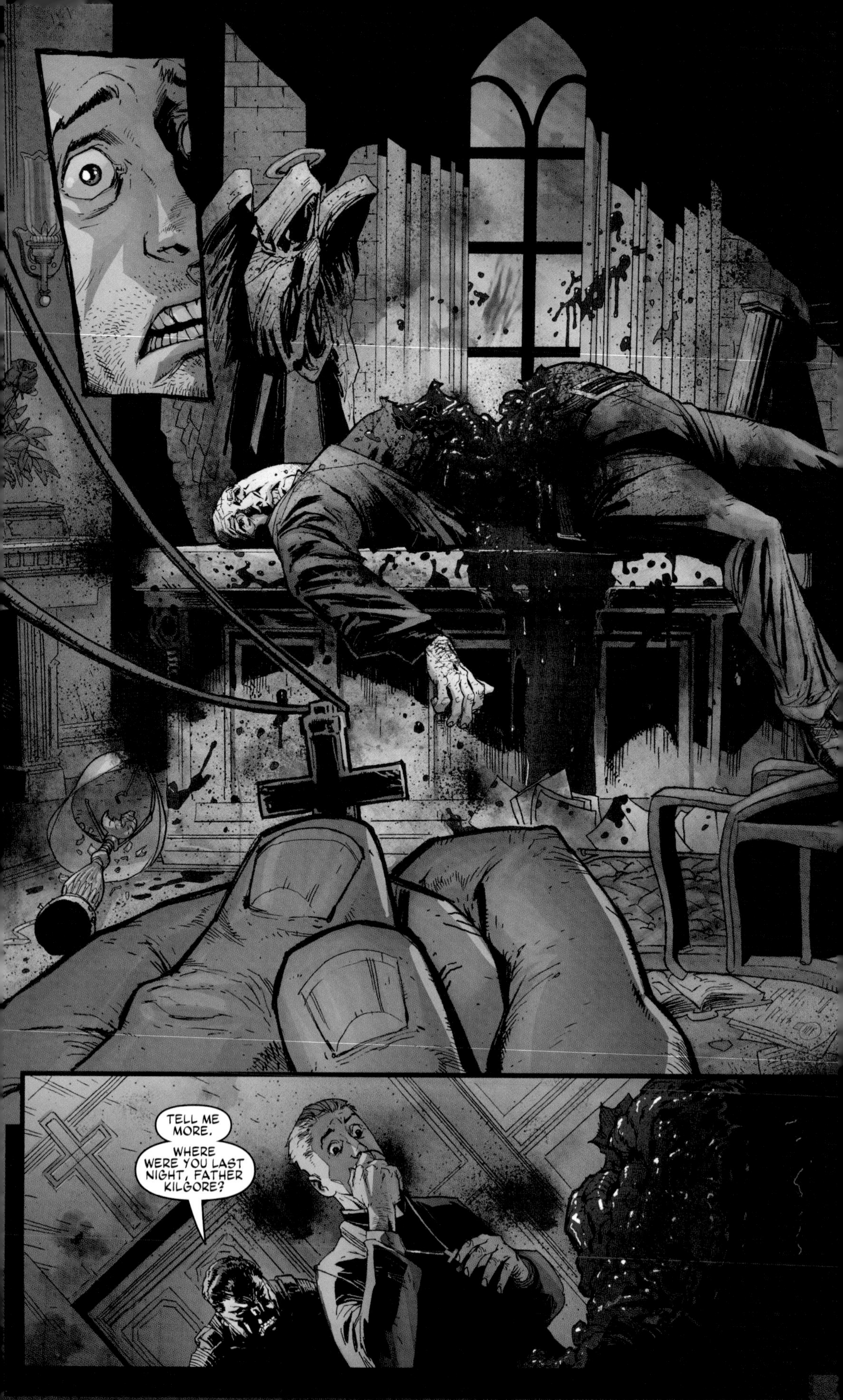
TELL ME MORE.
WHERE WERE YOU LAST NIGHT, FATHER KILGORE?

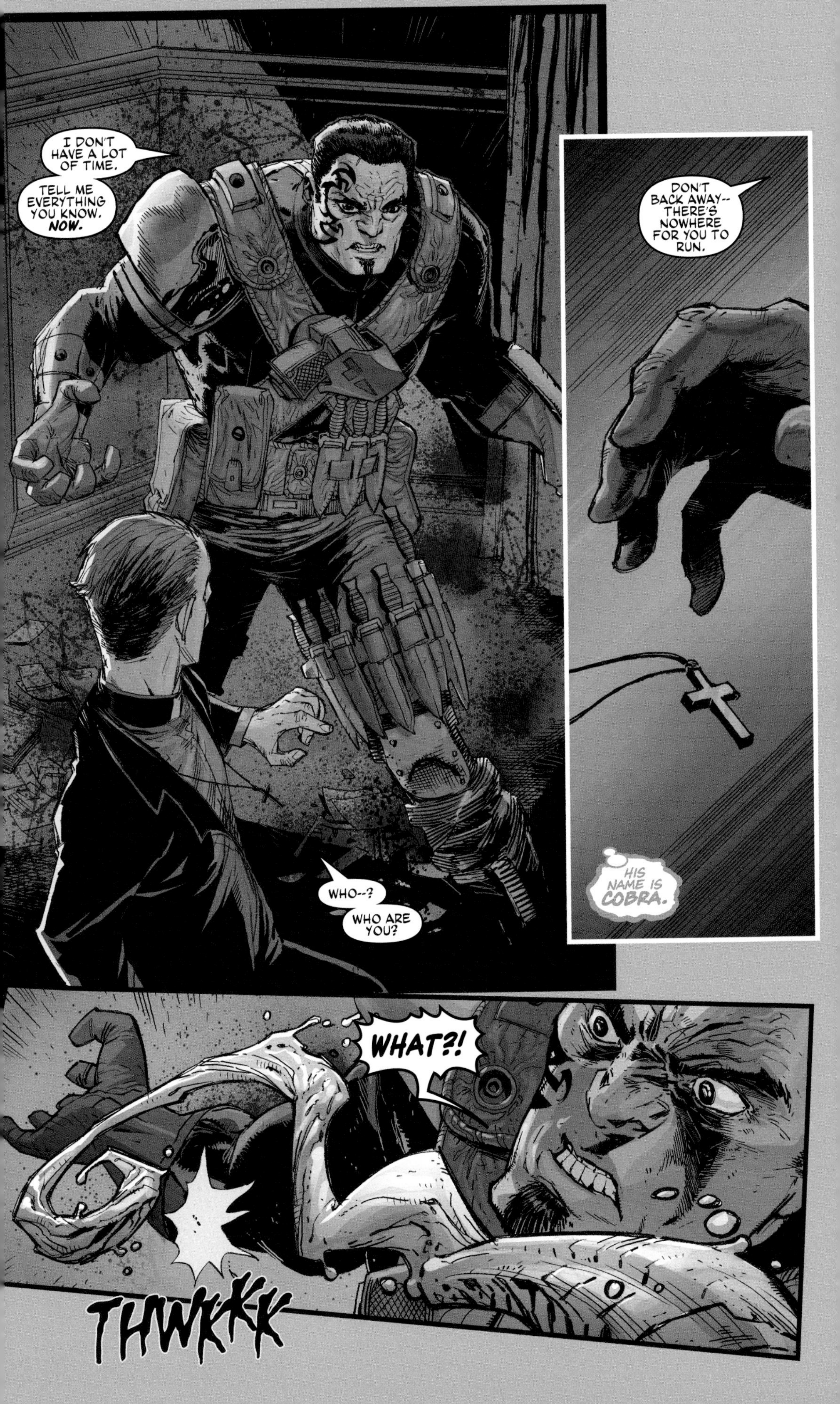
I DON'T HAVE A LOT OF TIME.
TELL ME EVERYTHING YOU KNOW. **NOW.**
WHO--?
WHO ARE YOU?
DON'T BACK AWAY-- THERE'S NOWHERE FOR YOU TO RUN.
HIS NAME IS COBRA.
WHAT?!
THWKKK

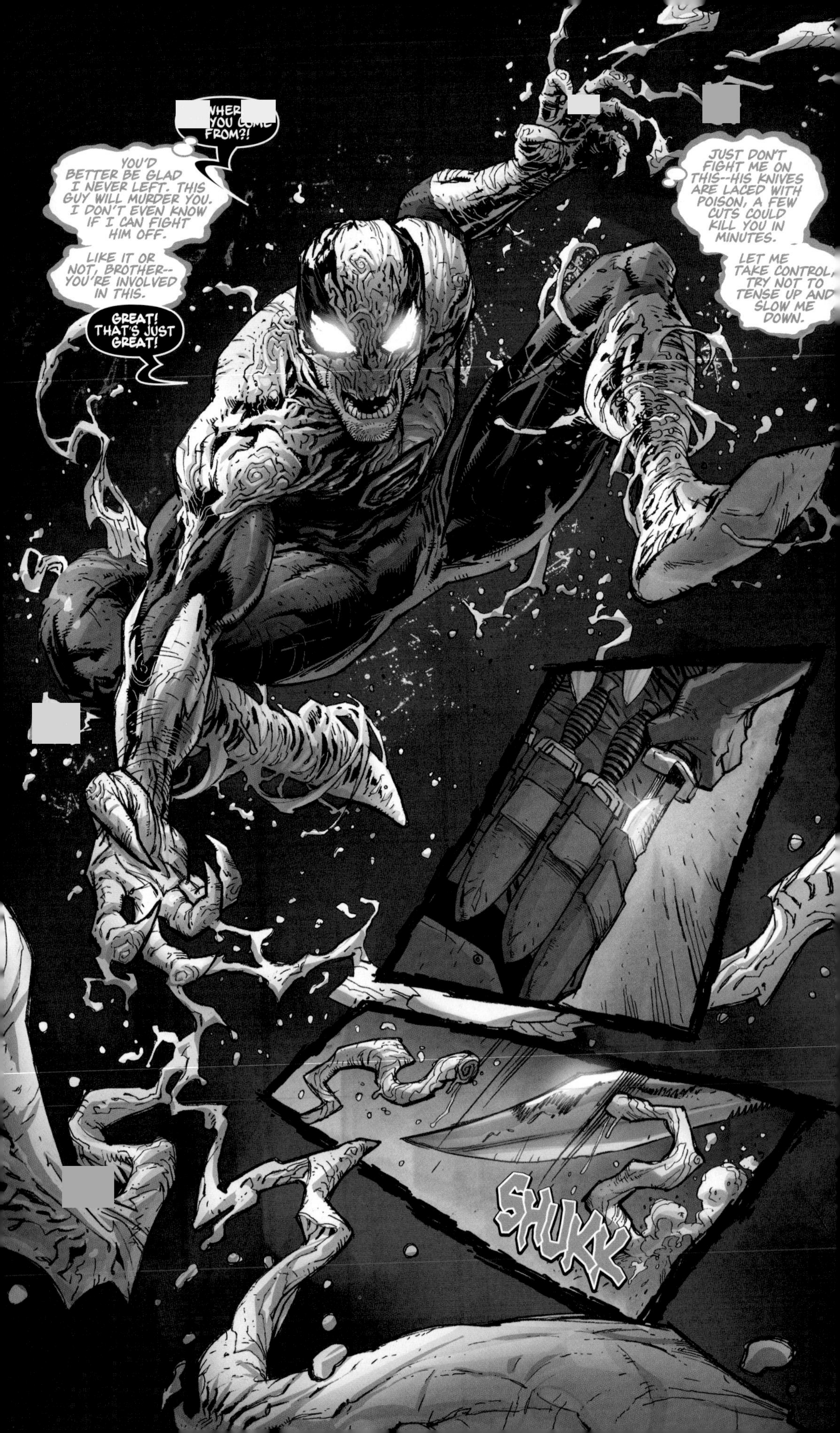

WHER YOU COME FROM?!
YOU'D BETTER BE GLAD I NEVER LEFT. THIS GUY WILL MURDER YOU. I DON'T EVEN KNOW IF I CAN FIGHT HIM OFF.
LIKE IT OR NOT, BROTHER--YOU'RE INVOLVED IN THIS.
GREAT! THAT'S JUST GREAT!
JUST DON'T FIGHT ME ON THIS--HIS KNIVES ARE LACED WITH POISON, A FEW CUTS COULD KILL YOU IN MINUTES.
LET ME TAKE CONTROL, TRY NOT TO TENSE UP AND SLOW ME DOWN.
SHUKK

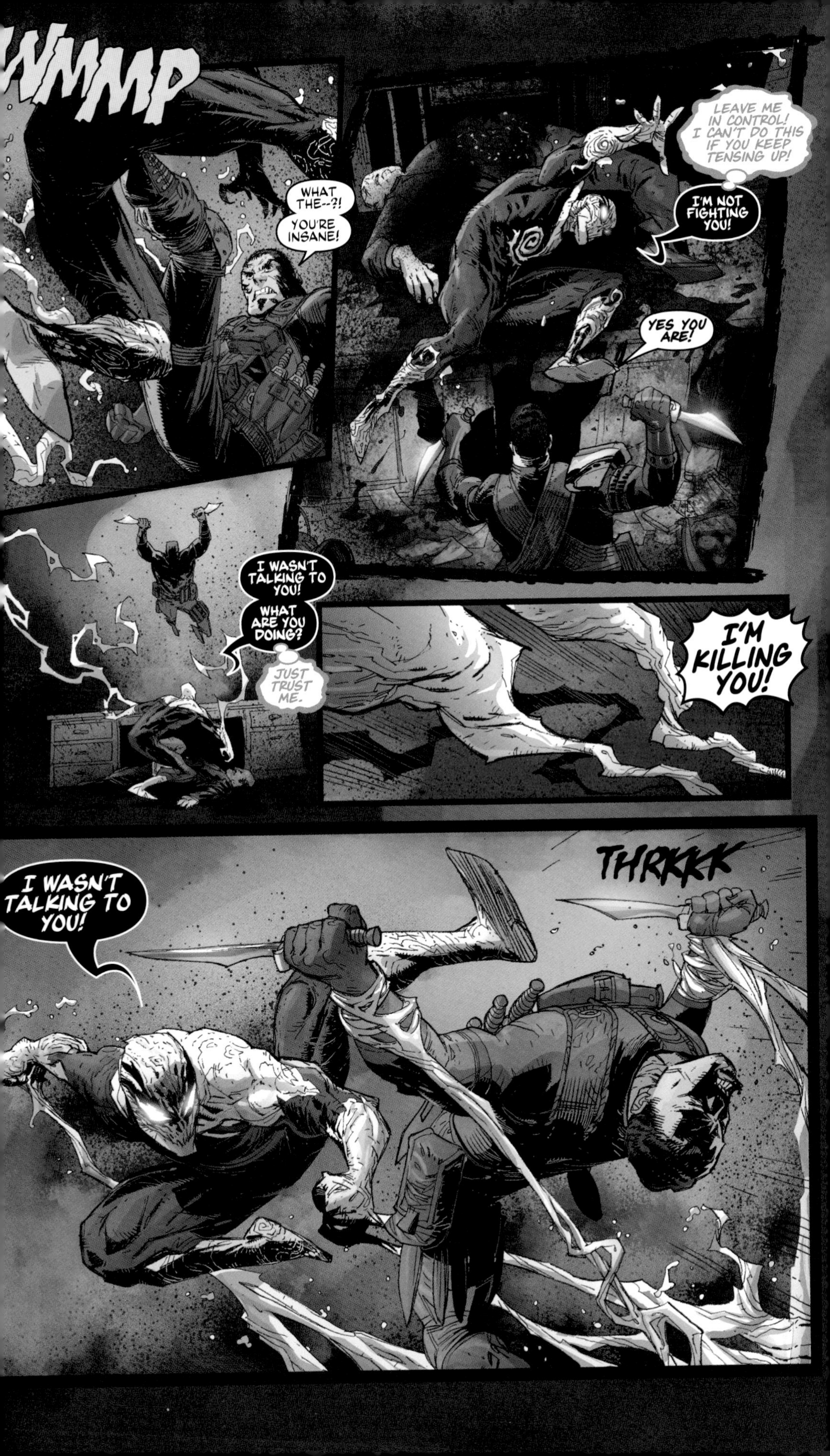

WMMP
WHAT THE--?!
YOU'RE INSANE!
LEAVE ME IN CONTROL! I CAN'T DO THIS IF YOU KEEP TENSING UP!
I'M NOT FIGHTING YOU!
YES YOU ARE!
I WASN'T TALKING TO YOU!
WHAT ARE YOU DOING?
JUST TRUST ME.
I'M KILLING YOU!
THRKKK
I WASN'T TALKING TO YOU!

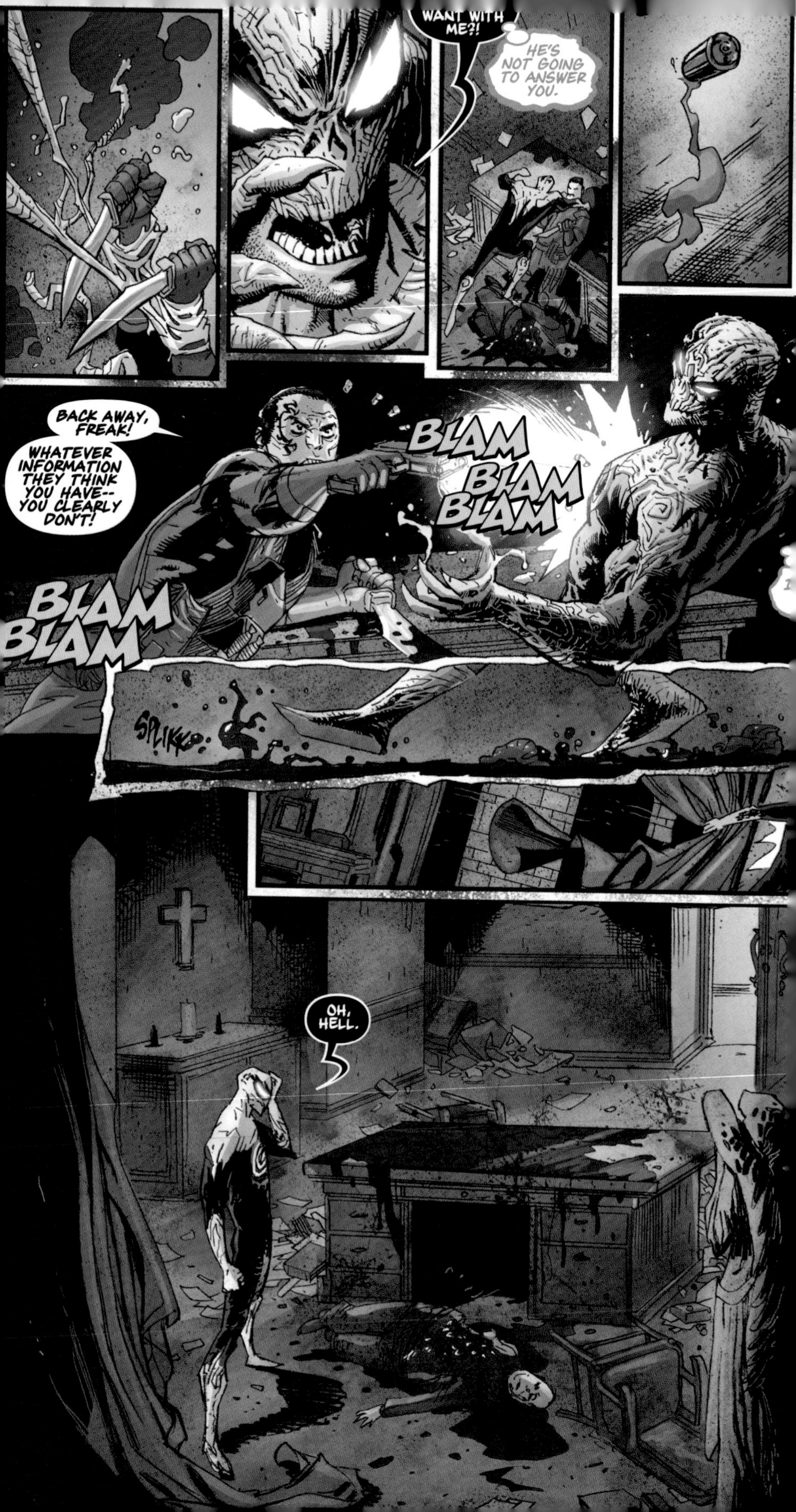
WANT WITH ME?!
HE'S NOT GOING TO ANSWER YOU.
BACK AWAY, FREAK!
WHATEVER INFORMATION THEY THINK YOU HAVE-- YOU CLEARLY DON'T!
BLAM BLAM BLAM
BLAM BLAM
SPLIKK
OH, HELL.

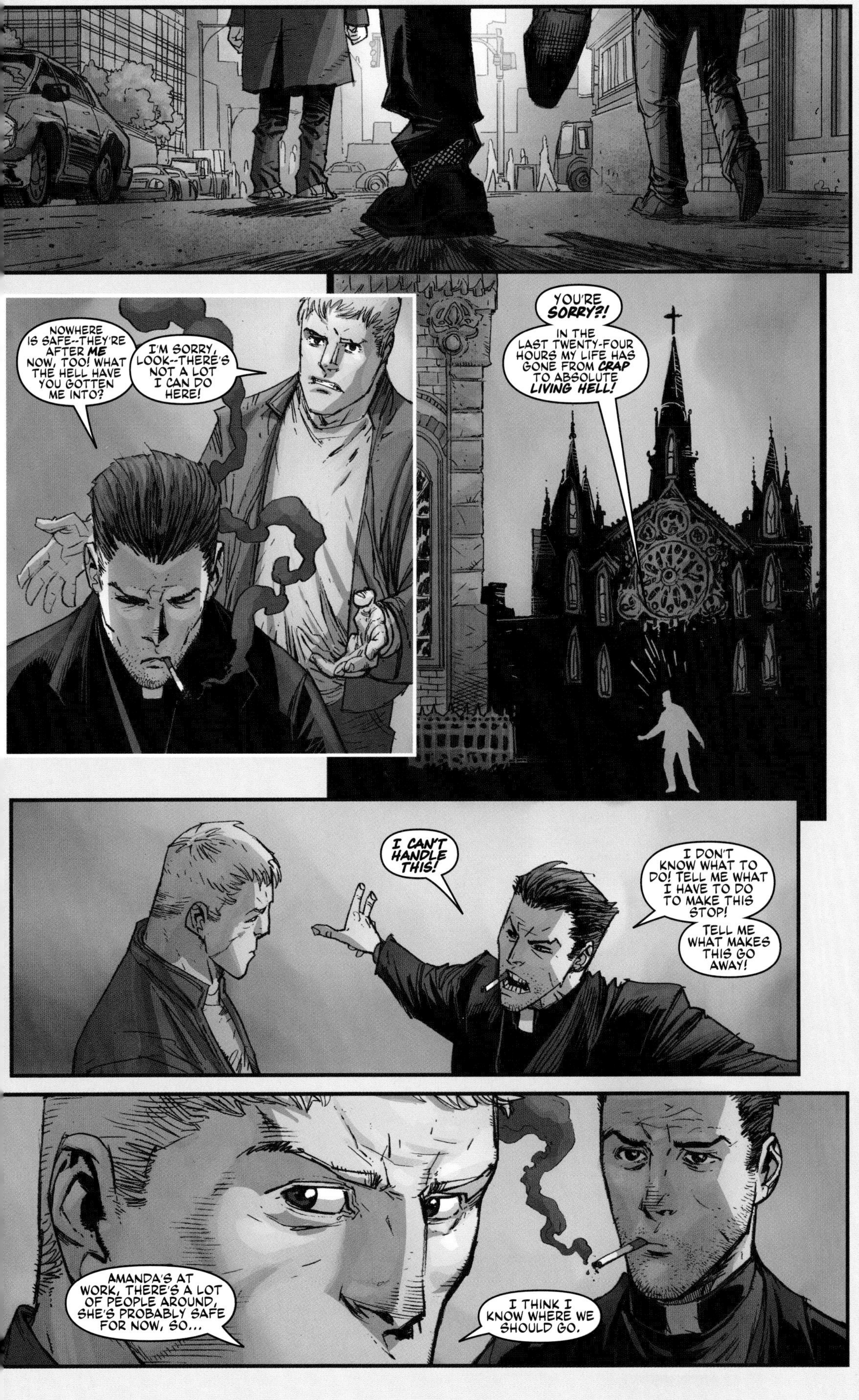
NOWHERE IS SAFE--THEY'RE AFTER ME NOW, TOO! WHAT THE HELL HAVE YOU GOTTEN ME INTO?
I'M SORRY, LOOK--THERE'S NOT A LOT I CAN DO HERE!
YOU'RE SORRY?!
IN THE LAST TWENTY-FOUR HOURS MY LIFE HAS GONE FROM CRAP TO ABSOLUTE LIVING HELL!
I CAN'T HANDLE THIS!
I DON'T KNOW WHAT TO DO! TELL ME WHAT I HAVE TO DO TO MAKE THIS STOP!
TELL ME WHAT MAKES THIS GO AWAY!
AMANDA'S AT WORK, THERE'S A LOT OF PEOPLE AROUND, SHE'S PROBABLY SAFE FOR NOW, SO...
I THINK I KNOW WHERE WE SHOULD GO.

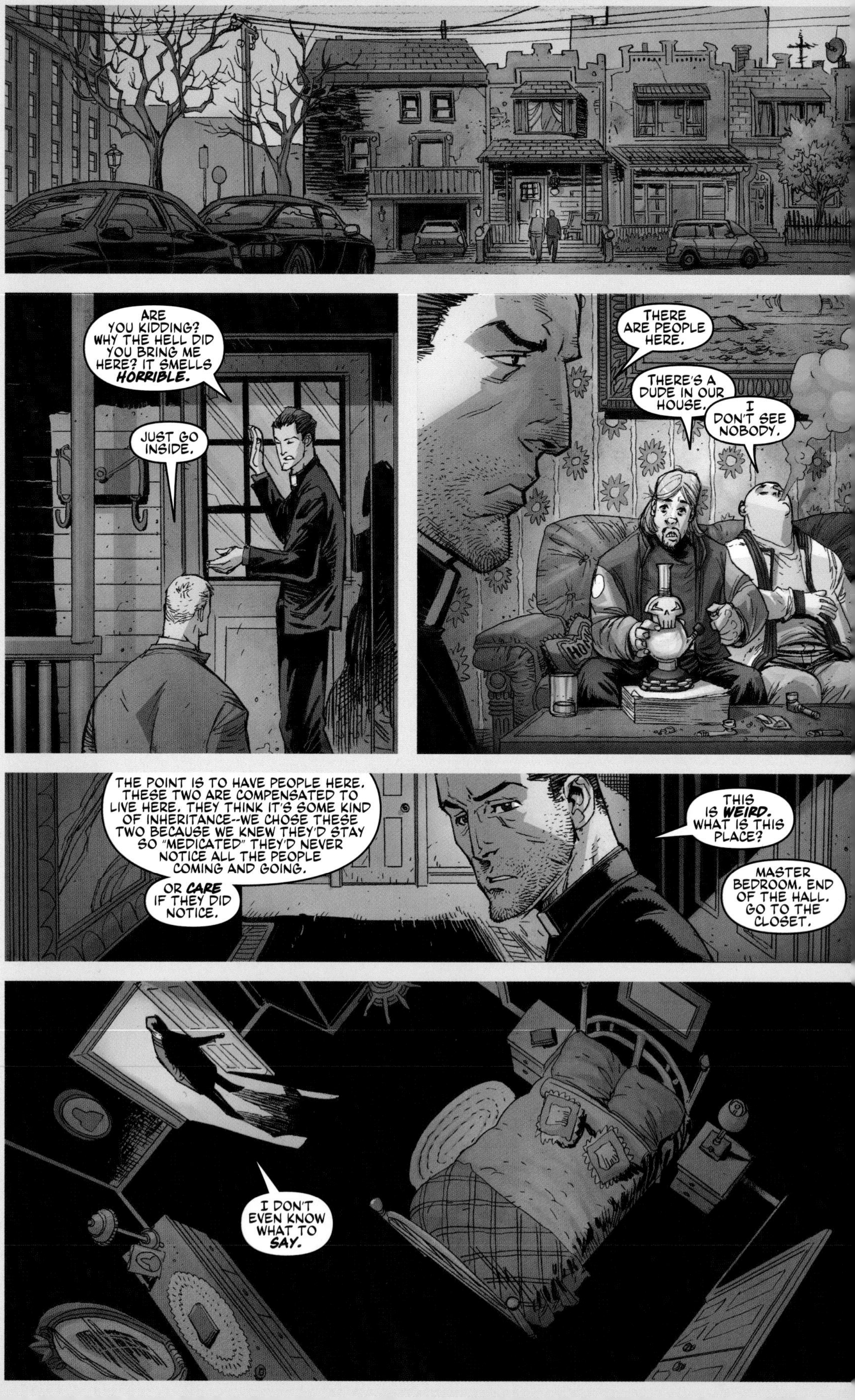
ARE YOU KIDDING? WHY THE HELL DID YOU BRING ME HERE? IT SMELLS HORRIBLE.
JUST GO INSIDE.
THERE ARE PEOPLE HERE.
THERE'S A DUDE IN OUR HOUSE.
I DON'T SEE NOBODY.
THE POINT IS TO HAVE PEOPLE HERE. THESE TWO ARE COMPENSATED TO LIVE HERE. THEY THINK IT'S SOME KIND OF INHERITANCE--WE CHOSE THESE TWO BECAUSE WE KNEW THEY'D STAY SO "MEDICATED" THEY'D NEVER NOTICE ALL THE PEOPLE COMING AND GOING.
OR CARE IF THEY DID NOTICE.
THIS IS WEIRD. WHAT IS THIS PLACE?
MASTER BEDROOM, END OF THE HALL. GO TO THE CLOSET.
I DON'T EVEN KNOW WHAT TO SAY.

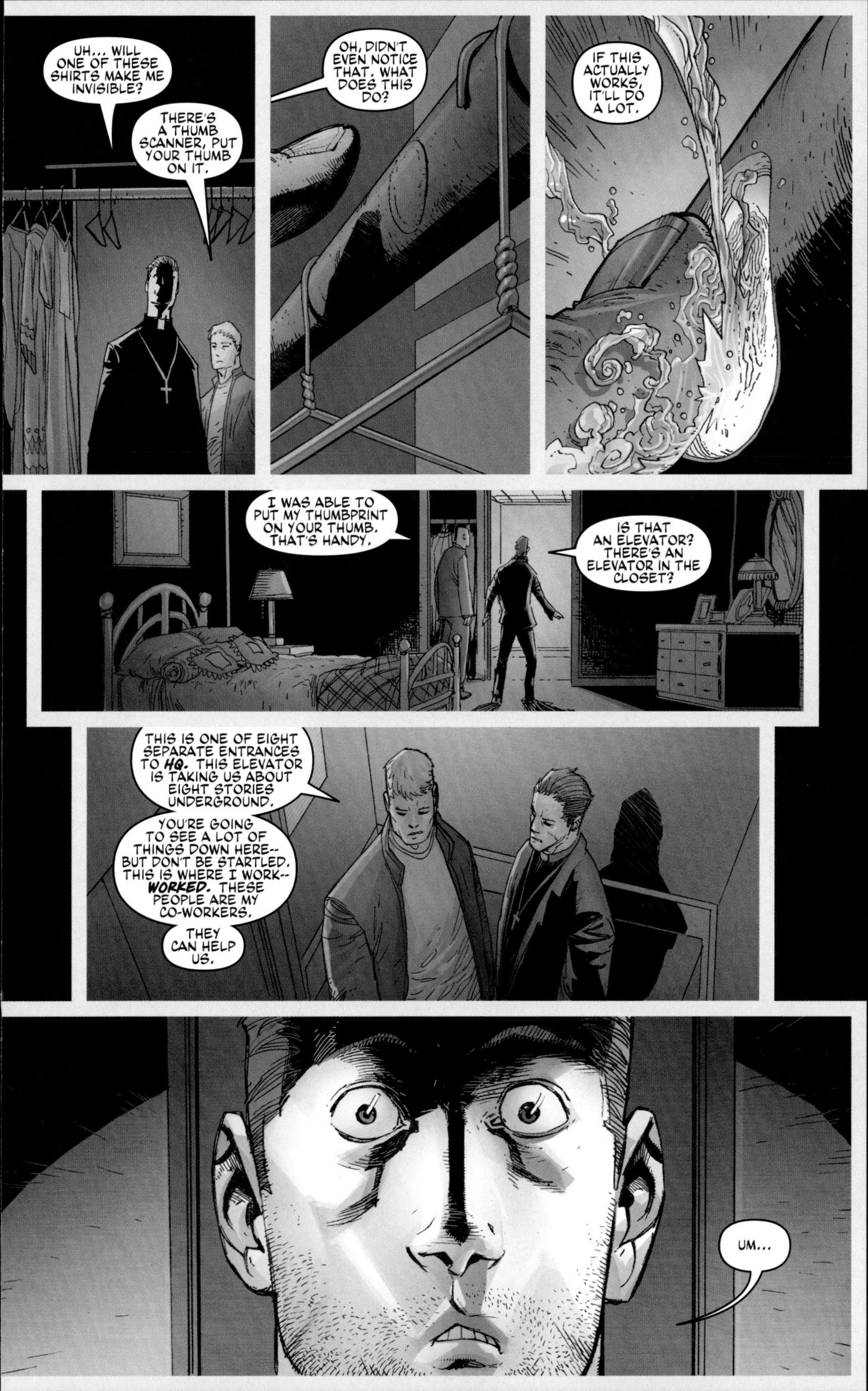
UH... WILL ONE OF THESE SHIRTS MAKE ME INVISIBLE?
THERE'S A THUMB SCANNER, PUT YOUR THUMB ON IT.
OH, DIDN'T EVEN NOTICE THAT. WHAT DOES THIS DO?
IF THIS ACTUALLY WORKS, IT'LL DO A LOT.
I WAS ABLE TO PUT MY THUMBPRINT ON YOUR THUMB. THAT'S HANDY.
IS THAT AN ELEVATOR? THERE'S AN ELEVATOR IN THE CLOSET?
THIS IS ONE OF EIGHT SEPARATE ENTRANCES TO HQ. THIS ELEVATOR IS TAKING US ABOUT EIGHT STORIES UNDERGROUND.
YOU'RE GOING TO SEE A LOT OF THINGS DOWN HERE-- BUT DON'T BE STARTLED. THIS IS WHERE I WORK-- WORKED. THESE PEOPLE ARE MY CO-WORKERS.
THEY CAN HELP US.
UM...

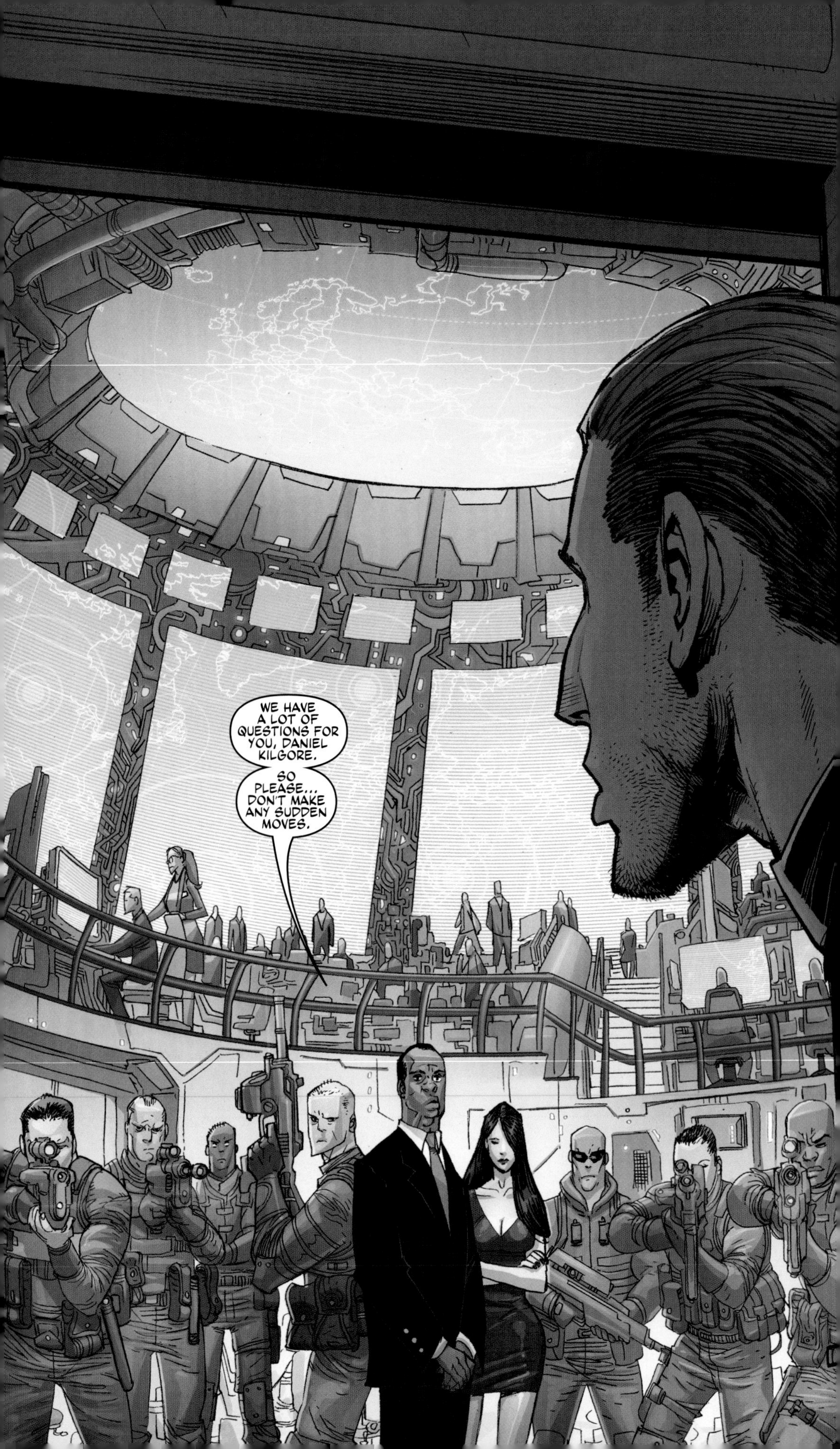
WE HAVE A LOT OF QUESTIONS FOR YOU, DANIEL KILGORE.
SO PLEASE... DON'T MAKE ANY SUDDEN MOVES.

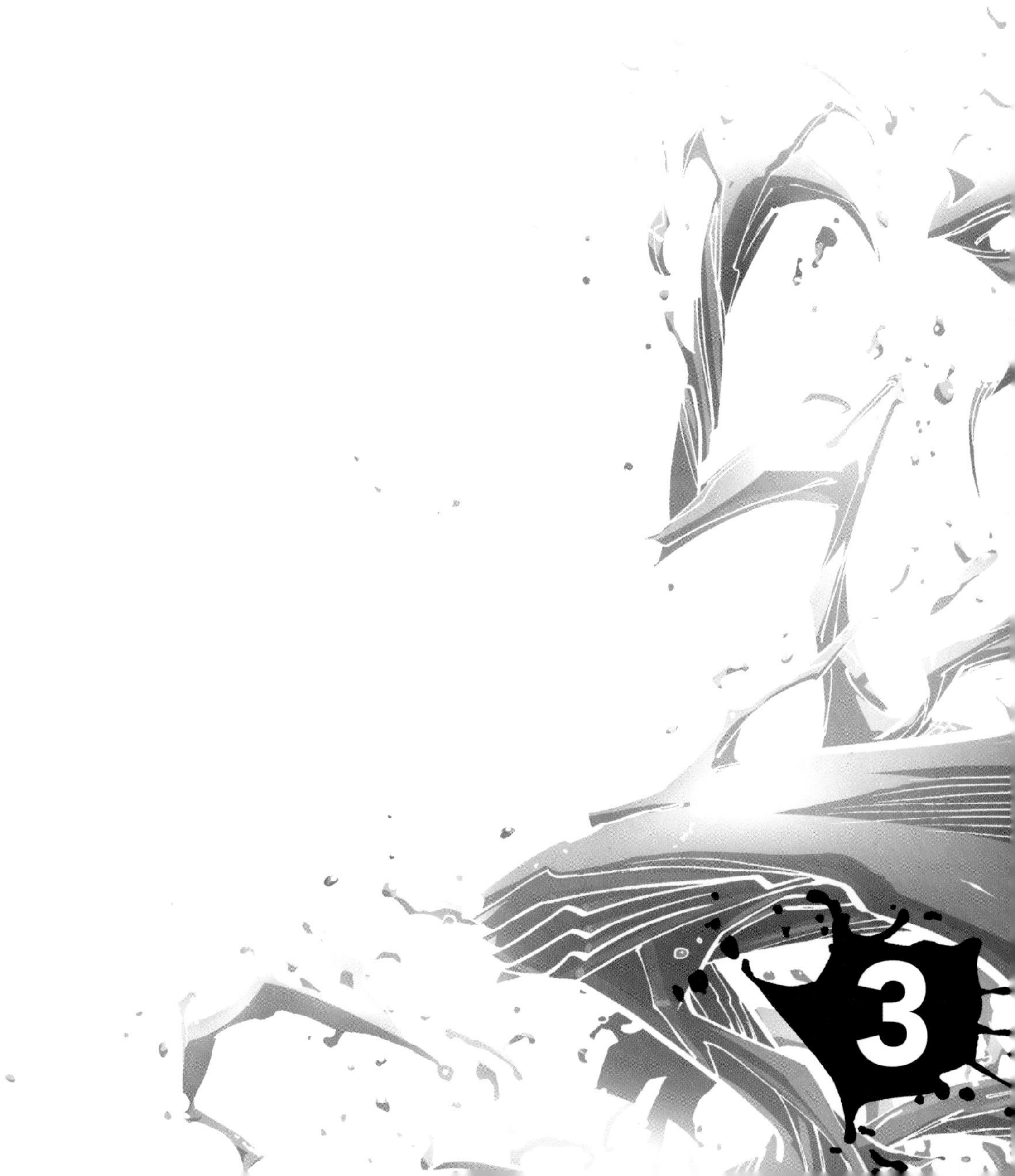
3

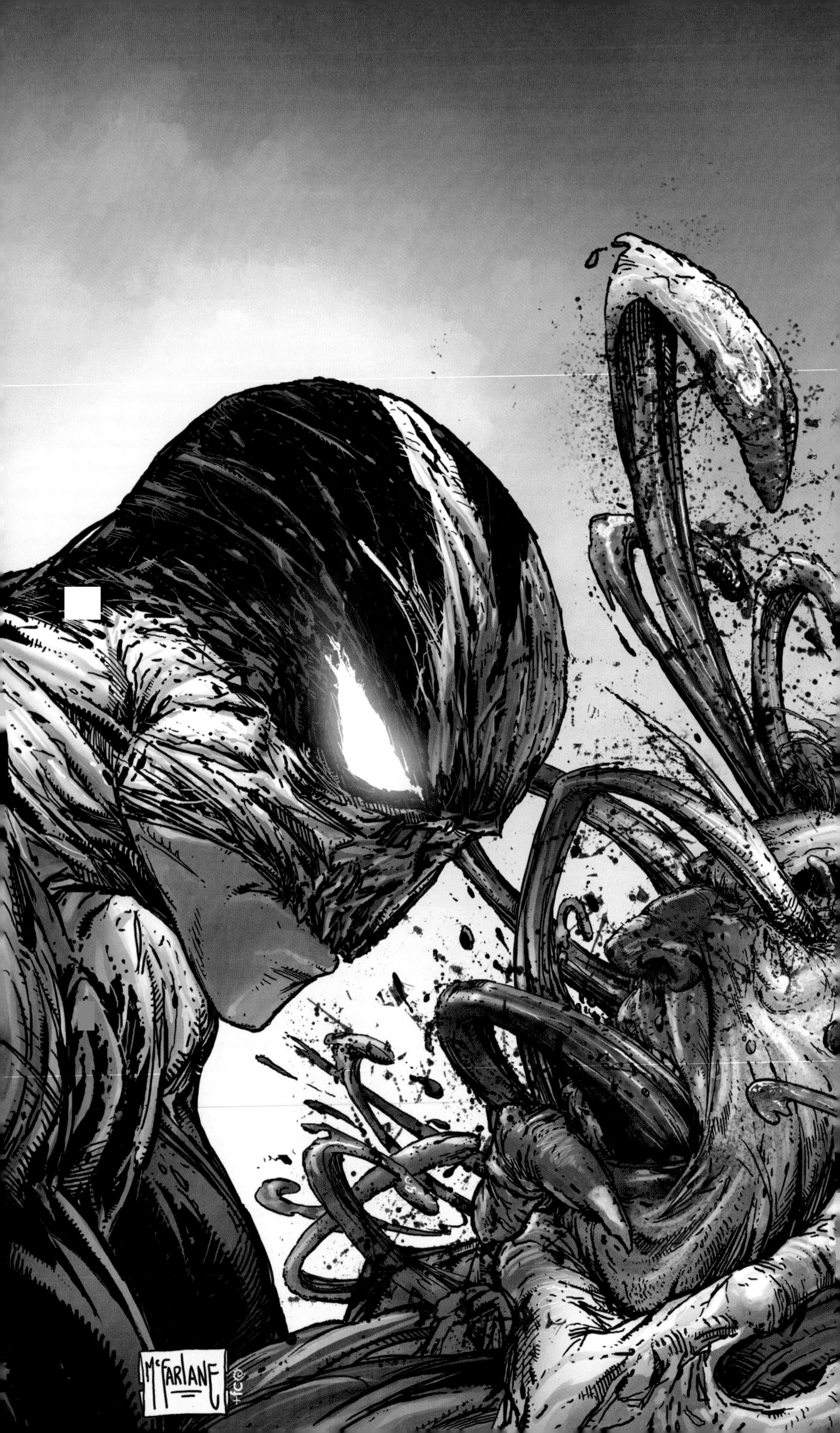
McFARLANE

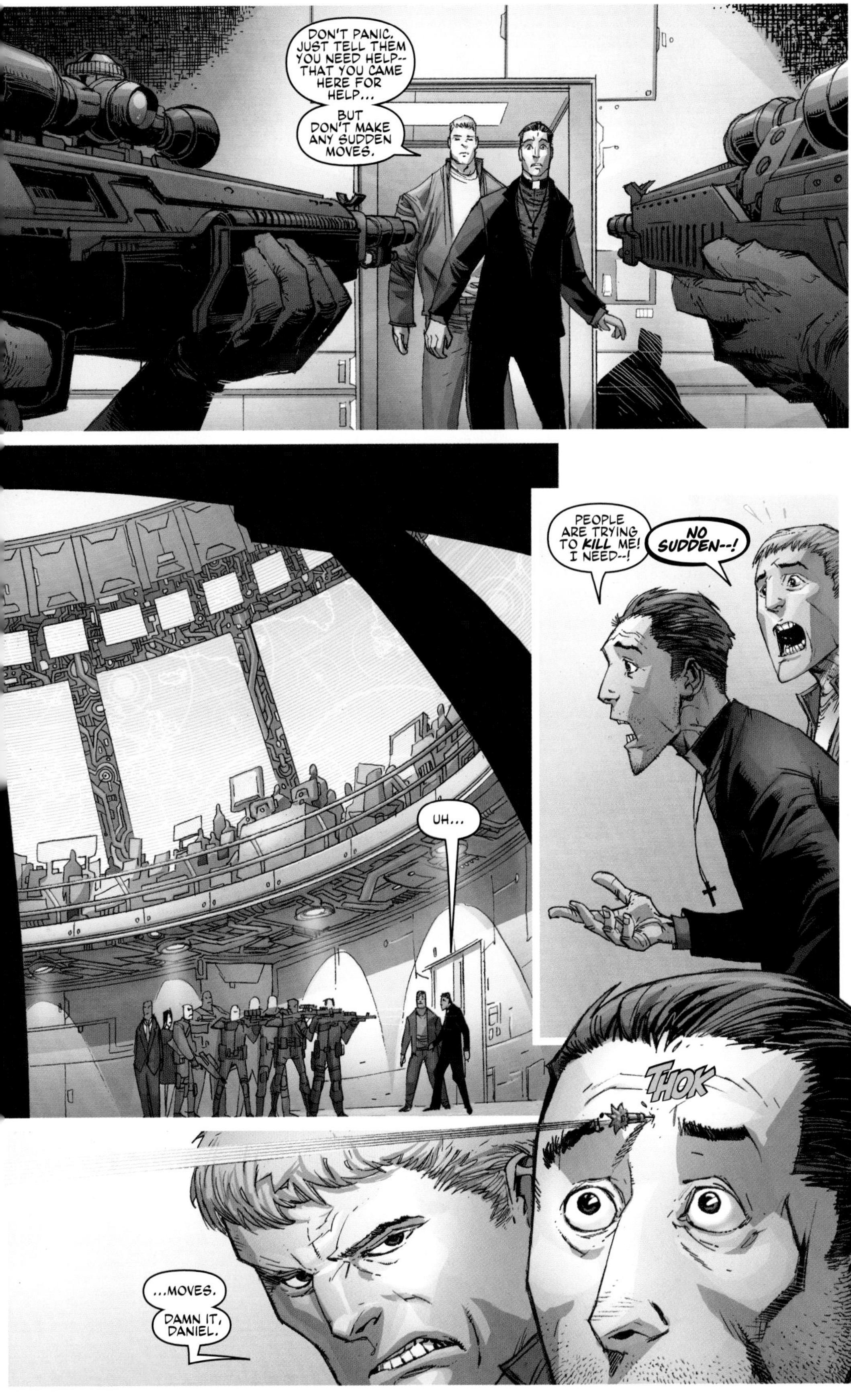
DON'T PANIC. JUST TELL THEM YOU NEED HELP-- THAT YOU CAME HERE FOR HELP...
BUT DON'T MAKE ANY SUDDEN MOVES.
UH...
PEOPLE ARE TRYING TO KILL ME! I NEED--!
NO SUDDEN--!
THOK
...MOVES.
DAMN IT, DANIEL.

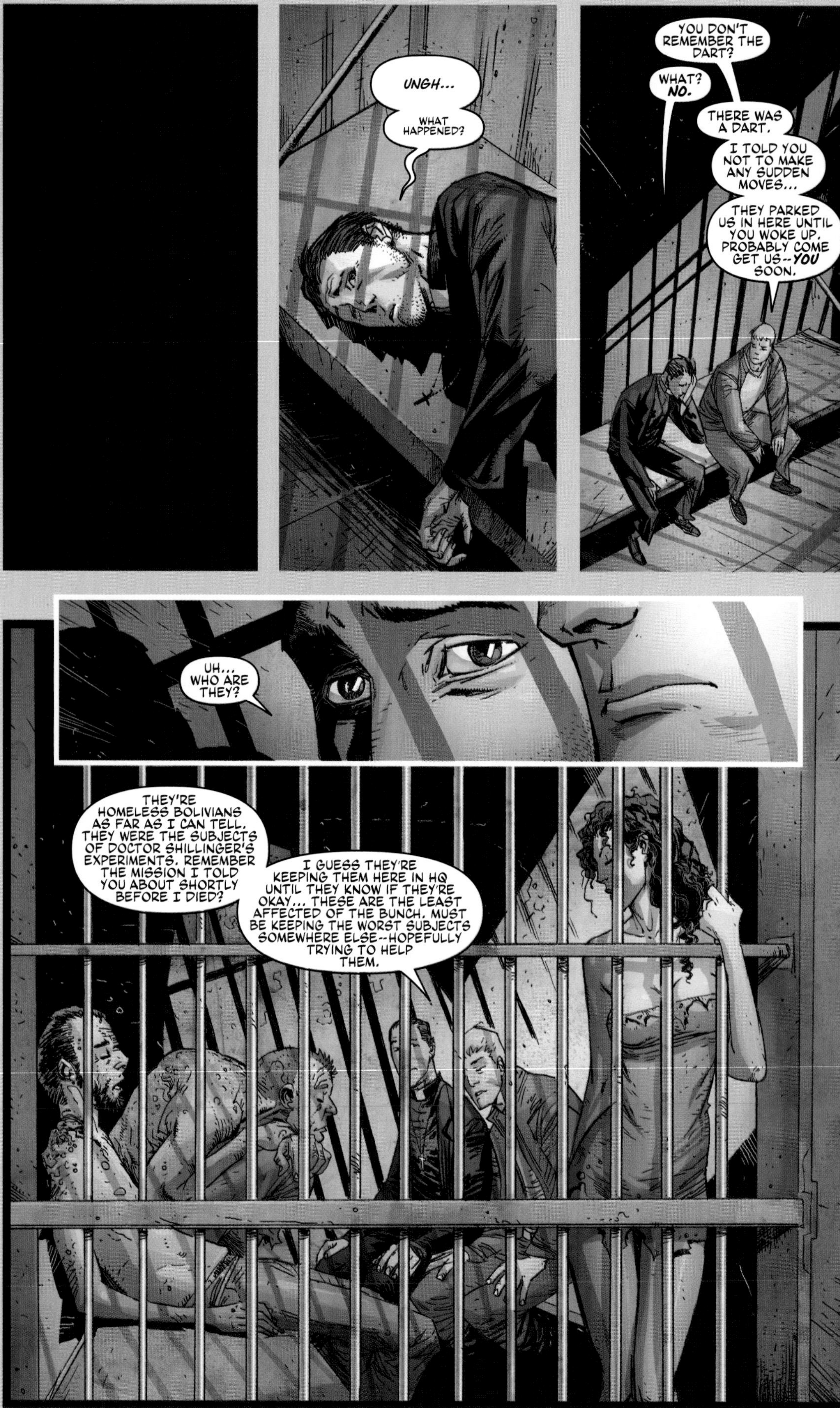
UNGH...
WHAT HAPPENED?
YOU DON'T REMEMBER THE DART?
WHAT? NO.
THERE WAS A DART.
I TOLD YOU NOT TO MAKE ANY SUDDEN MOVES...
THEY PARKED US IN HERE UNTIL YOU WOKE UP. PROBABLY COME GET US--YOU SOON.
UH... WHO ARE THEY?
THEY'RE HOMELESS BOLIVIANS AS FAR AS I CAN TELL. THEY WERE THE SUBJECTS OF DOCTOR SHILLINGER'S EXPERIMENTS. REMEMBER THE MISSION I TOLD YOU ABOUT SHORTLY BEFORE I DIED?
I GUESS THEY'RE KEEPING THEM HERE IN HQ UNTIL THEY KNOW IF THEY'RE OKAY... THESE ARE THE LEAST AFFECTED OF THE BUNCH. MUST BE KEEPING THE WORST SUBJECTS SOMEWHERE ELSE--HOPEFULLY TRYING TO HELP THEM.

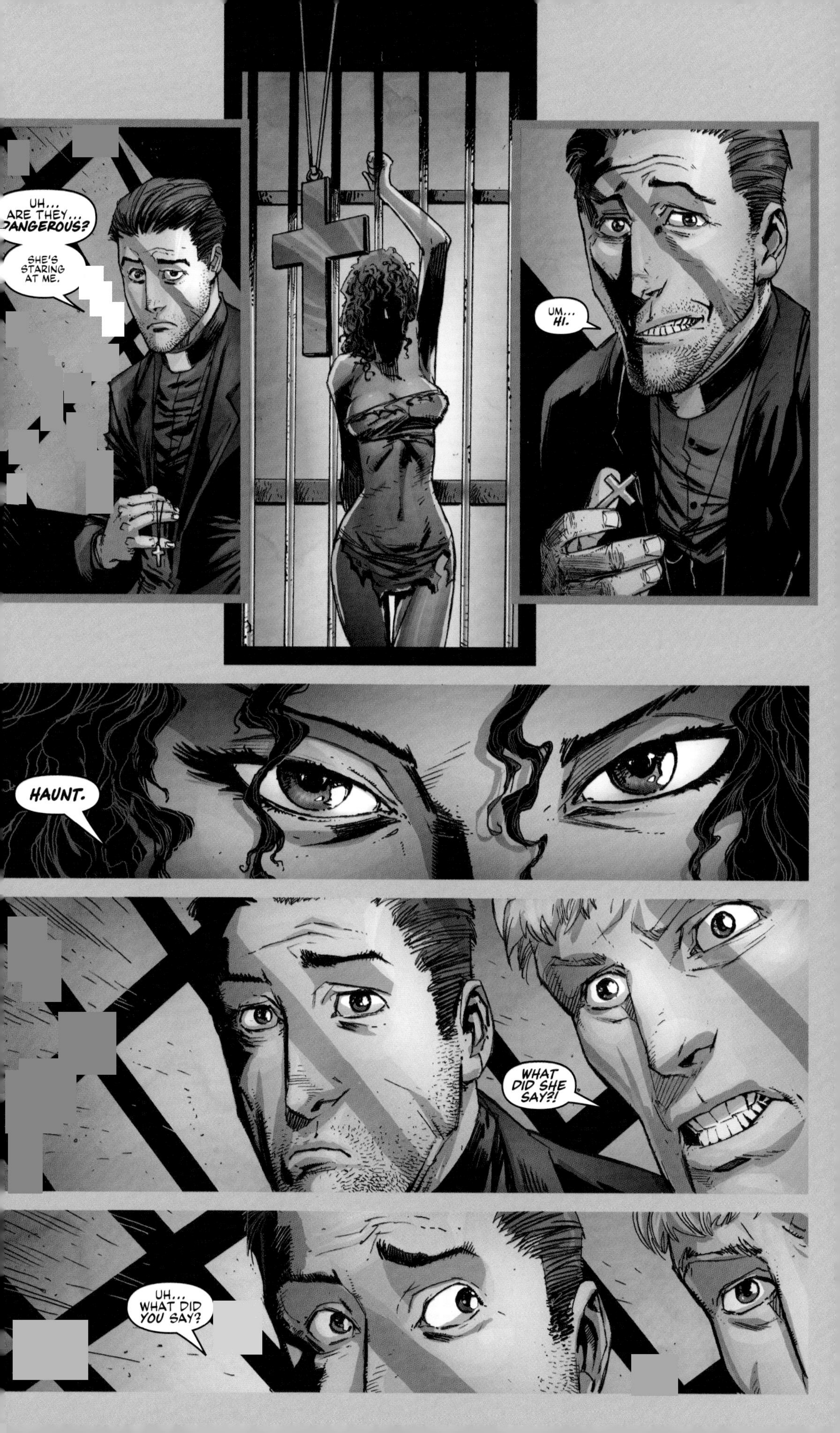
UH... ARE THEY... DANGEROUS?
SHE'S STARING AT ME.
UM... HI.
HAUNT.
WHAT DID SHE SAY?!
UH... WHAT DID YOU SAY?

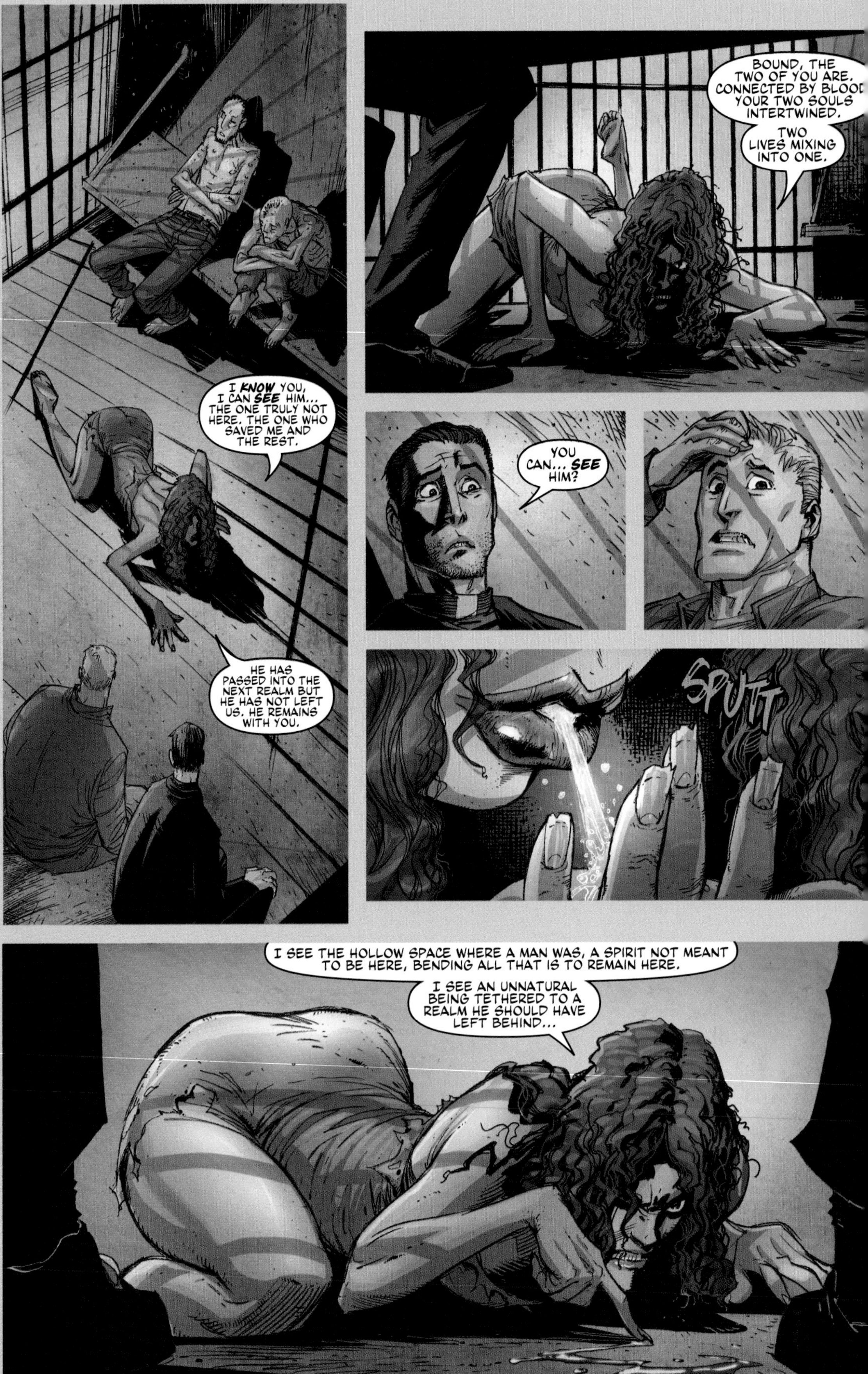

I KNOW YOU, I CAN SEE HIM... THE ONE TRULY NOT HERE. THE ONE WHO SAVED ME AND THE REST.
HE HAS PASSED INTO THE NEXT REALM BUT HE HAS NOT LEFT US. HE REMAINS WITH YOU.
BOUND, THE TWO OF YOU ARE. CONNECTED BY BLOOD YOUR TWO SOULS INTERTWINED.
TWO LIVES MIXING INTO ONE.
YOU CAN... SEE HIM?
SPUTT
I SEE THE HOLLOW SPACE WHERE A MAN WAS, A SPIRIT NOT MEANT TO BE HERE, BENDING ALL THAT IS TO REMAIN HERE.
I SEE AN UNNATURAL BEING TETHERED TO A REALM HE SHOULD HAVE LEFT BEHIND...

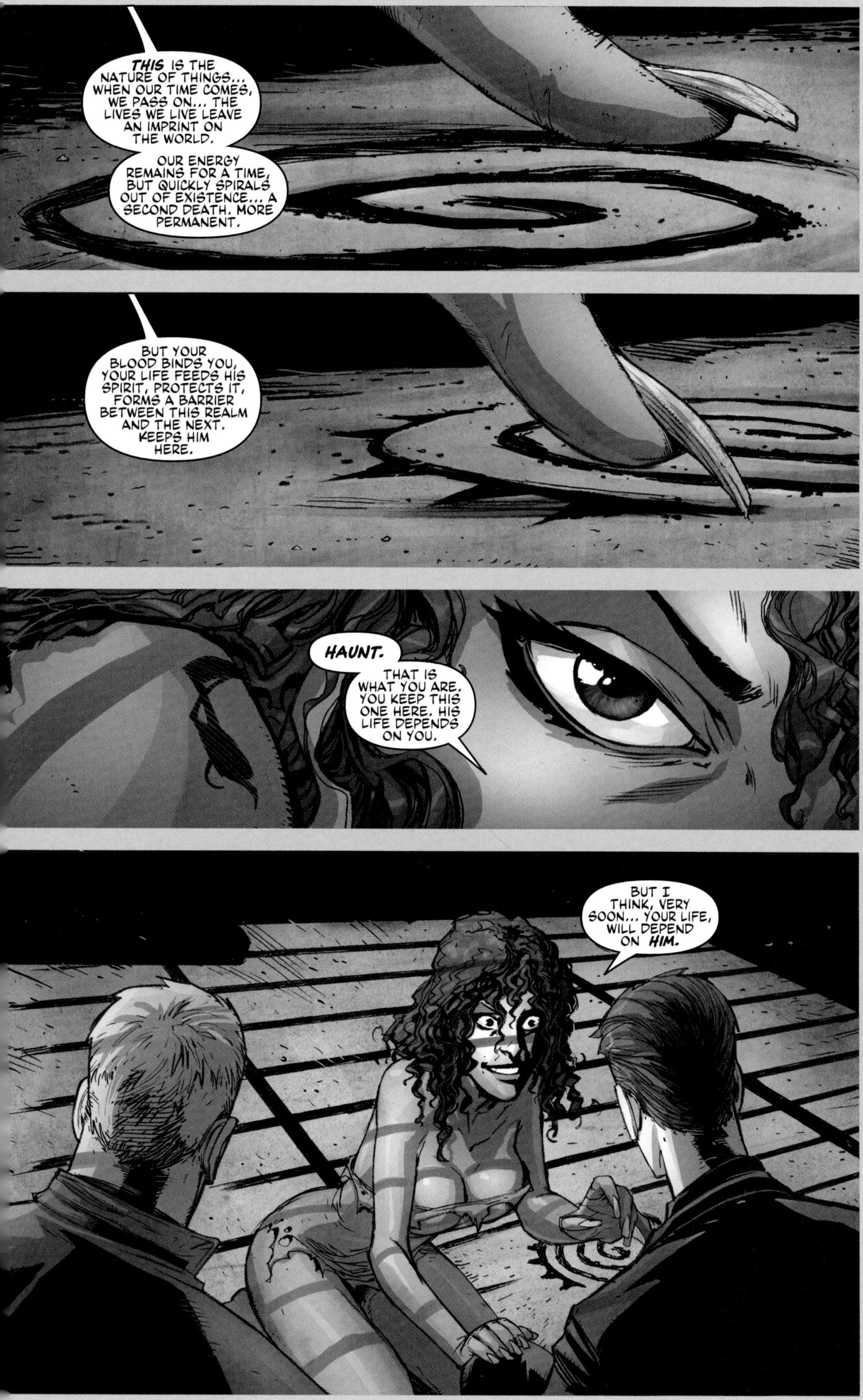
THIS IS THE NATURE OF THINGS... WHEN OUR TIME COMES, WE PASS ON... THE LIVES WE LIVE LEAVE AN IMPRINT ON THE WORLD.
OUR ENERGY REMAINS FOR A TIME, BUT QUICKLY SPIRALS OUT OF EXISTENCE... A SECOND DEATH. MORE PERMANENT.
BUT YOUR BLOOD BINDS YOU, YOUR LIFE FEEDS HIS SPIRIT, PROTECTS IT, FORMS A BARRIER BETWEEN THIS REALM AND THE NEXT. KEEPS HIM HERE.
HAUNT.
THAT IS WHAT YOU ARE. YOU KEEP THIS ONE HERE. HIS LIFE DEPENDS ON YOU.
BUT I THINK, VERY SOON... YOUR LIFE, WILL DEPEND ON HIM.

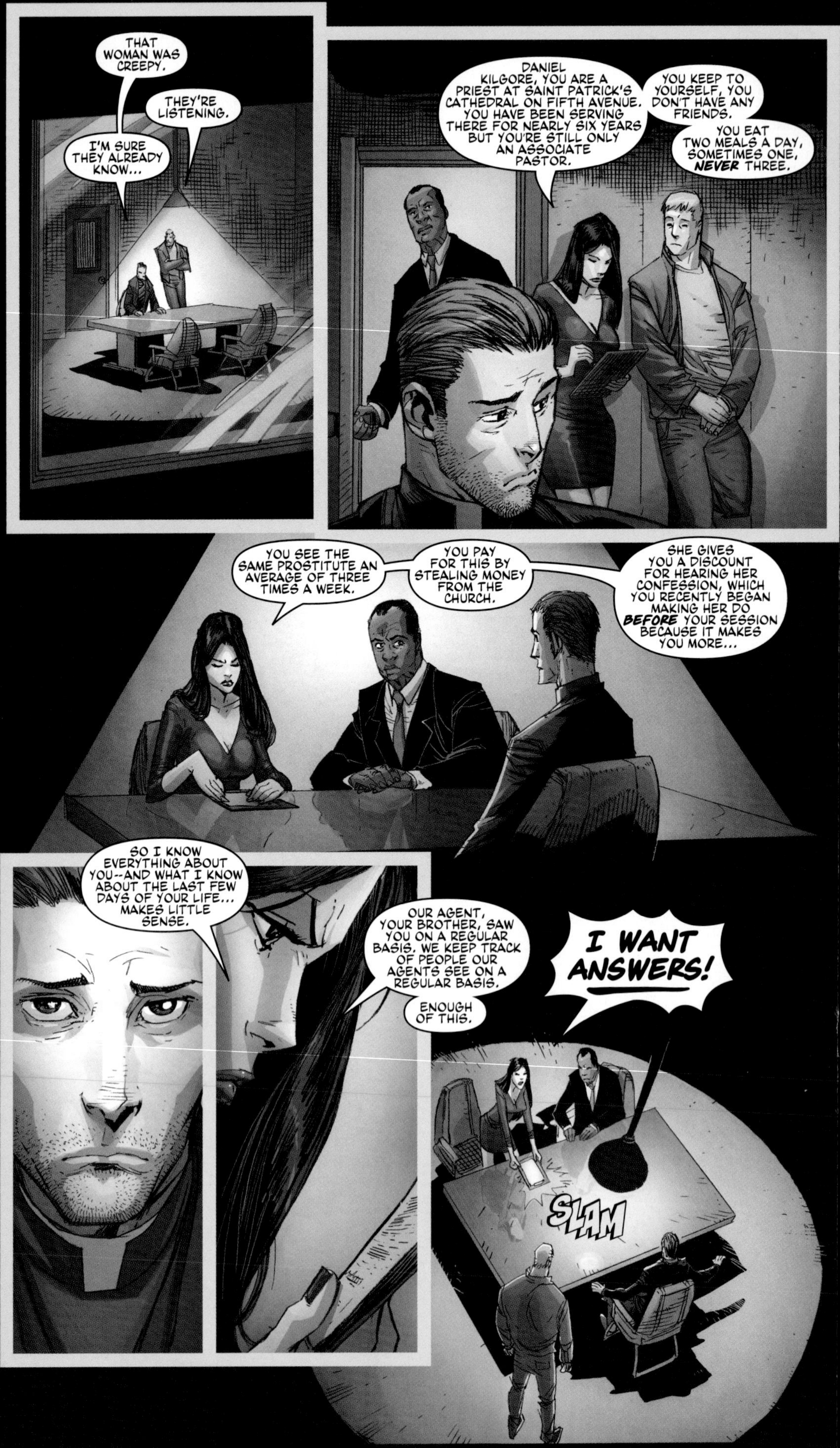

THAT WOMAN WAS CREEPY.
THEY'RE LISTENING.
I'M SURE THEY ALREADY KNOW...
DANIEL KILGORE, YOU ARE A PRIEST AT SAINT PATRICK'S CATHEDRAL ON FIFTH AVENUE. YOU HAVE BEEN SERVING THERE FOR NEARLY SIX YEARS BUT YOU'RE STILL ONLY AN ASSOCIATE PASTOR.
YOU KEEP TO YOURSELF, YOU DON'T HAVE ANY FRIENDS.
YOU EAT TWO MEALS A DAY, SOMETIMES ONE, **NEVER** THREE.
YOU SEE THE SAME PROSTITUTE AN AVERAGE OF THREE TIMES A WEEK.
YOU PAY FOR THIS BY STEALING MONEY FROM THE CHURCH.
SHE GIVES YOU A DISCOUNT FOR HEARING HER CONFESSION, WHICH YOU RECENTLY BEGAN MAKING HER DO **BEFORE** YOUR SESSION BECAUSE IT MAKES YOU MORE...
SO I KNOW EVERYTHING ABOUT YOU--AND WHAT I KNOW ABOUT THE LAST FEW DAYS OF YOUR LIFE... MAKES LITTLE SENSE.
OUR AGENT, YOUR BROTHER, SAW YOU ON A REGULAR BASIS. WE KEEP TRACK OF PEOPLE OUR AGENTS SEE ON A REGULAR BASIS.
ENOUGH OF THIS.
I WANT ANSWERS!
SLAM

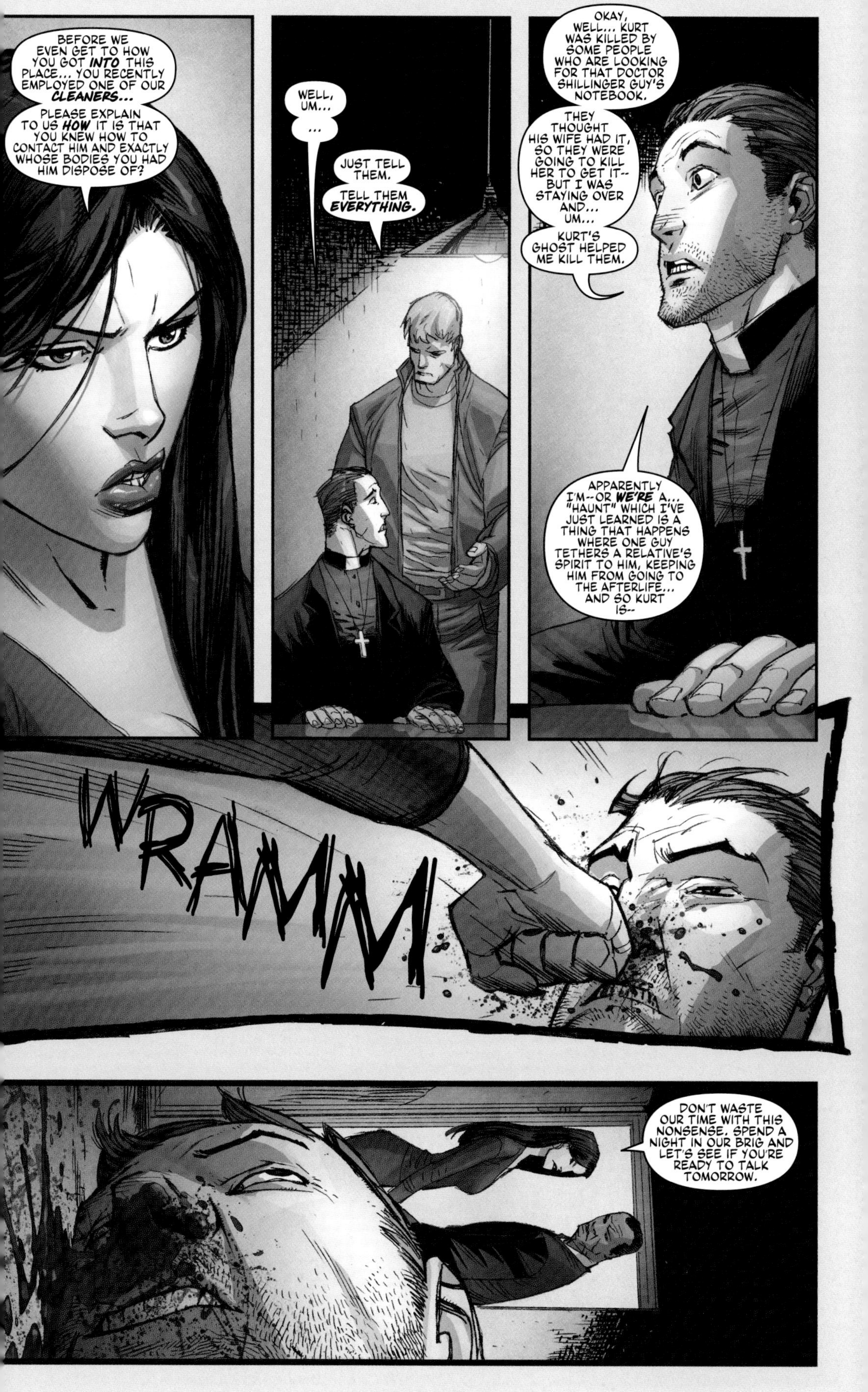
BEFORE WE EVEN GET TO HOW YOU GOT INTO THIS PLACE... YOU RECENTLY EMPLOYED ONE OF OUR CLEANERS...
PLEASE EXPLAIN TO US HOW IT IS THAT YOU KNEW HOW TO CONTACT HIM AND EXACTLY WHOSE BODIES YOU HAD HIM DISPOSE OF?
WELL, UM...
...
JUST TELL THEM.
TELL THEM EVERYTHING.
OKAY, WELL... KURT WAS KILLED BY SOME PEOPLE WHO ARE LOOKING FOR THAT DOCTOR SHILLINGER GUY'S NOTEBOOK.
THEY THOUGHT HIS WIFE HAD IT, SO THEY WERE GOING TO KILL HER TO GET IT-- BUT I WAS STAYING OVER AND... UM...
KURT'S GHOST HELPED ME KILL THEM.
APPARENTLY I'M--OR WE'RE A... "HAUNT" WHICH I'VE JUST LEARNED IS A THING THAT HAPPENS WHERE ONE GUY TETHERS A RELATIVE'S SPIRIT TO HIM, KEEPING HIM FROM GOING TO THE AFTERLIFE... AND SO KURT IS--
WRAMM
DON'T WASTE OUR TIME WITH THIS NONSENSE. SPEND A NIGHT IN OUR BRIG AND LET'S SEE IF YOU'RE READY TO TALK TOMORROW.

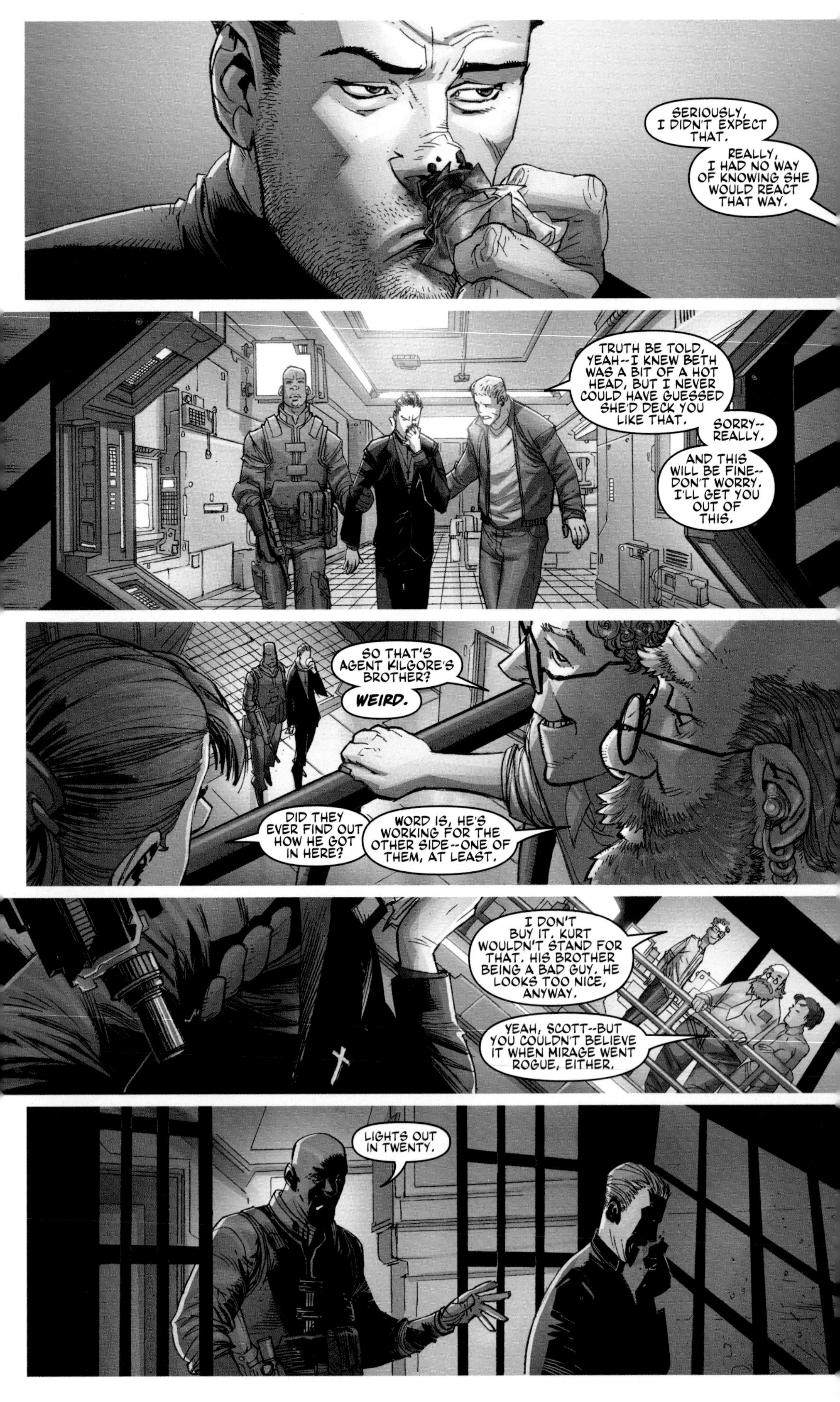
SERIOUSLY, I DIDN'T EXPECT THAT.
REALLY, I HAD NO WAY OF KNOWING SHE WOULD REACT THAT WAY.
TRUTH BE TOLD, YEAH--I KNEW BETH WAS A BIT OF A HOT HEAD, BUT I NEVER COULD HAVE GUESSED SHE'D DECK YOU LIKE THAT.
SORRY--REALLY.
AND THIS WILL BE FINE--DON'T WORRY. I'LL GET YOU OUT OF THIS.
SO THAT'S AGENT KILGORE'S BROTHER?
WEIRD.
DID THEY EVER FIND OUT HOW HE GOT IN HERE?
WORD IS, HE'S WORKING FOR THE OTHER SIDE--ONE OF THEM, AT LEAST.
I DON'T BUY IT. KURT WOULDN'T STAND FOR THAT. HIS BROTHER BEING A BAD GUY. HE LOOKS TOO NICE, ANYWAY.
YEAH, SCOTT--BUT YOU COULDN'T BELIEVE IT WHEN MIRAGE WENT ROGUE, EITHER.
LIGHTS OUT IN TWENTY.

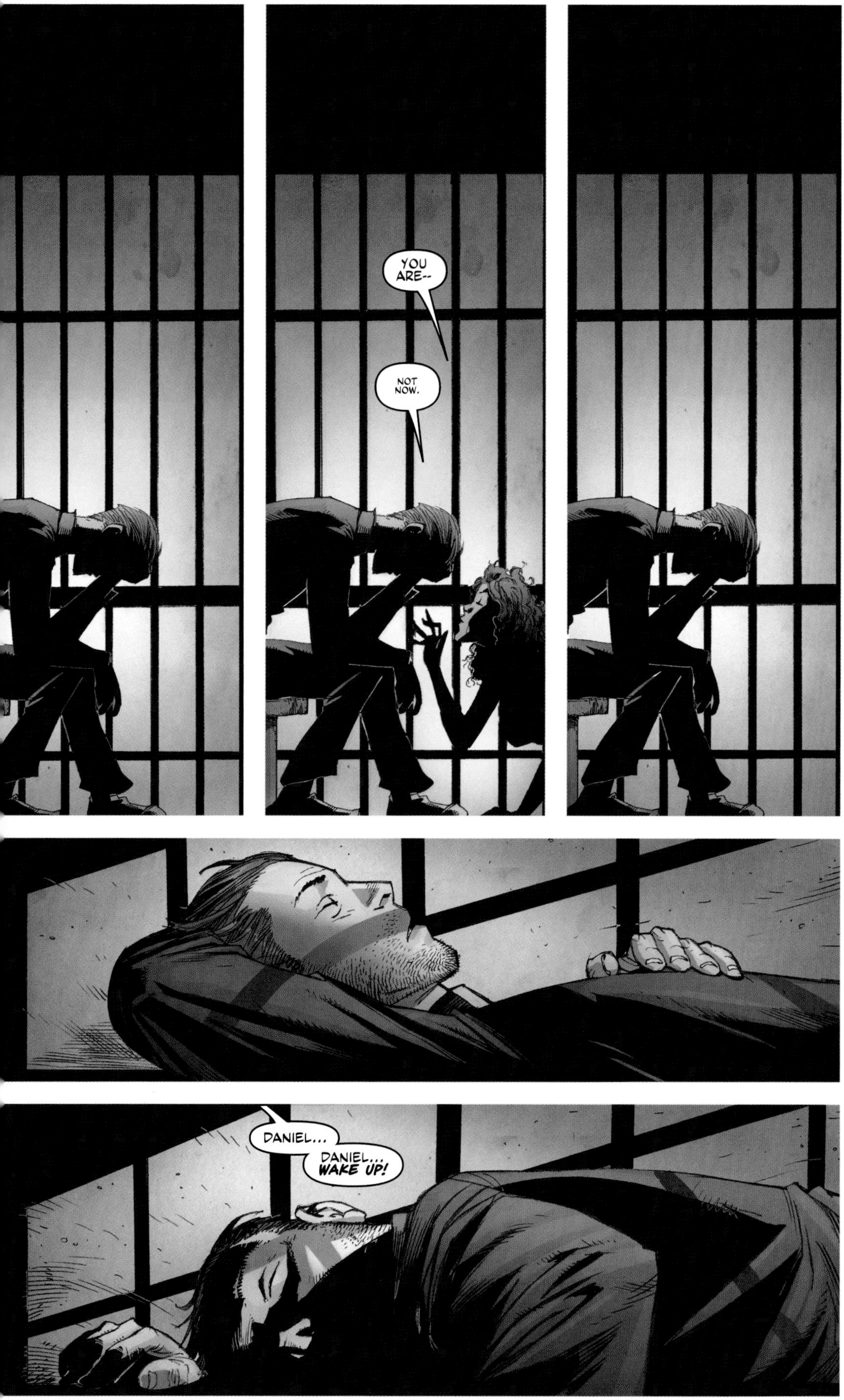
YOU ARE--
NOT NOW.
DANIEL...
DANIEL... WAKE UP!

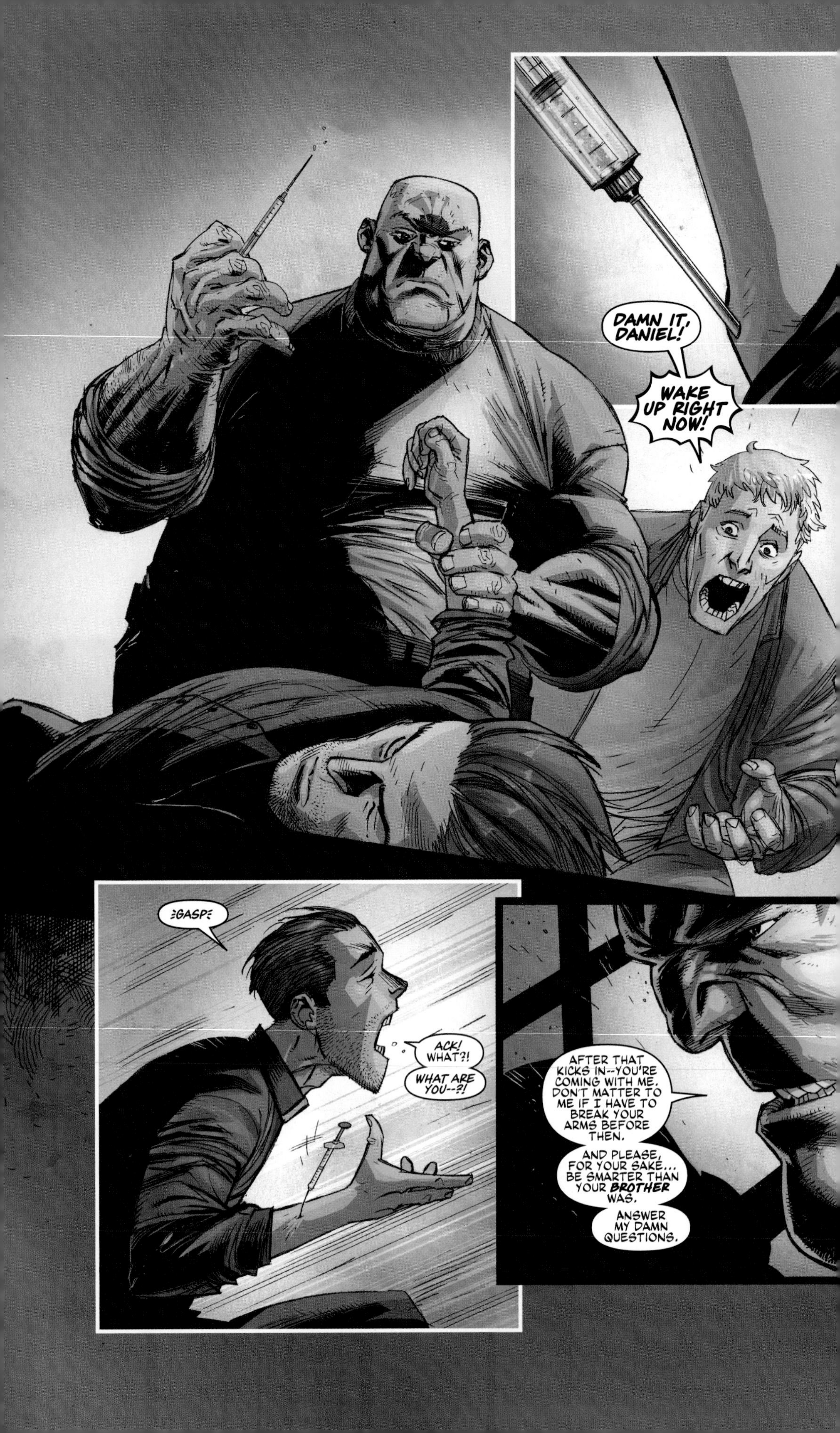
DAMN IT, DANIEL!
WAKE UP RIGHT NOW!
GASP
ACK! WHAT?!
WHAT ARE YOU--?!
AFTER THAT KICKS IN--YOU'RE COMING WITH ME. DON'T MATTER TO ME IF I HAVE TO BREAK YOUR ARMS BEFORE THEN.
AND PLEASE, FOR YOUR SAKE... BE SMARTER THAN YOUR BROTHER WAS.
ANSWER MY DAMN QUESTIONS.

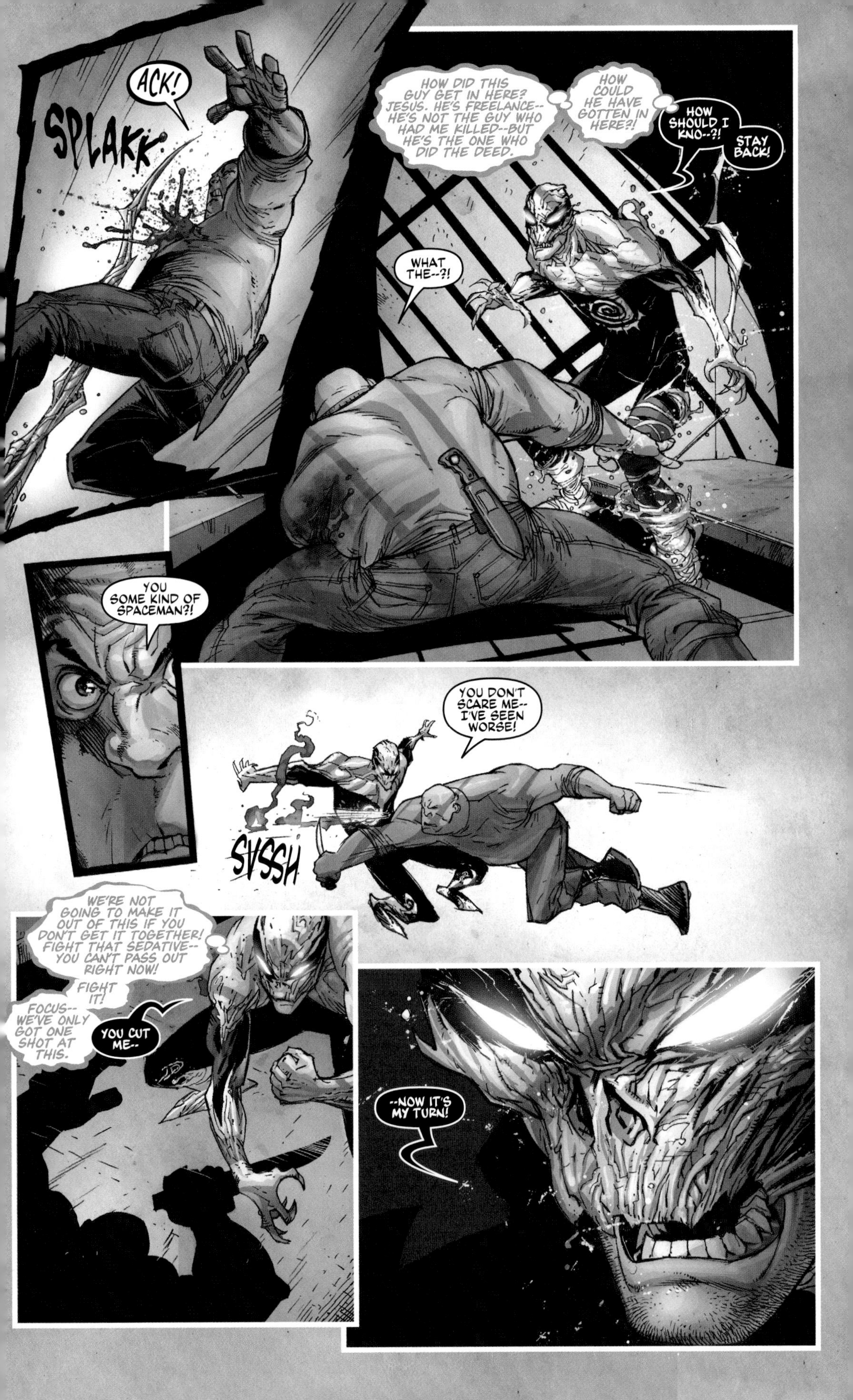
SPLAKK
ACK!
HOW DID THIS GUY GET IN HERE? JESUS. HE'S FREELANCE-- HE'S NOT THE GUY WHO HAD ME KILLED--BUT HE'S THE ONE WHO DID THE DEED.
HOW COULD HE HAVE GOTTEN IN HERE?!
HOW SHOULD I KNO--?!
STAY BACK!
WHAT THE--?!
YOU SOME KIND OF SPACEMAN?!
YOU DON'T SCARE ME-- I'VE SEEN WORSE!
SVSSH
WE'RE NOT GOING TO MAKE IT OUT OF THIS IF YOU DON'T GET IT TOGETHER! FIGHT THAT SEDATIVE-- YOU CAN'T PASS OUT RIGHT NOW!
FIGHT IT!
FOCUS-- WE'VE ONLY GOT ONE SHOT AT THIS.
YOU CUT ME--
--NOW IT'S MY TURN!

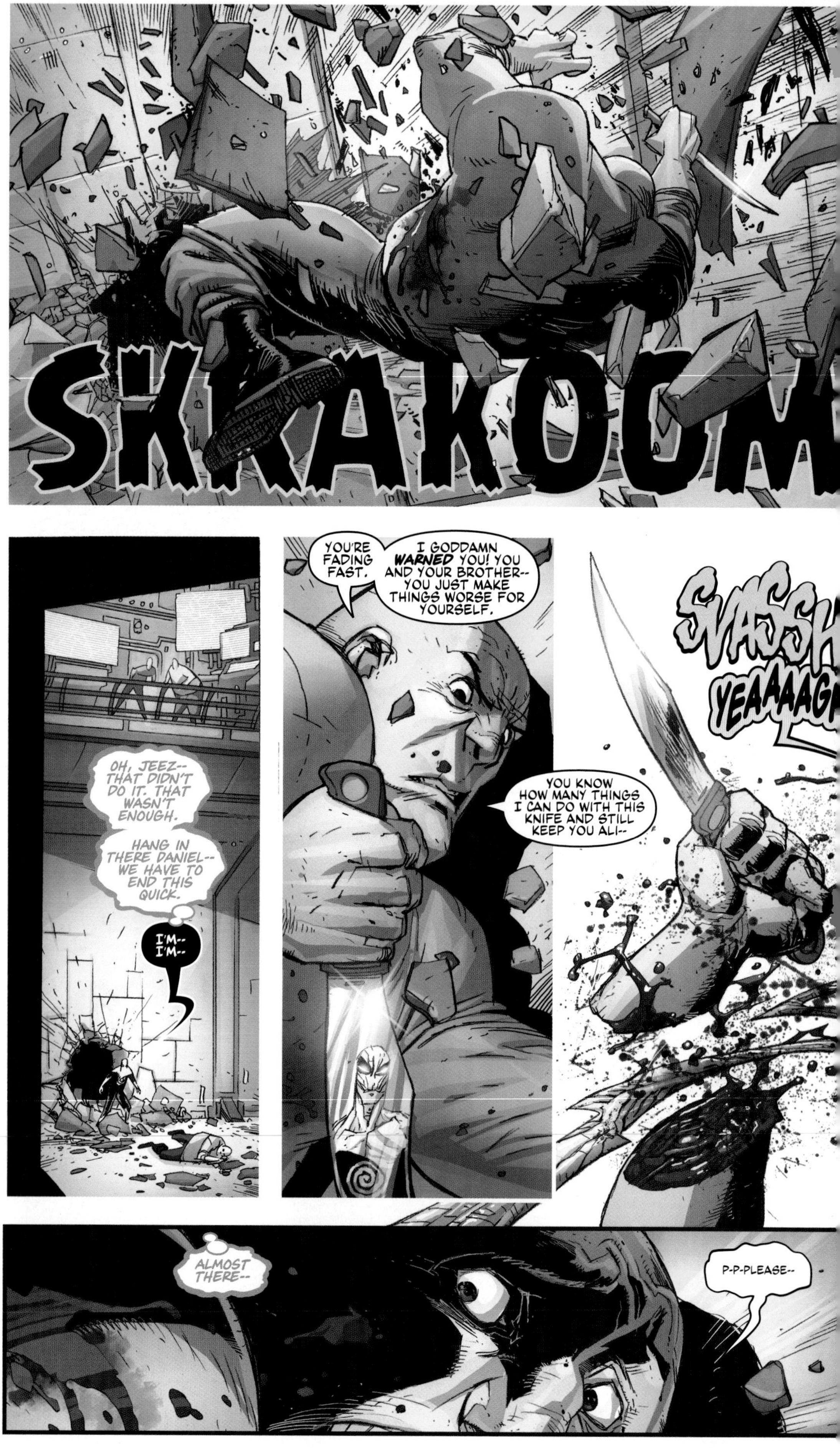
SKRAKOOM
OH, JEEZ-- THAT DIDN'T DO IT. THAT WASN'T ENOUGH.
HANG IN THERE DANIEL-- WE HAVE TO END THIS QUICK.
I'M-- I'M--
YOU'RE FADING FAST.
I GODDAMN WARNED YOU! YOU AND YOUR BROTHER-- YOU JUST MAKE THINGS WORSE FOR YOURSELF.
YOU KNOW HOW MANY THINGS I CAN DO WITH THIS KNIFE AND STILL KEEP YOU ALI--
ALMOST THERE--
P-P-PLEASE--

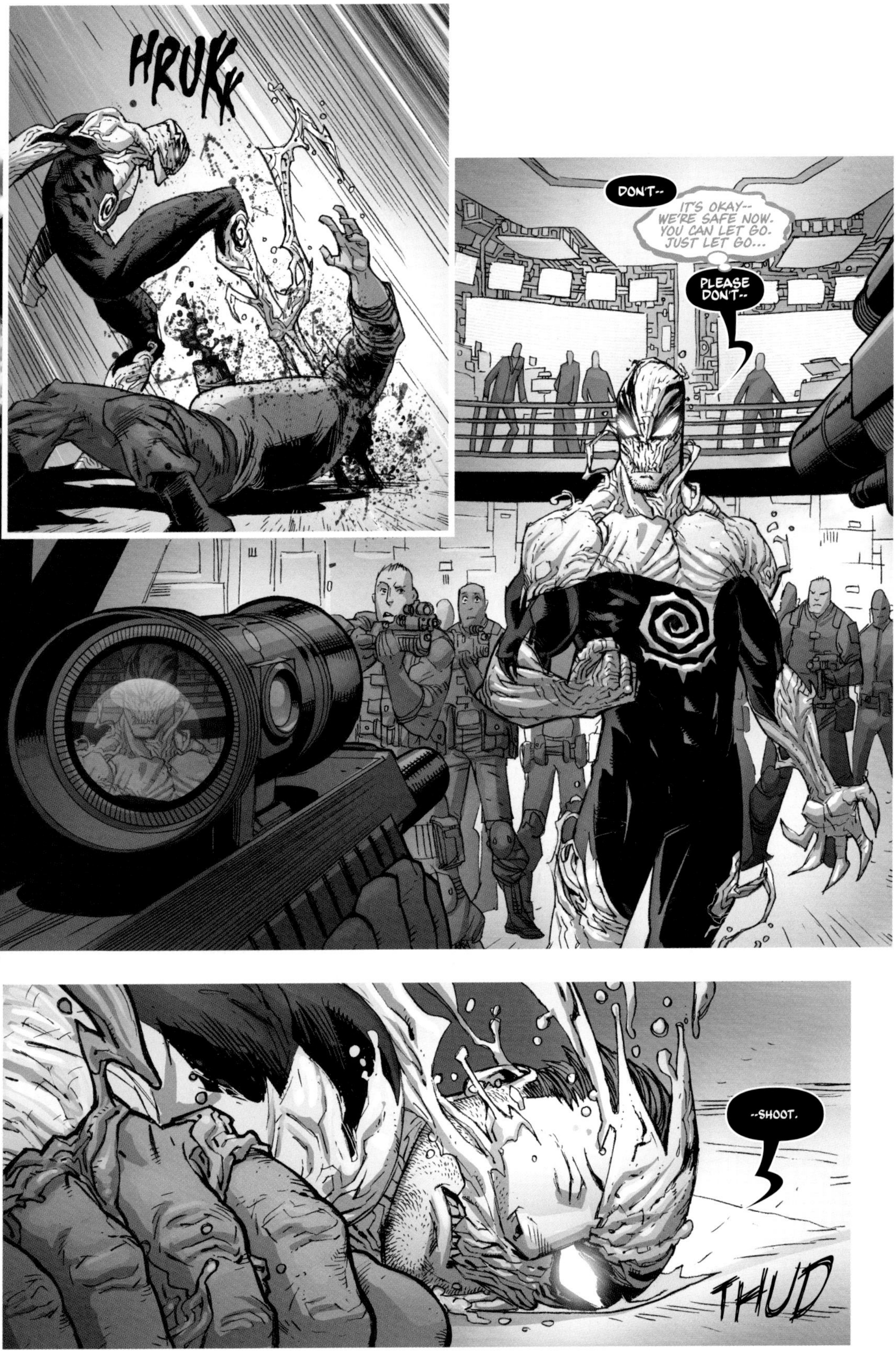
HRUKK
DON'T--
IT'S OKAY-- WE'RE SAFE NOW. YOU CAN LET GO. JUST LET GO...
PLEASE DON'T--
--SHOOT.
THUD

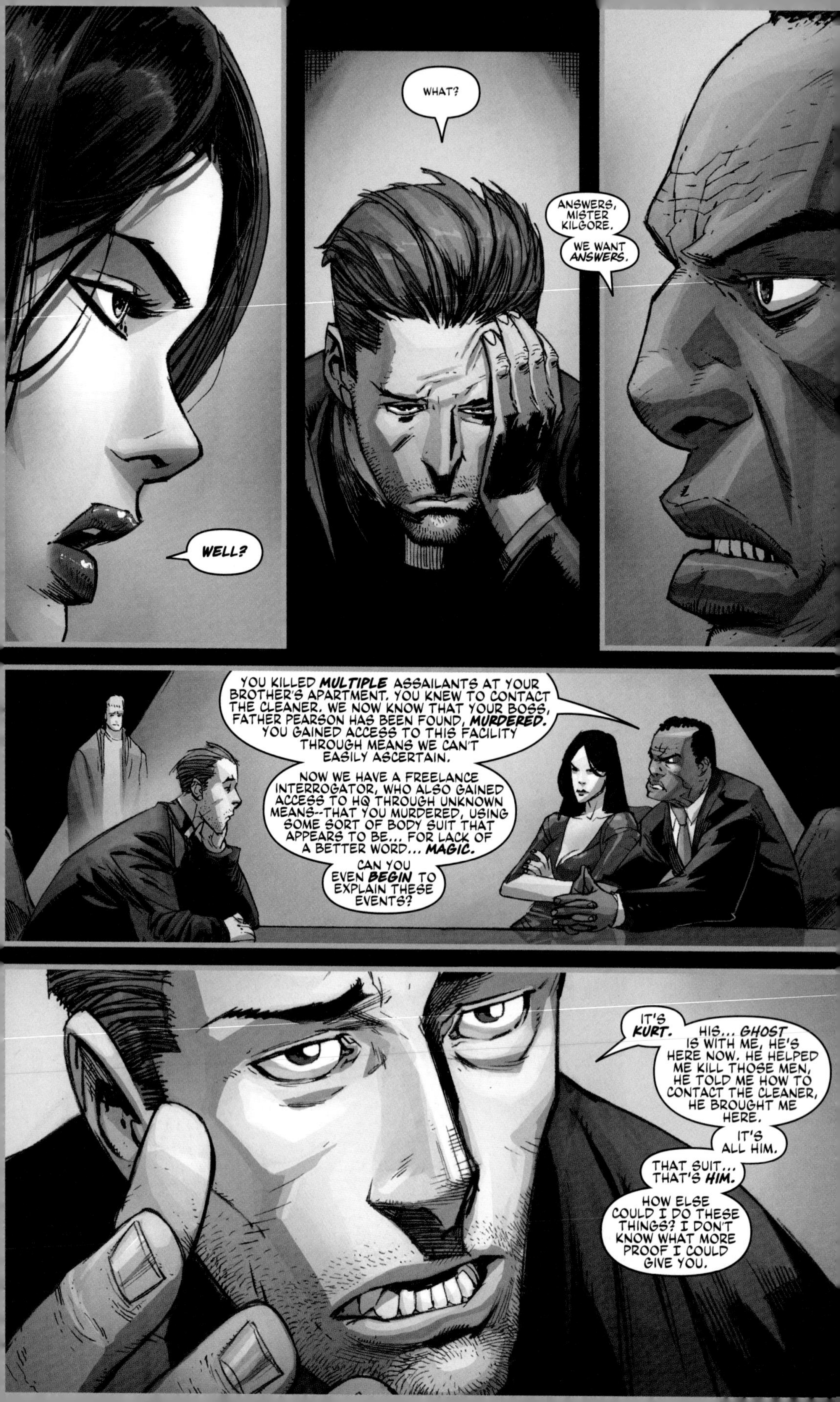
WELL?
WHAT?
ANSWERS, MISTER KILGORE.
WE WANT ANSWERS.
YOU KILLED MULTIPLE ASSAILANTS AT YOUR BROTHER'S APARTMENT. YOU KNEW TO CONTACT THE CLEANER. WE NOW KNOW THAT YOUR BOSS, FATHER PEARSON HAS BEEN FOUND, MURDERED. YOU GAINED ACCESS TO THIS FACILITY THROUGH MEANS WE CAN'T EASILY ASCERTAIN.
NOW WE HAVE A FREELANCE INTERROGATOR, WHO ALSO GAINED ACCESS TO HQ THROUGH UNKNOWN MEANS--THAT YOU MURDERED, USING SOME SORT OF BODY SUIT THAT APPEARS TO BE... FOR LACK OF A BETTER WORD... MAGIC.
CAN YOU EVEN BEGIN TO EXPLAIN THESE EVENTS?
IT'S KURT.
HIS... GHOST IS WITH ME, HE'S HERE NOW. HE HELPED ME KILL THOSE MEN, HE TOLD ME HOW TO CONTACT THE CLEANER, HE BROUGHT ME HERE.
IT'S ALL HIM.
THAT SUIT... THAT'S HIM.
HOW ELSE COULD I DO THESE THINGS? I DON'T KNOW WHAT MORE PROOF I COULD GIVE YOU.

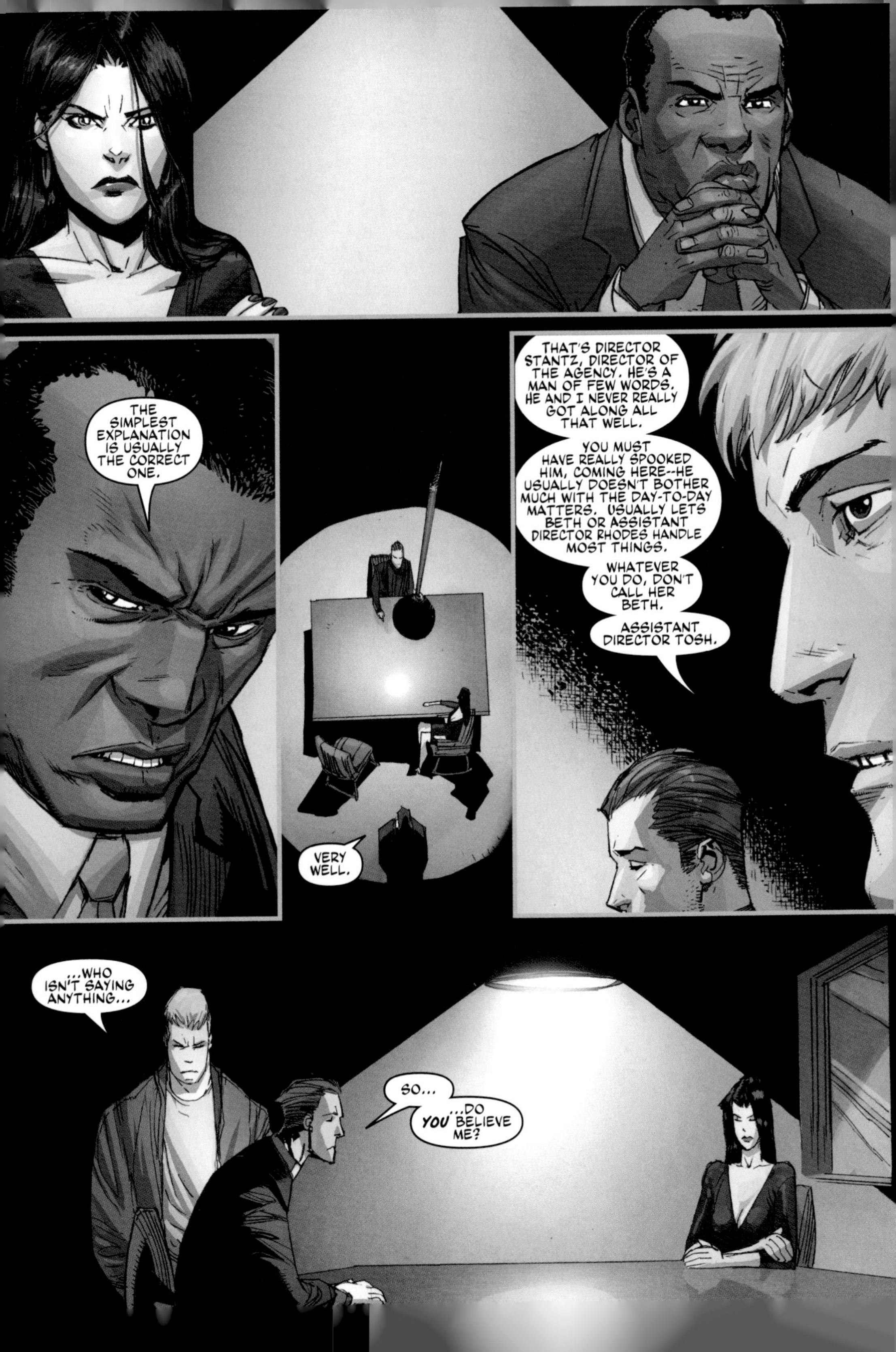
THE SIMPLEST EXPLANATION IS USUALLY THE CORRECT ONE.
VERY WELL.
THAT'S DIRECTOR STANTZ, DIRECTOR OF THE AGENCY. HE'S A MAN OF FEW WORDS. HE AND I NEVER REALLY GOT ALONG ALL THAT WELL.
YOU MUST HAVE REALLY SPOOKED HIM, COMING HERE--HE USUALLY DOESN'T BOTHER MUCH WITH THE DAY-TO-DAY MATTERS. USUALLY LETS BETH OR ASSISTANT DIRECTOR RHODES HANDLE MOST THINGS.
WHATEVER YOU DO, DON'T CALL HER BETH.
ASSISTANT DIRECTOR TOSH.
...WHO ISN'T SAYING ANYTHING...
SO...
...DO *YOU* BELIEVE ME?

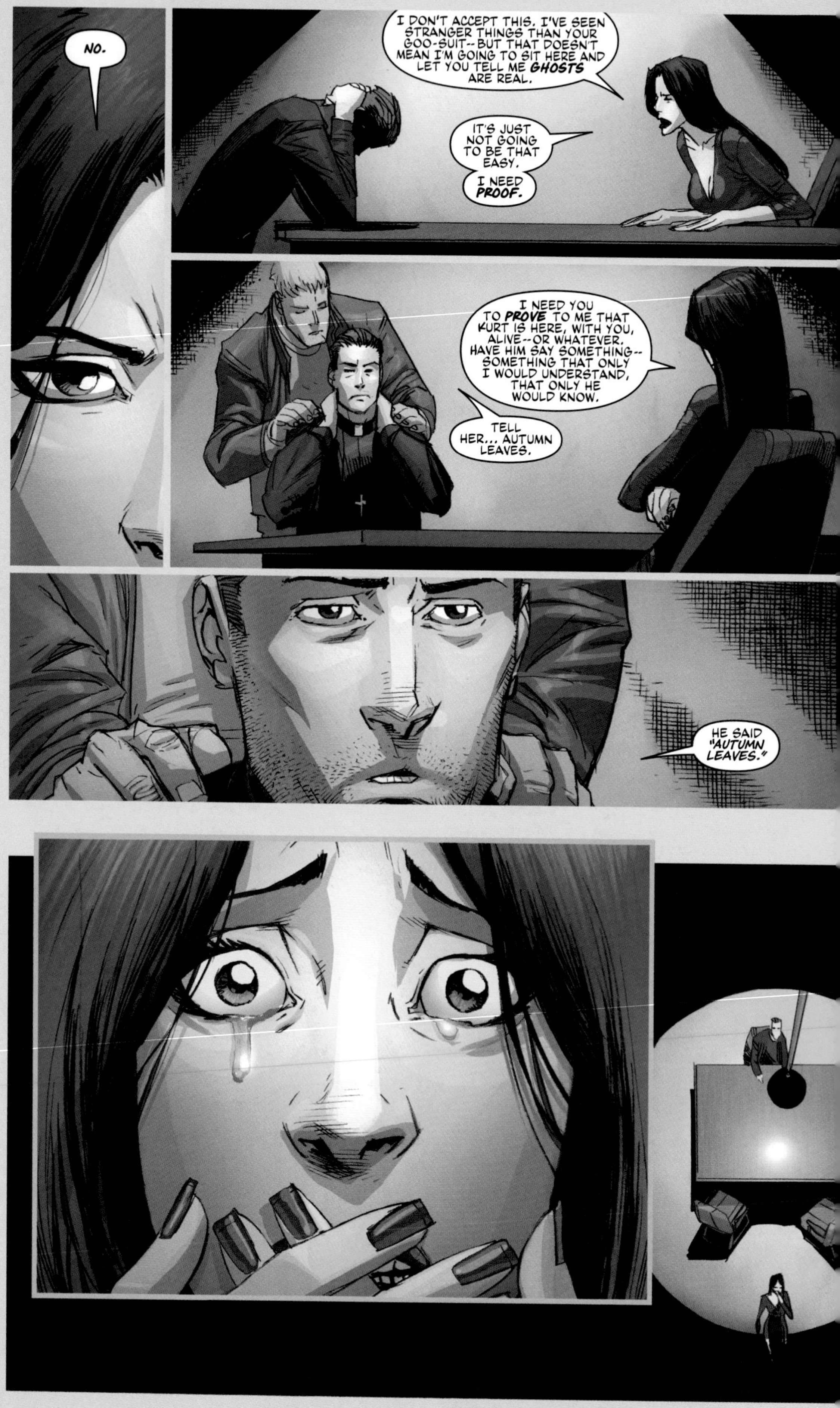

NO.
I DON'T ACCEPT THIS. I'VE SEEN STRANGER THINGS THAN YOUR GOO-SUIT--BUT THAT DOESN'T MEAN I'M GOING TO SIT HERE AND LET YOU TELL ME GHOSTS ARE REAL.
IT'S JUST NOT GOING TO BE THAT EASY.
I NEED PROOF.
I NEED YOU TO PROVE TO ME THAT KURT IS HERE, WITH YOU, ALIVE--OR WHATEVER. HAVE HIM SAY SOMETHING--SOMETHING THAT ONLY I WOULD UNDERSTAND, THAT ONLY HE WOULD KNOW.
TELL HER... AUTUMN LEAVES.
HE SAID "AUTUMN LEAVES."

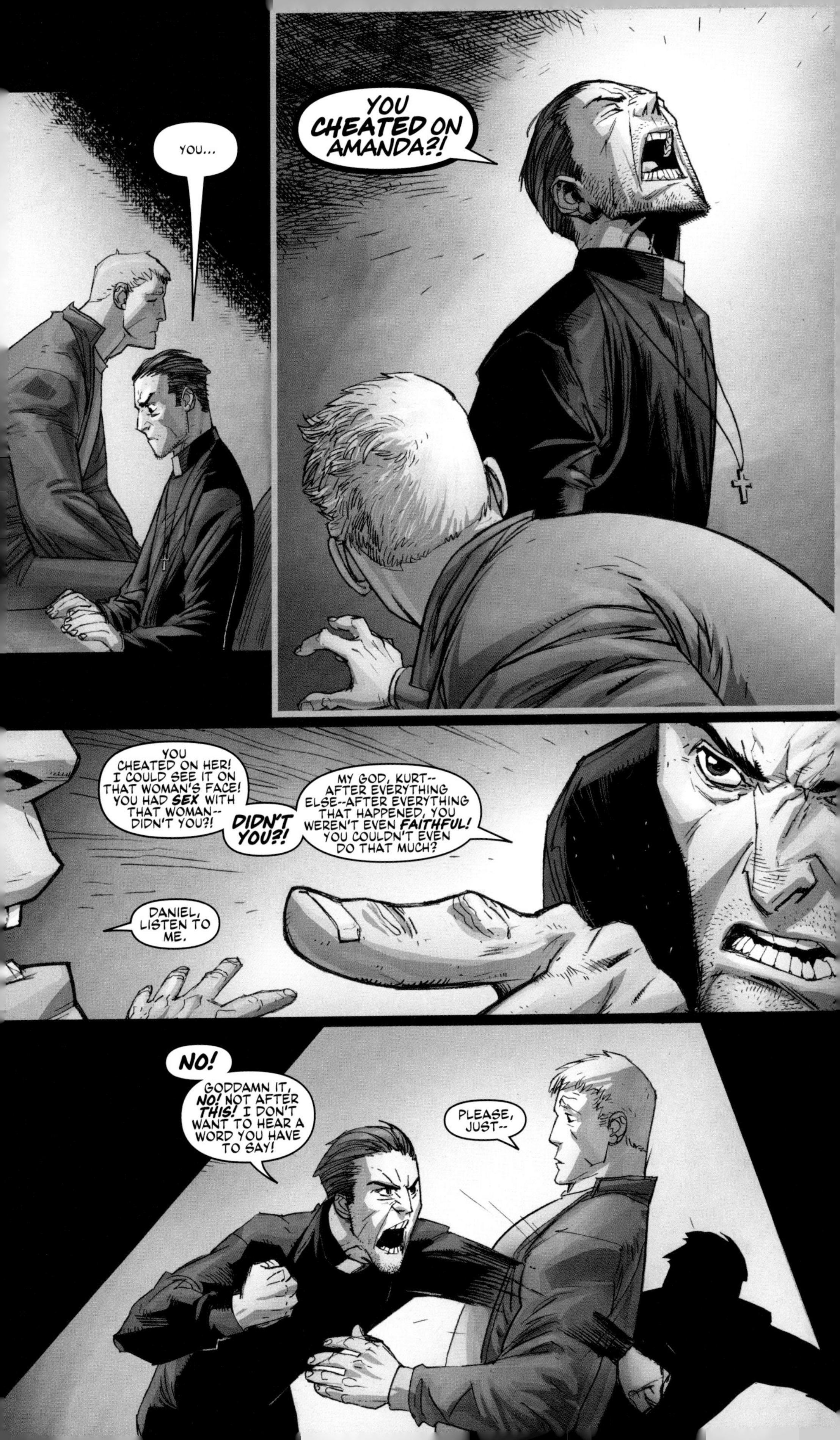
YOU...
YOU CHEATED ON AMANDA?!
YOU CHEATED ON HER! I COULD SEE IT ON THAT WOMAN'S FACE! YOU HAD SEX WITH THAT WOMAN-- DIDN'T YOU?!
DIDN'T YOU?!
MY GOD, KURT-- AFTER EVERYTHING ELSE--AFTER EVERYTHING THAT HAPPENED, YOU WEREN'T EVEN FAITHFUL! YOU COULDN'T EVEN DO THAT MUCH?
DANIEL, LISTEN TO ME.
NO!
GODDAMN IT, NO! NOT AFTER THIS! I DON'T WANT TO HEAR A WORD YOU HAVE TO SAY!
PLEASE, JUST--

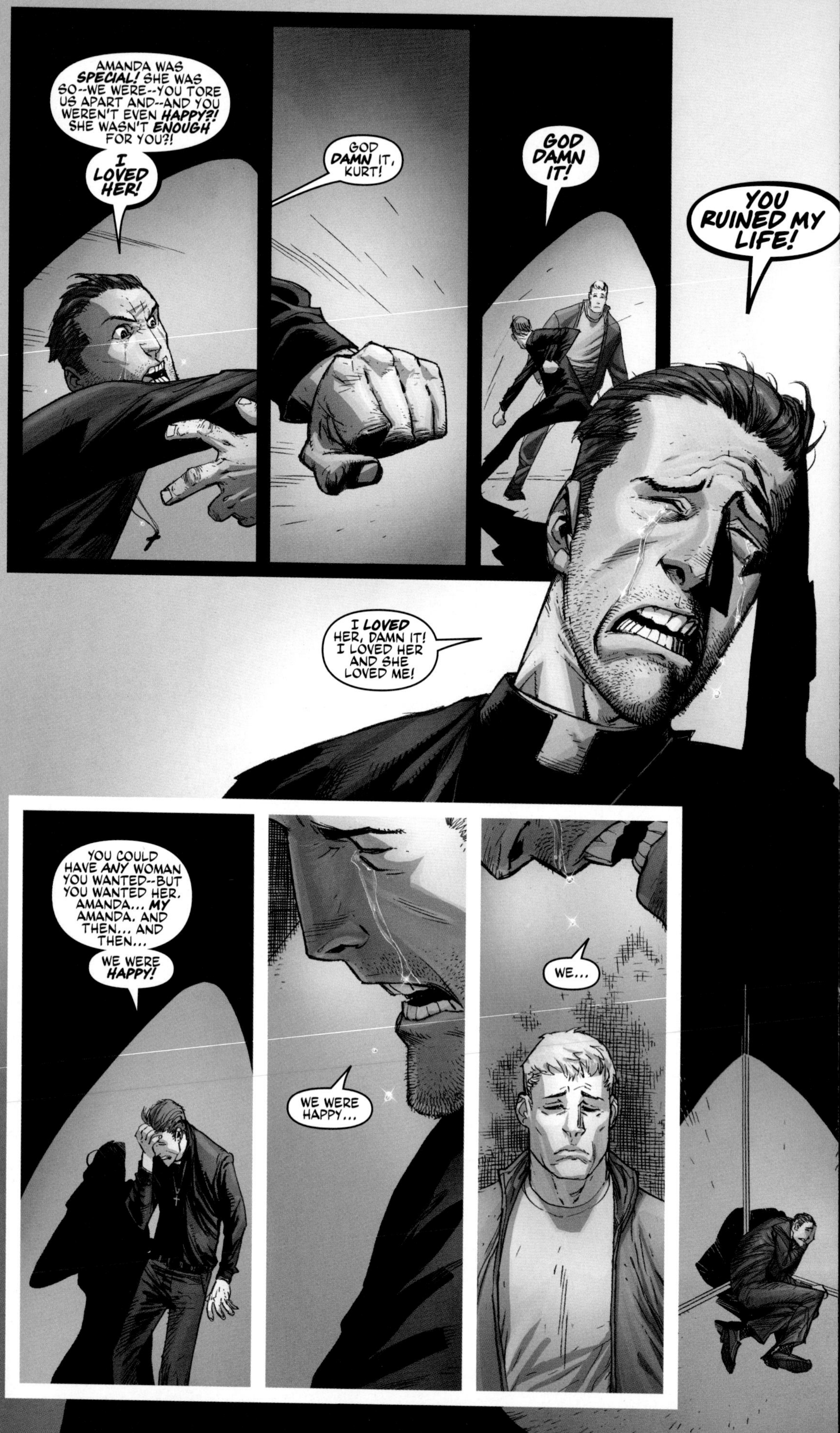
AMANDA WAS SPECIAL! SHE WAS SO--WE WERE--YOU TORE US APART AND--AND YOU WEREN'T EVEN HAPPY?! SHE WASN'T ENOUGH FOR YOU?!
I LOVED HER!
GOD DAMN IT, KURT!
GOD DAMN IT!
YOU RUINED MY LIFE!
I LOVED HER, DAMN IT! I LOVED HER AND SHE LOVED ME!
YOU COULD HAVE ANY WOMAN YOU WANTED--BUT YOU WANTED HER. AMANDA... MY AMANDA. AND THEN... AND THEN...
WE WERE HAPPY!
WE WERE HAPPY...
WE...

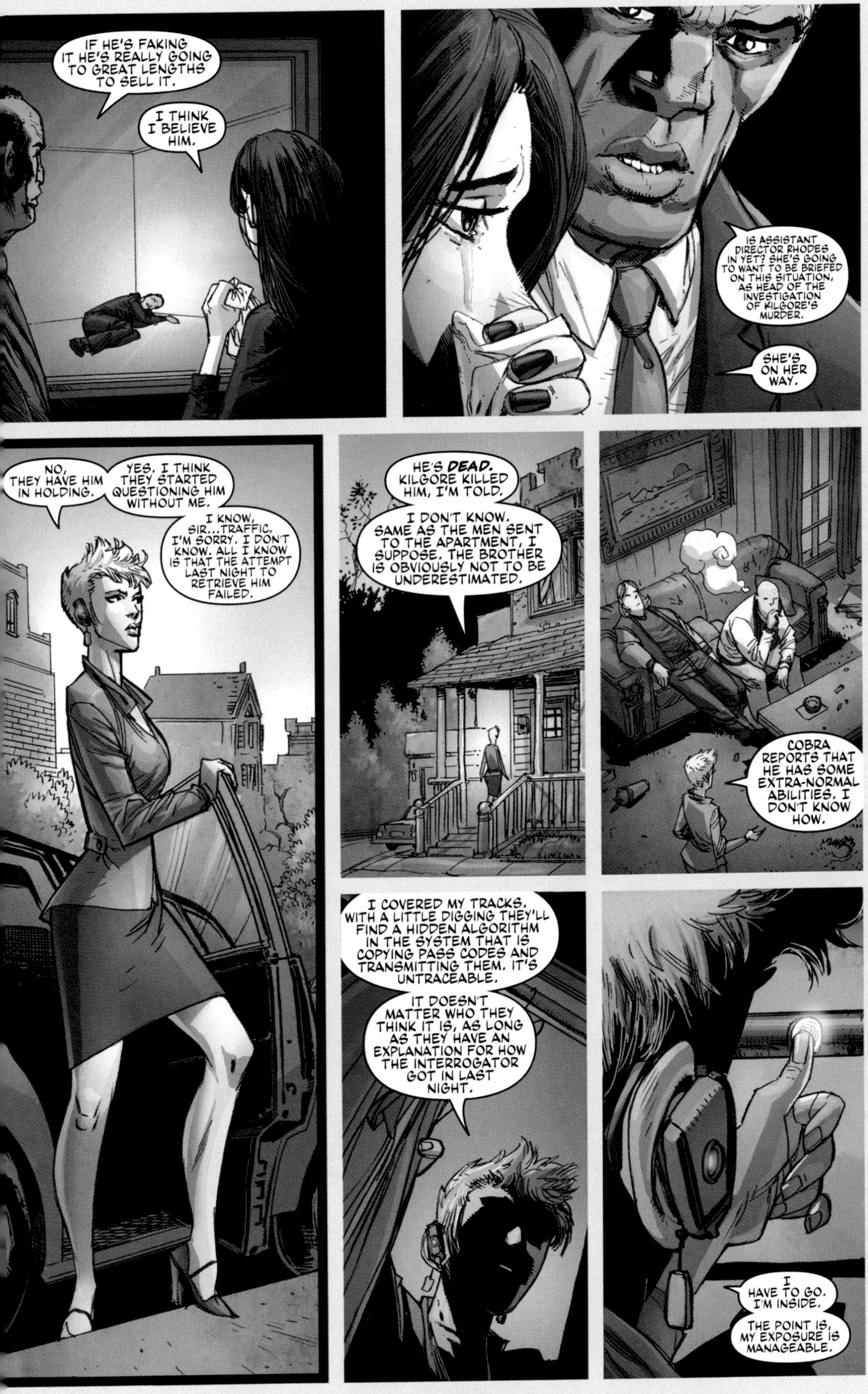
IF HE'S FAKING IT HE'S REALLY GOING TO GREAT LENGTHS TO SELL IT.
I THINK I BELIEVE HIM.
IS ASSISTANT DIRECTOR RHODES IN YET? SHE'S GOING TO WANT TO BE BRIEFED ON THIS SITUATION, AS HEAD OF THE INVESTIGATION OF KILGORE'S MURDER.
SHE'S ON HER WAY.
NO, THEY HAVE HIM IN HOLDING.
YES. I THINK THEY STARTED QUESTIONING HIM WITHOUT ME.
I KNOW, SIR...TRAFFIC. I'M SORRY. I DON'T KNOW. ALL I KNOW IS THAT THE ATTEMPT LAST NIGHT TO RETRIEVE HIM FAILED.
HE'S DEAD. KILGORE KILLED HIM, I'M TOLD.
I DON'T KNOW. SAME AS THE MEN SENT TO THE APARTMENT, I SUPPOSE. THE BROTHER IS OBVIOUSLY NOT TO BE UNDERESTIMATED.
COBRA REPORTS THAT HE HAS SOME EXTRA-NORMAL ABILITIES. I DON'T KNOW HOW.
I COVERED MY TRACKS. WITH A LITTLE DIGGING THEY'LL FIND A HIDDEN ALGORITHM IN THE SYSTEM THAT IS COPYING PASS CODES AND TRANSMITTING THEM. IT'S UNTRACEABLE.
IT DOESN'T MATTER WHO THEY THINK IT IS, AS LONG AS THEY HAVE AN EXPLANATION FOR HOW THE INTERROGATOR GOT IN LAST NIGHT.
I HAVE TO GO. I'M INSIDE.
THE POINT IS, MY EXPOSURE IS MANAGEABLE.

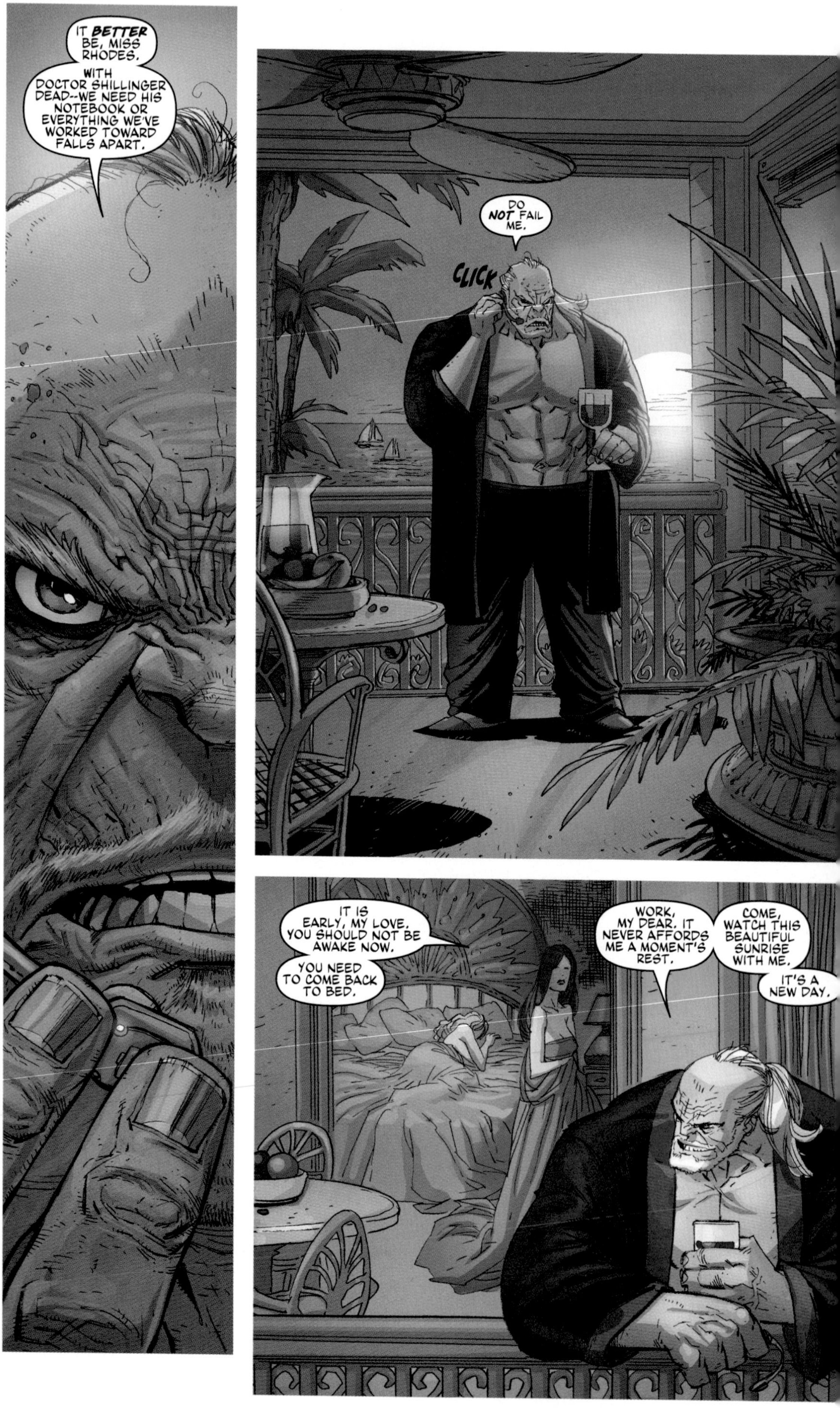
IT BETTER BE, MISS RHODES.
WITH DOCTOR SHILLINGER DEAD--WE NEED HIS NOTEBOOK OR EVERYTHING WE'VE WORKED TOWARD FALLS APART.
DO NOT FAIL ME.
CLICK
IT IS EARLY, MY LOVE. YOU SHOULD NOT BE AWAKE NOW.
YOU NEED TO COME BACK TO BED.
WORK, MY DEAR. IT NEVER AFFORDS ME A MOMENT'S REST.
COME, WATCH THIS BEAUTIFUL SUNRISE WITH ME.
IT'S A NEW DAY.

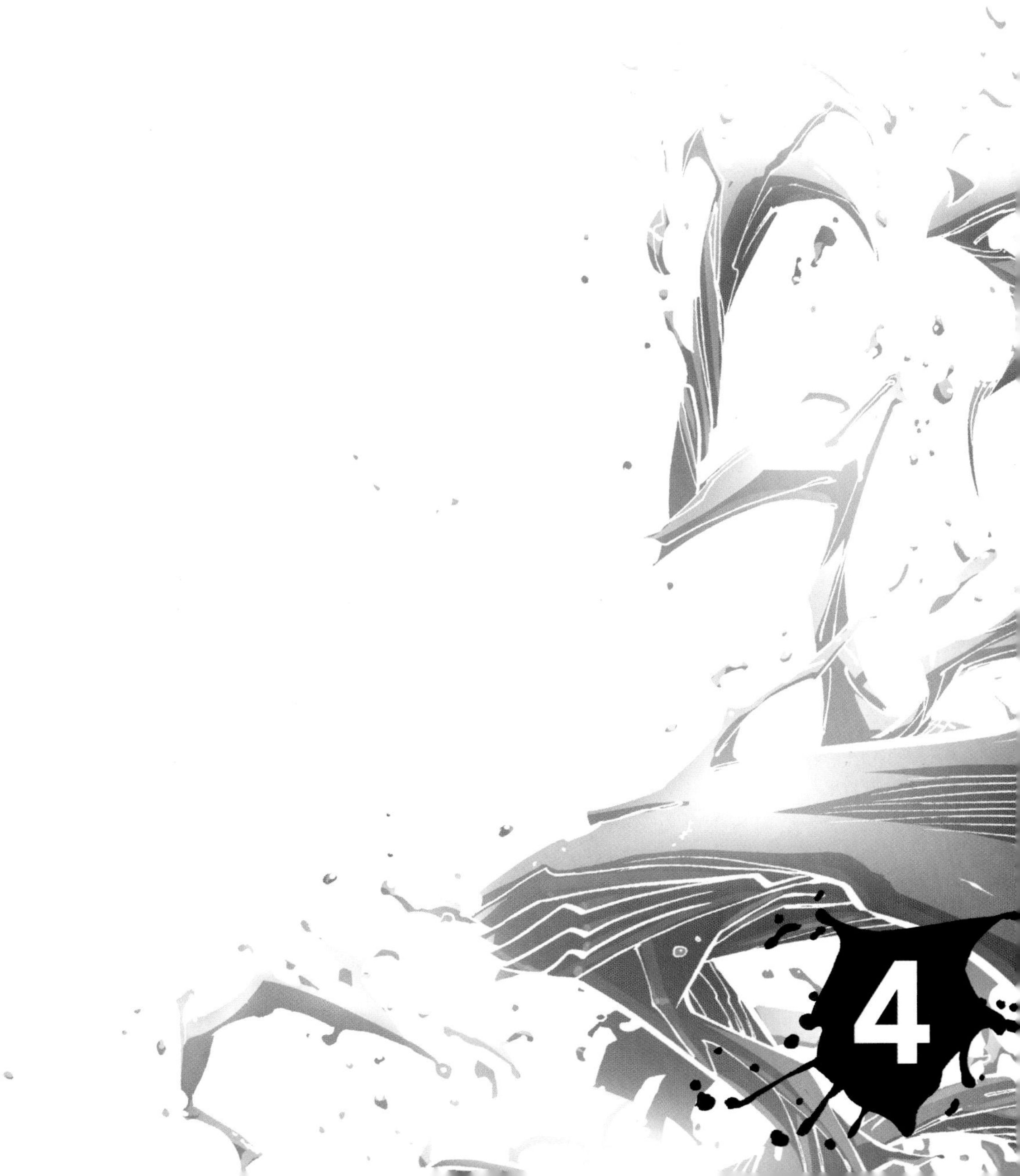
4

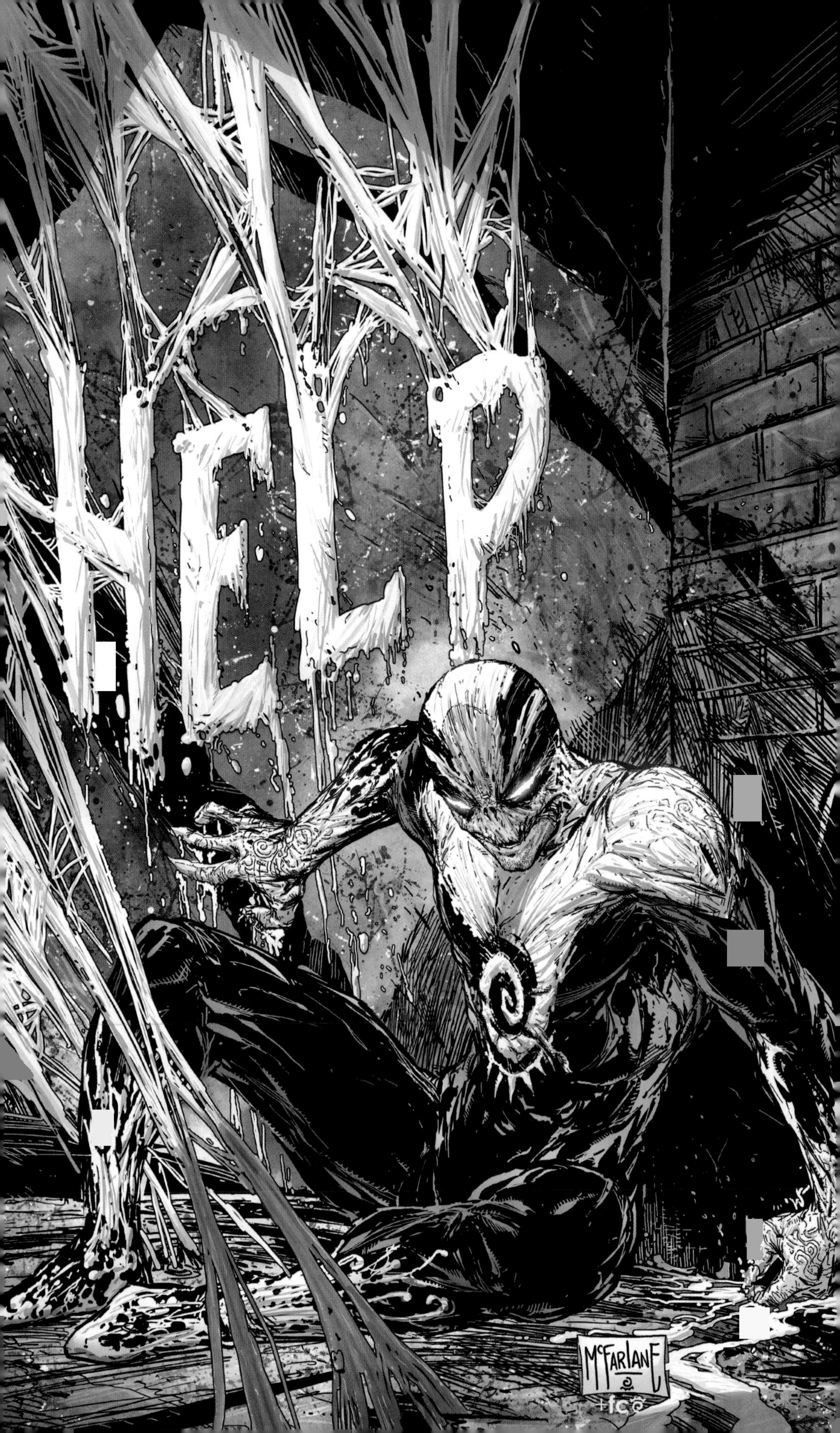
HELP
McFARLANE

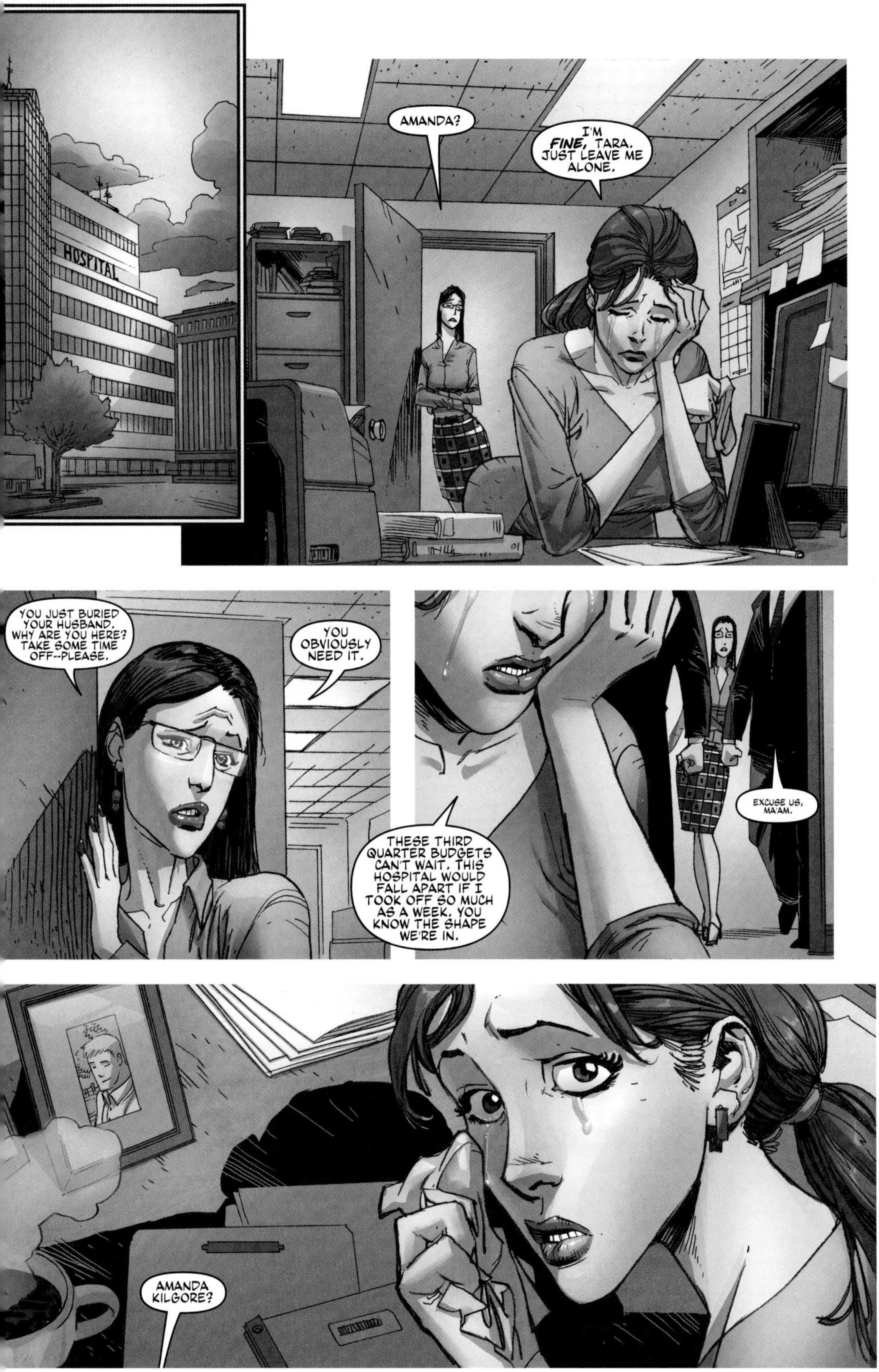
HOSPITAL
AMANDA?
I'M FINE, TARA. JUST LEAVE ME ALONE.
YOU JUST BURIED YOUR HUSBAND. WHY ARE YOU HERE? TAKE SOME TIME OFF--PLEASE.
YOU OBVIOUSLY NEED IT.
THESE THIRD QUARTER BUDGETS CAN'T WAIT. THIS HOSPITAL WOULD FALL APART IF I TOOK OFF SO MUCH AS A WEEK. YOU KNOW THE SHAPE WE'RE IN.
EXCUSE US, MA'AM.
AMANDA KILGORE?

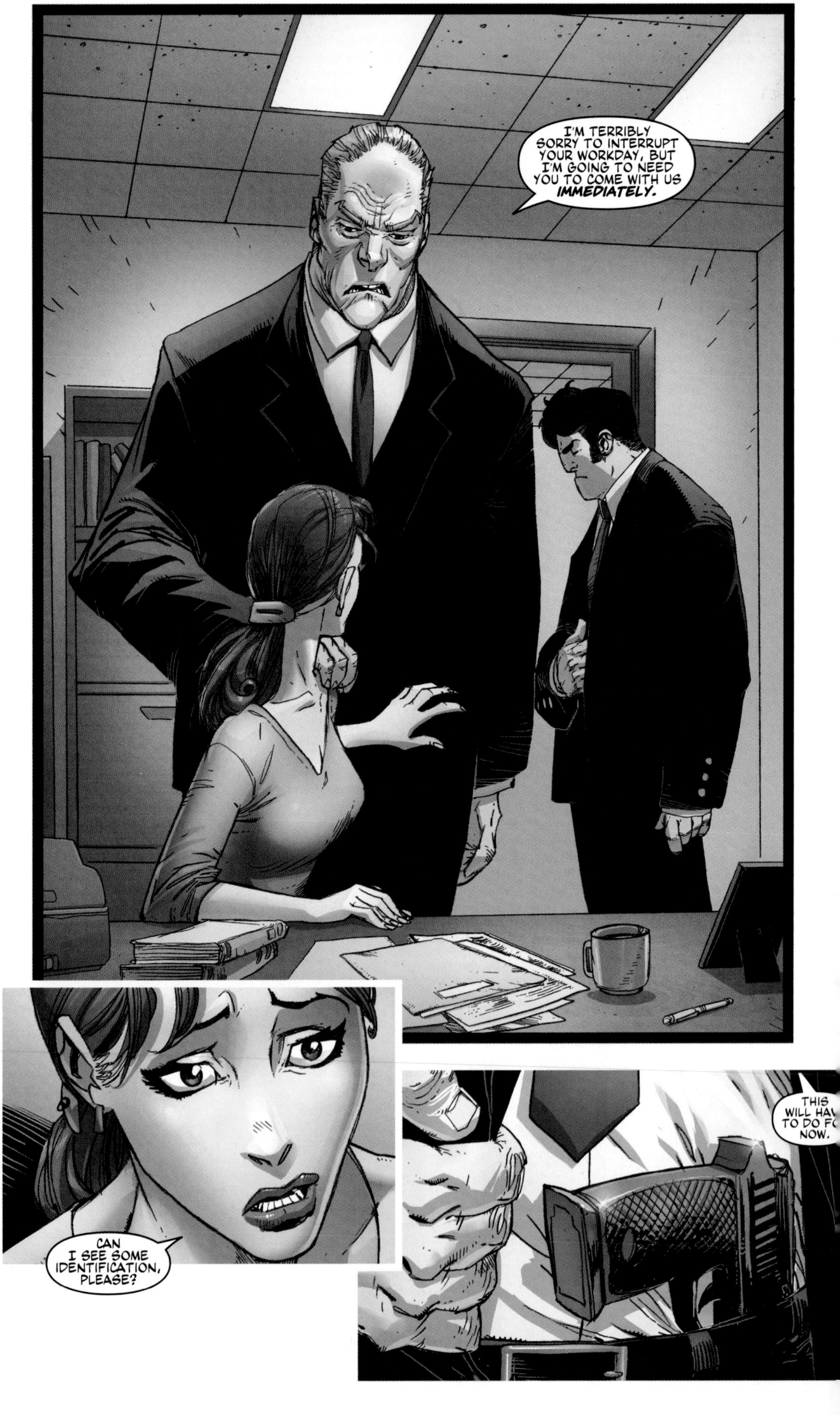

I'M TERRIBLY SORRY TO INTERRUPT YOUR WORKDAY, BUT I'M GOING TO NEED YOU TO COME WITH US ***IMMEDIATELY.***
CAN I SEE SOME IDENTIFICATION, PLEASE?

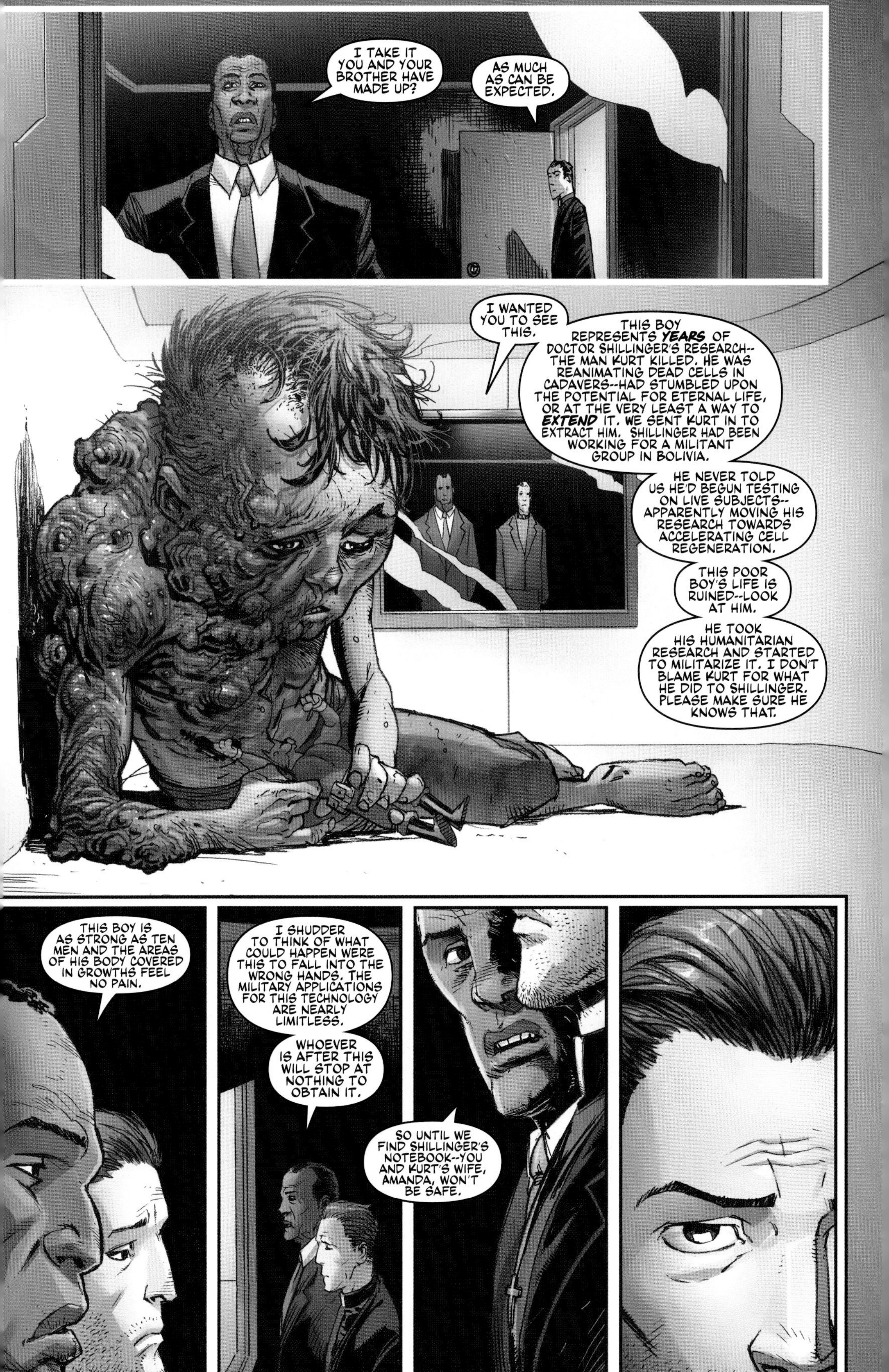
I TAKE IT YOU AND YOUR BROTHER HAVE MADE UP?
AS MUCH AS CAN BE EXPECTED.
I WANTED YOU TO SEE THIS.
THIS BOY REPRESENTS *YEARS* OF DOCTOR SHILLINGER'S RESEARCH--THE MAN KURT KILLED. HE WAS REANIMATING DEAD CELLS IN CADAVERS--HAD STUMBLED UPON THE POTENTIAL FOR ETERNAL LIFE, OR AT THE VERY LEAST A WAY TO *EXTEND* IT. WE SENT KURT IN TO EXTRACT HIM. SHILLINGER HAD BEEN WORKING FOR A MILITANT GROUP IN BOLIVIA.
HE NEVER TOLD US HE'D BEGUN TESTING ON LIVE SUBJECTS--APPARENTLY MOVING HIS RESEARCH TOWARDS ACCELERATING CELL REGENERATION.
THIS POOR BOY'S LIFE IS RUINED--LOOK AT HIM.
HE TOOK HIS HUMANITARIAN RESEARCH AND STARTED TO MILITARIZE IT. I DON'T BLAME KURT FOR WHAT HE DID TO SHILLINGER. PLEASE MAKE SURE HE KNOWS THAT.
THIS BOY IS AS STRONG AS TEN MEN AND THE AREAS OF HIS BODY COVERED IN GROWTHS FEEL NO PAIN.
I SHUDDER TO THINK OF WHAT COULD HAPPEN WERE THIS TO FALL INTO THE WRONG HANDS. THE MILITARY APPLICATIONS FOR THIS TECHNOLOGY ARE NEARLY LIMITLESS.
WHOEVER IS AFTER THIS WILL STOP AT NOTHING TO OBTAIN IT.
SO UNTIL WE FIND SHILLINGER'S NOTEBOOK--YOU AND KURT'S WIFE, AMANDA, WON'T BE SAFE.

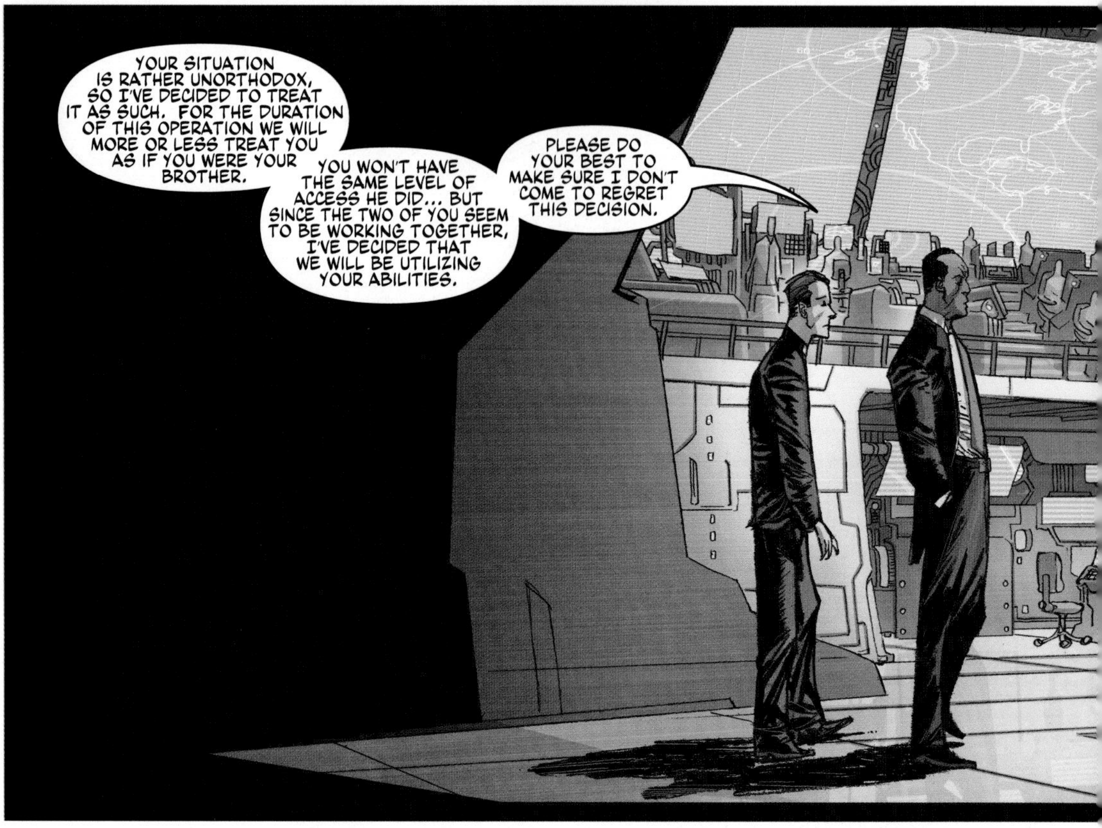
YOUR SITUATION IS RATHER UNORTHODOX, SO I'VE DECIDED TO TREAT IT AS SUCH. FOR THE DURATION OF THIS OPERATION WE WILL MORE OR LESS TREAT YOU AS IF YOU WERE YOUR BROTHER.
YOU WON'T HAVE THE SAME LEVEL OF ACCESS HE DID... BUT SINCE THE TWO OF YOU SEEM TO BE WORKING TOGETHER, I'VE DECIDED THAT WE WILL BE UTILIZING YOUR ABILITIES.
PLEASE DO YOUR BEST TO MAKE SURE I DON'T COME TO REGRET THIS DECISION.

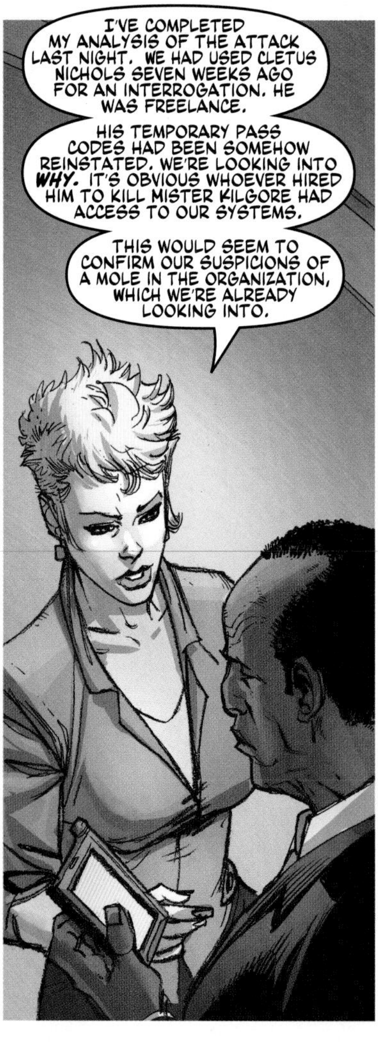
I'VE COMPLETED MY ANALYSIS OF THE ATTACK LAST NIGHT. WE HAD USED CLETUS NICHOLS SEVEN WEEKS AGO FOR AN INTERROGATION. HE WAS FREELANCE.
HIS TEMPORARY PASS CODES HAD BEEN SOMEHOW REINSTATED. WE'RE LOOKING INTO ***WHY***. IT'S OBVIOUS WHOEVER HIRED HIM TO KILL MISTER KILGORE HAD ACCESS TO OUR SYSTEMS.
THIS WOULD SEEM TO CONFIRM OUR SUSPICIONS OF A MOLE IN THE ORGANIZATION, WHICH WE'RE ALREADY LOOKING INTO.

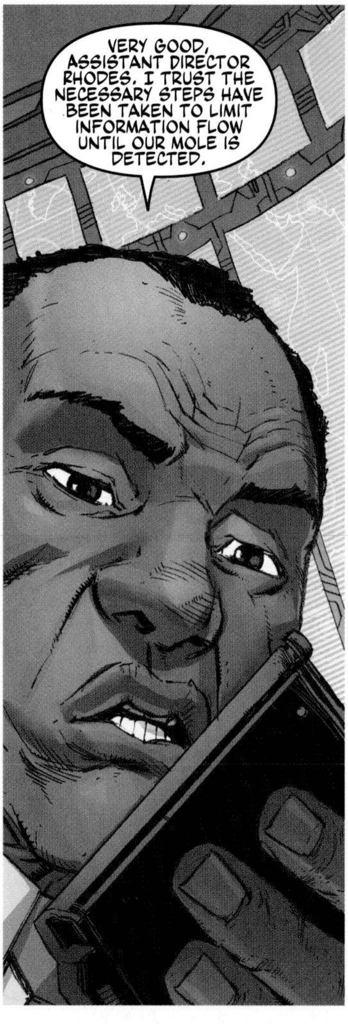
VERY GOOD, ASSISTANT DIRECTOR RHODES. I TRUST THE NECESSARY STEPS HAVE BEEN TAKEN TO LIMIT INFORMATION FLOW UNTIL OUR MOLE IS DETECTED.

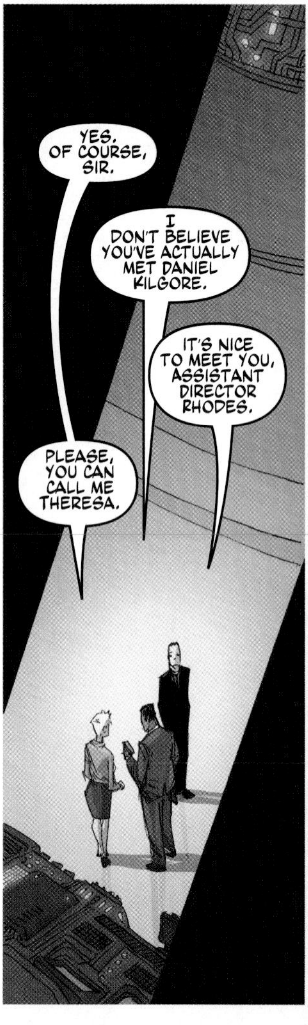
YES, OF COURSE, SIR.
I DON'T BELIEVE YOU'VE ACTUALLY MET DANIEL KILGORE.
IT'S NICE TO MEET YOU, ASSISTANT DIRECTOR RHODES.
PLEASE, YOU CAN CALL ME THERESA.

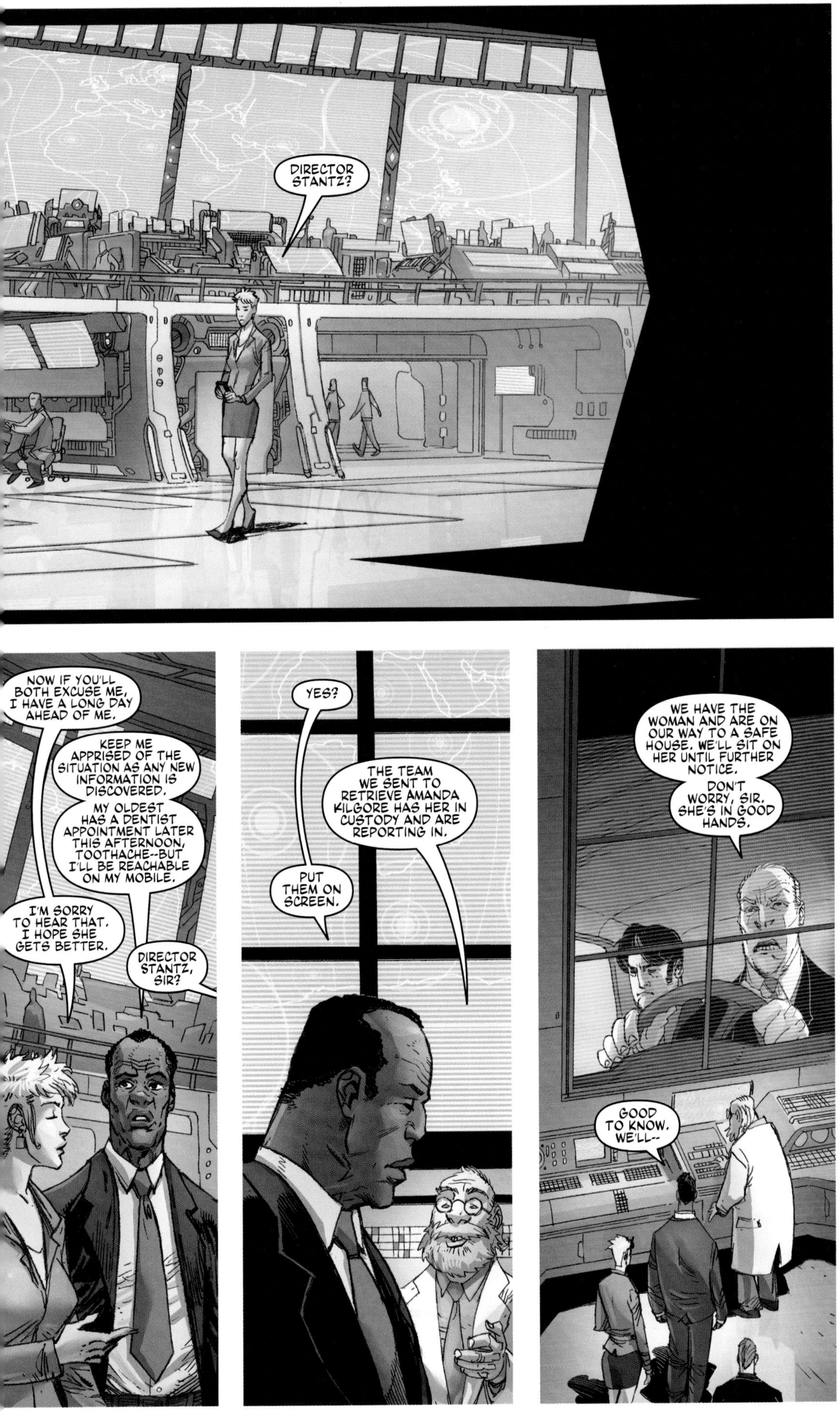
DIRECTOR STANTZ?
NOW IF YOU'LL BOTH EXCUSE ME, I HAVE A LONG DAY AHEAD OF ME.
KEEP ME APPRISED OF THE SITUATION AS ANY NEW INFORMATION IS DISCOVERED.
MY OLDEST HAS A DENTIST APPOINTMENT LATER THIS AFTERNOON, TOOTHACHE--BUT I'LL BE REACHABLE ON MY MOBILE.
I'M SORRY TO HEAR THAT. I HOPE SHE GETS BETTER.
DIRECTOR STANTZ, SIR?
YES?
THE TEAM WE SENT TO RETRIEVE AMANDA KILGORE HAS HER IN CUSTODY AND ARE REPORTING IN.
PUT THEM ON SCREEN.
WE HAVE THE WOMAN AND ARE ON OUR WAY TO A SAFE HOUSE. WE'LL SIT ON HER UNTIL FURTHER NOTICE.
DON'T WORRY, SIR. SHE'S IN GOOD HANDS.
GOOD TO KNOW. WE'LL--

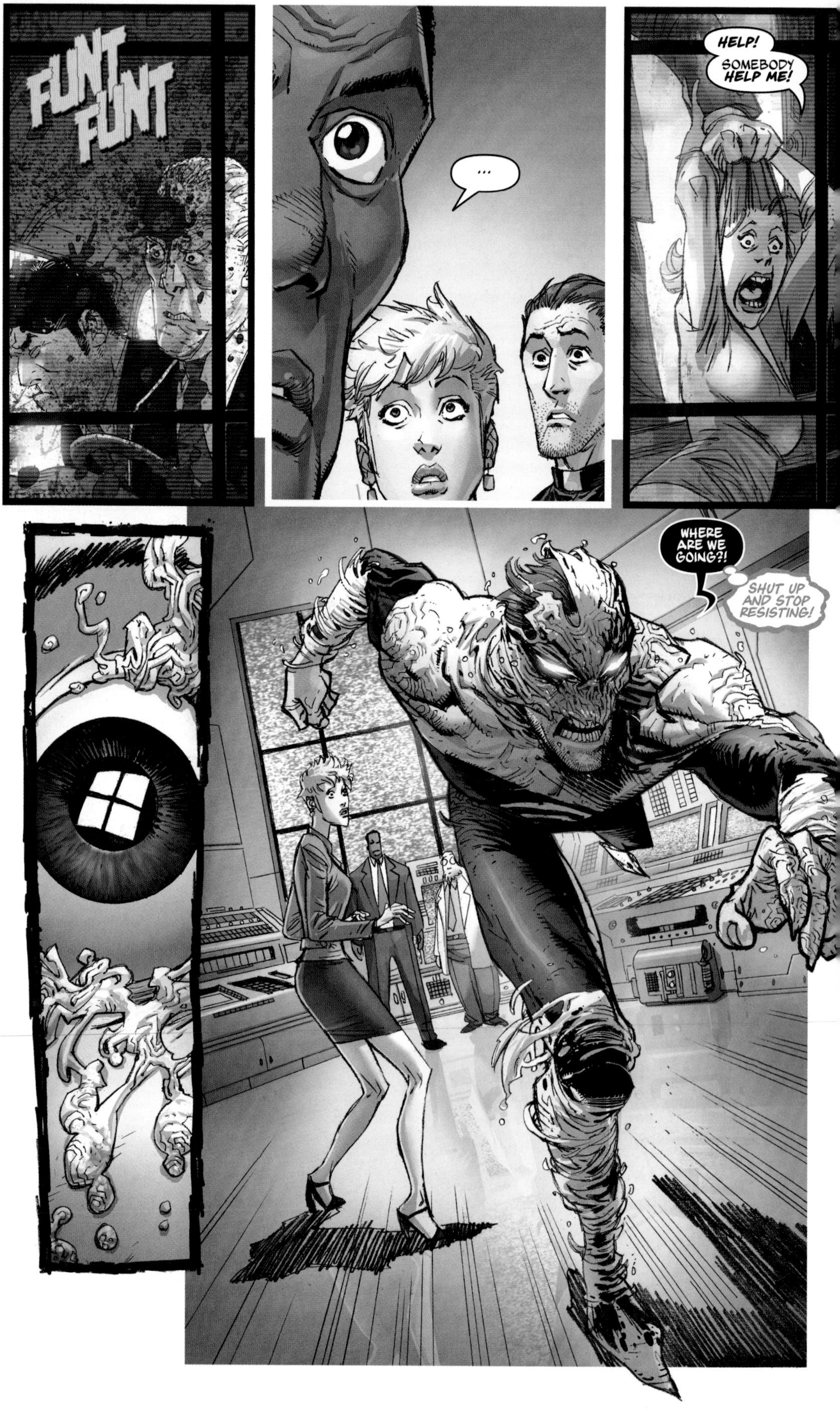
FUNT
FUNT
...
HELP!
SOMEBODY HELP ME!
WHERE ARE WE GOING?!
SHUT UP AND STOP RESISTING!

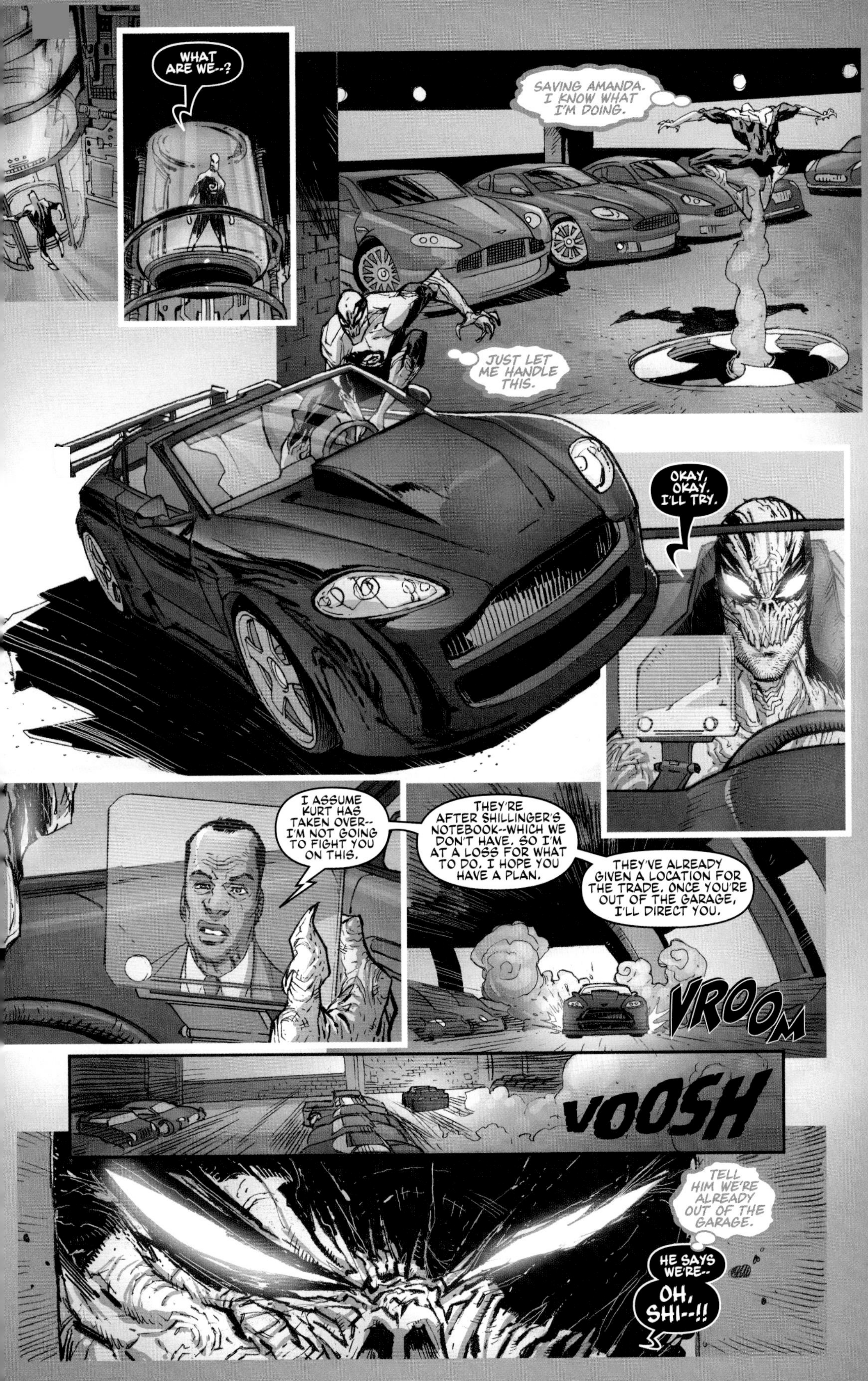

WHAT ARE WE--?
SAVING AMANDA. I KNOW WHAT I'M DOING.
JUST LET ME HANDLE THIS.
OKAY, OKAY. I'LL TRY.
I ASSUME KURT HAS TAKEN OVER-- I'M NOT GOING TO FIGHT YOU ON THIS.
THEY'RE AFTER SHILLINGER'S NOTEBOOK--WHICH WE DON'T HAVE. SO I'M AT A LOSS FOR WHAT TO DO. I HOPE YOU HAVE A PLAN.
THEY'VE ALREADY GIVEN A LOCATION FOR THE TRADE. ONCE YOU'RE OUT OF THE GARAGE, I'LL DIRECT YOU.
VROOM
VOOSH
TELL HIM WE'RE ALREADY OUT OF THE GARAGE.
HE SAYS WE'RE--
OH, SHI--!!

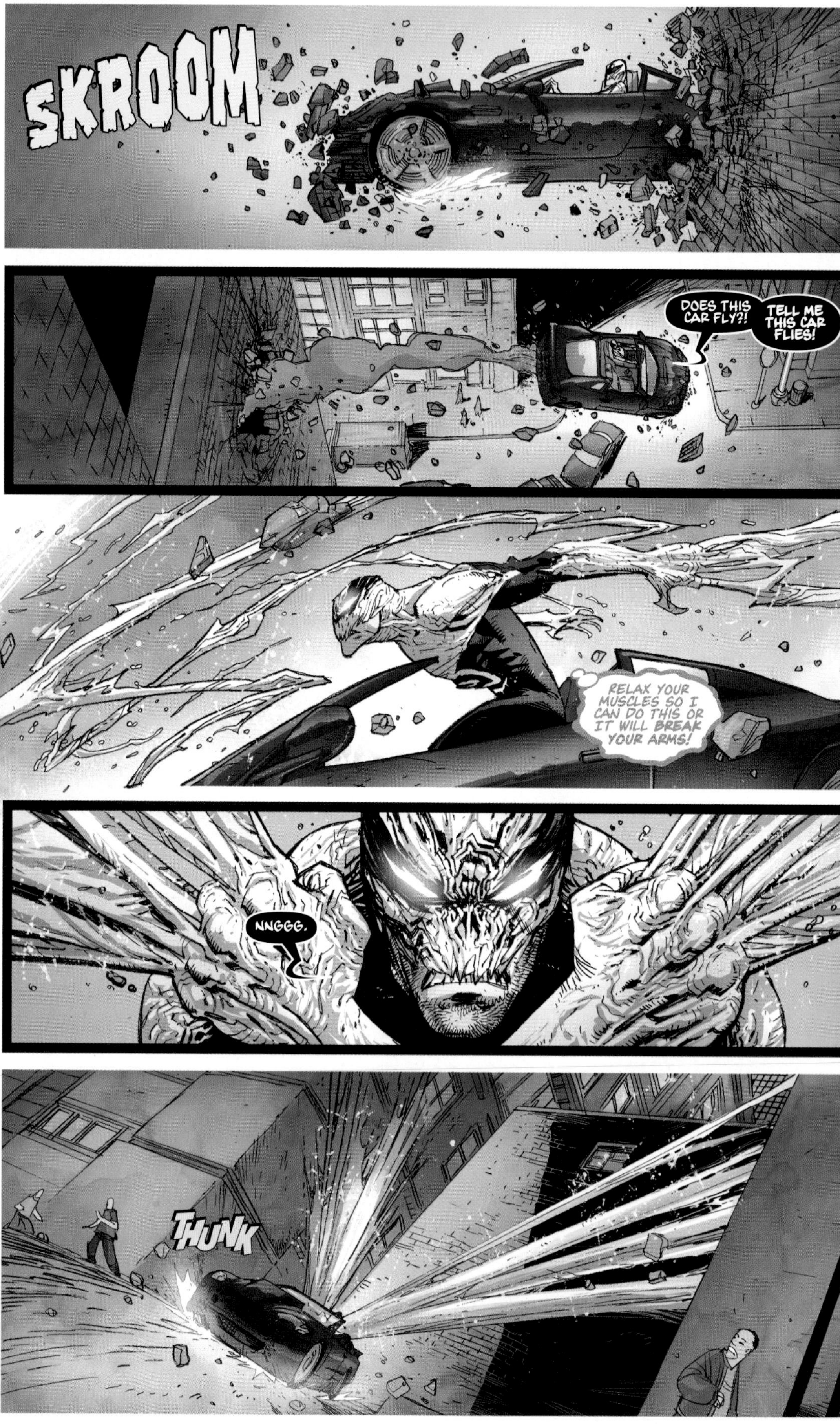
SKROOM
DOES THIS CAR FLY?!
TELL ME THIS CAR FLIES!
RELAX YOUR MUSCLES SO I CAN DO THIS OR IT WILL BREAK YOUR ARMS!
NNGGG.
THUNK

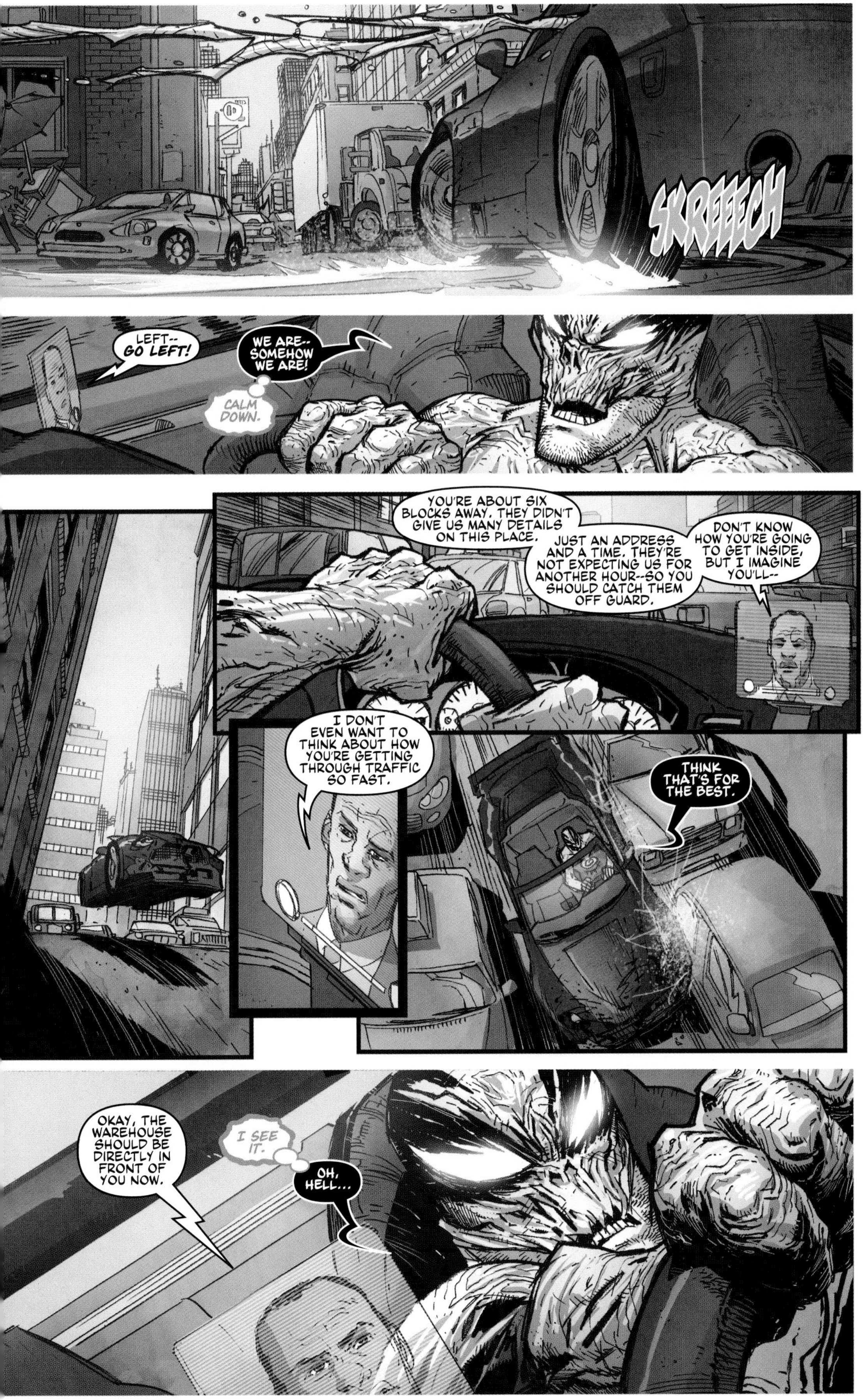
SKREEECH
LEFT--
GO LEFT!
WE ARE--
SOMEHOW
WE ARE!
CALM
DOWN.
YOU'RE ABOUT SIX BLOCKS AWAY. THEY DIDN'T GIVE US MANY DETAILS ON THIS PLACE.
JUST AN ADDRESS AND A TIME. THEY'RE NOT EXPECTING US FOR ANOTHER HOUR--SO YOU SHOULD CATCH THEM OFF GUARD.
DON'T KNOW HOW YOU'RE GOING TO GET INSIDE, BUT I IMAGINE YOU'LL--
I DON'T EVEN WANT TO THINK ABOUT HOW YOU'RE GETTING THROUGH TRAFFIC SO FAST.
THINK THAT'S FOR THE BEST.
OKAY, THE WAREHOUSE SHOULD BE DIRECTLY IN FRONT OF YOU NOW.
I SEE IT.
OH, HELL...

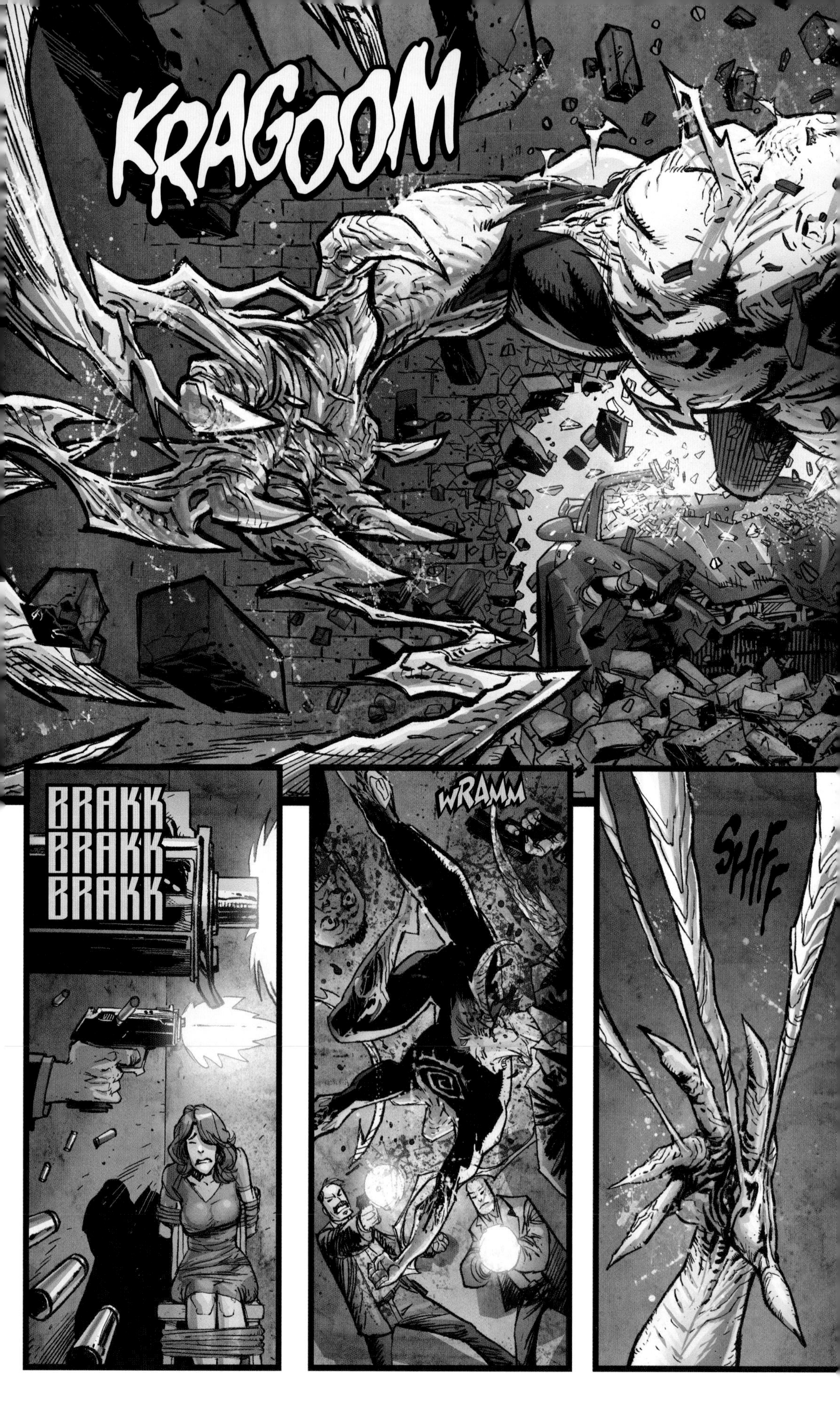
KRAGOOM
BRAKK
BRAKK
BRAKK
WRAMM
SHIFF

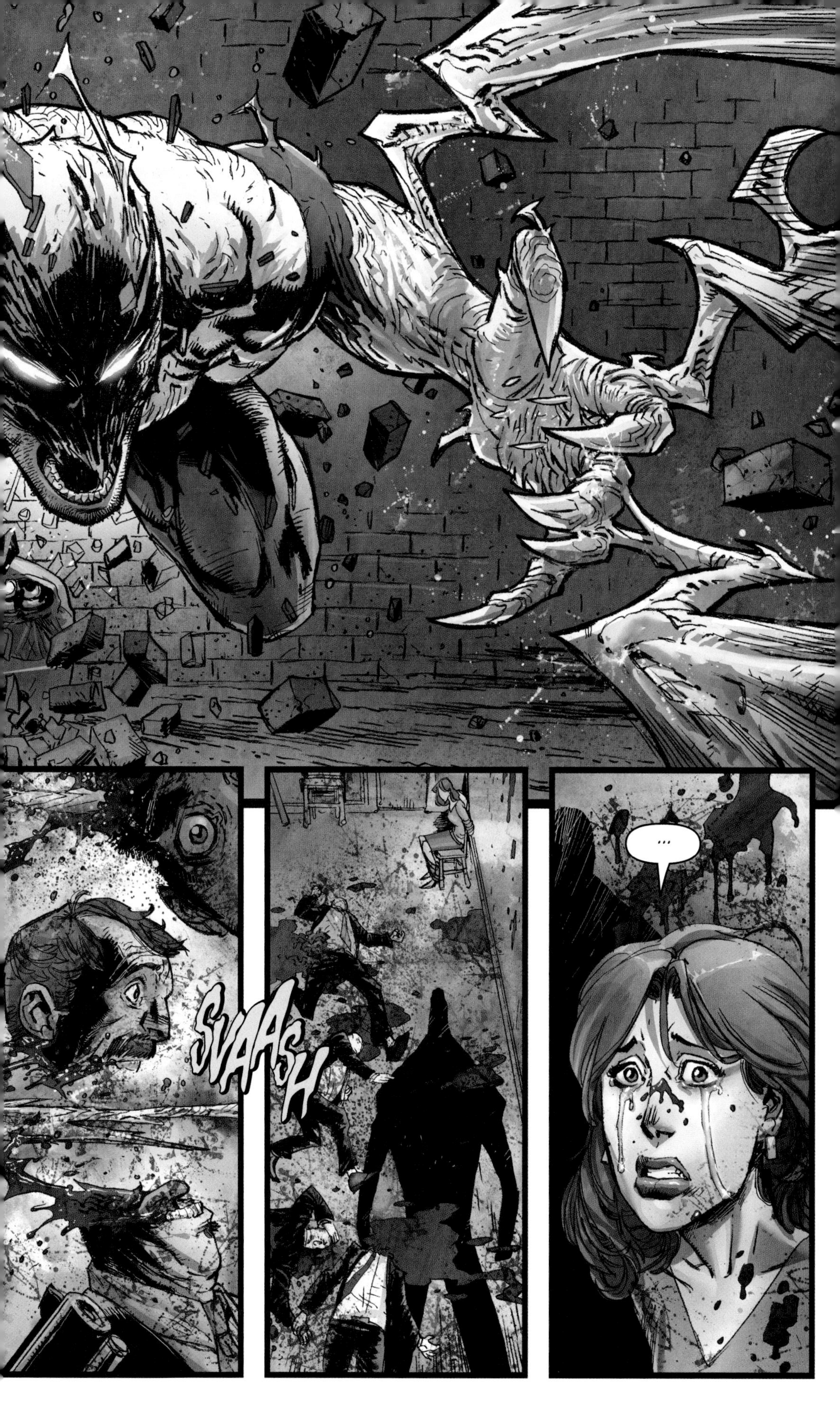
SVAASH
...

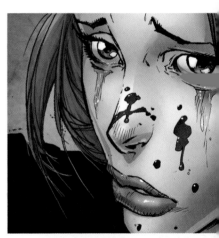

IT'S OKAY. YOU'RE SAF NOW.

SHRIIPP

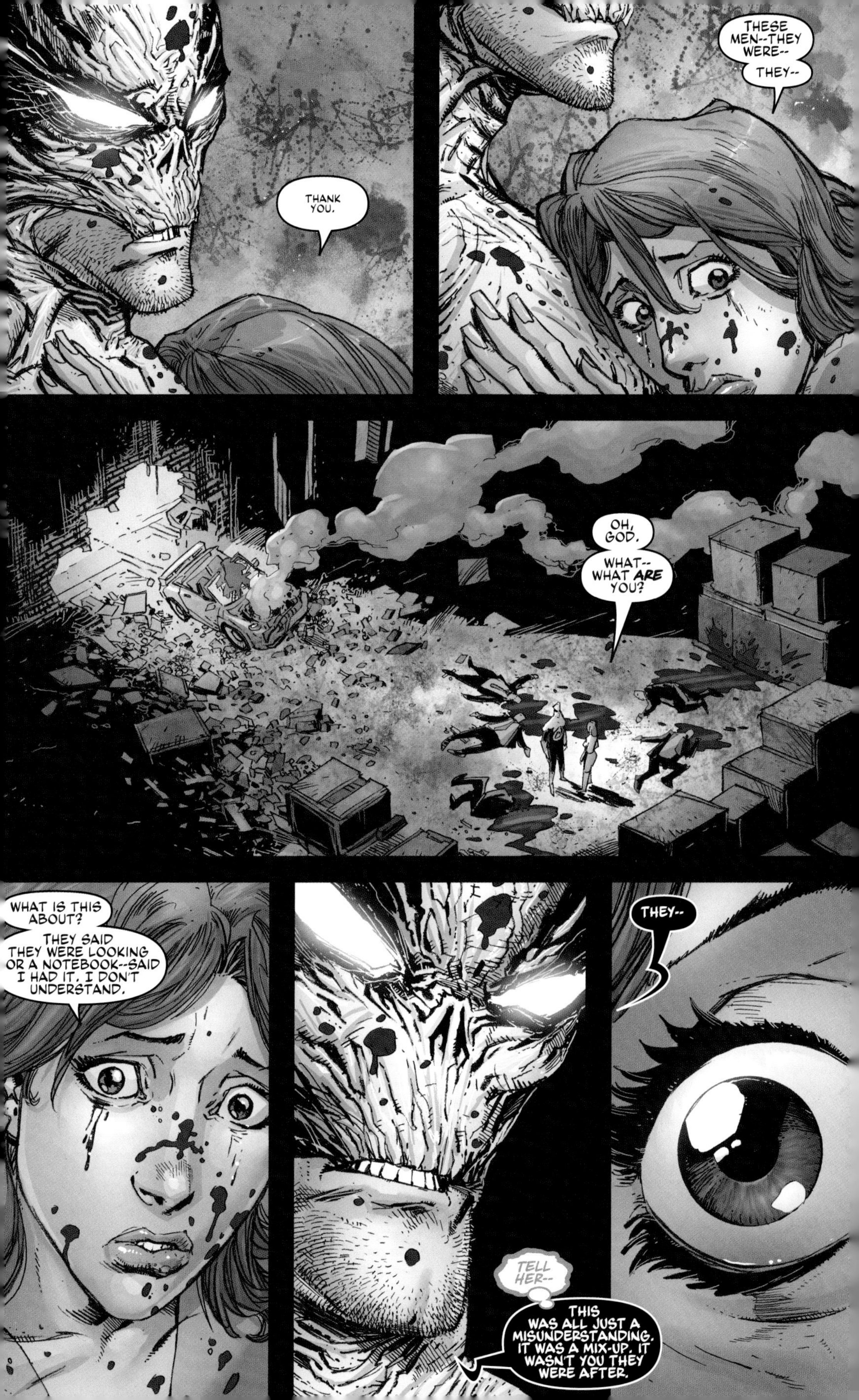
THANK YOU.
THESE MEN--THEY WERE--
THEY--
OH, GOD.
WHAT-- WHAT ARE YOU?
WHAT IS THIS ABOUT?
THEY SAID THEY WERE LOOKING OR A NOTEBOOK--SAID I HAD IT. I DON'T UNDERSTAND.
THEY--
TELL HER--
THIS WAS ALL JUST A MISUNDERSTANDING. IT WAS A MIX-UP. IT WASN'T YOU THEY WERE AFTER.

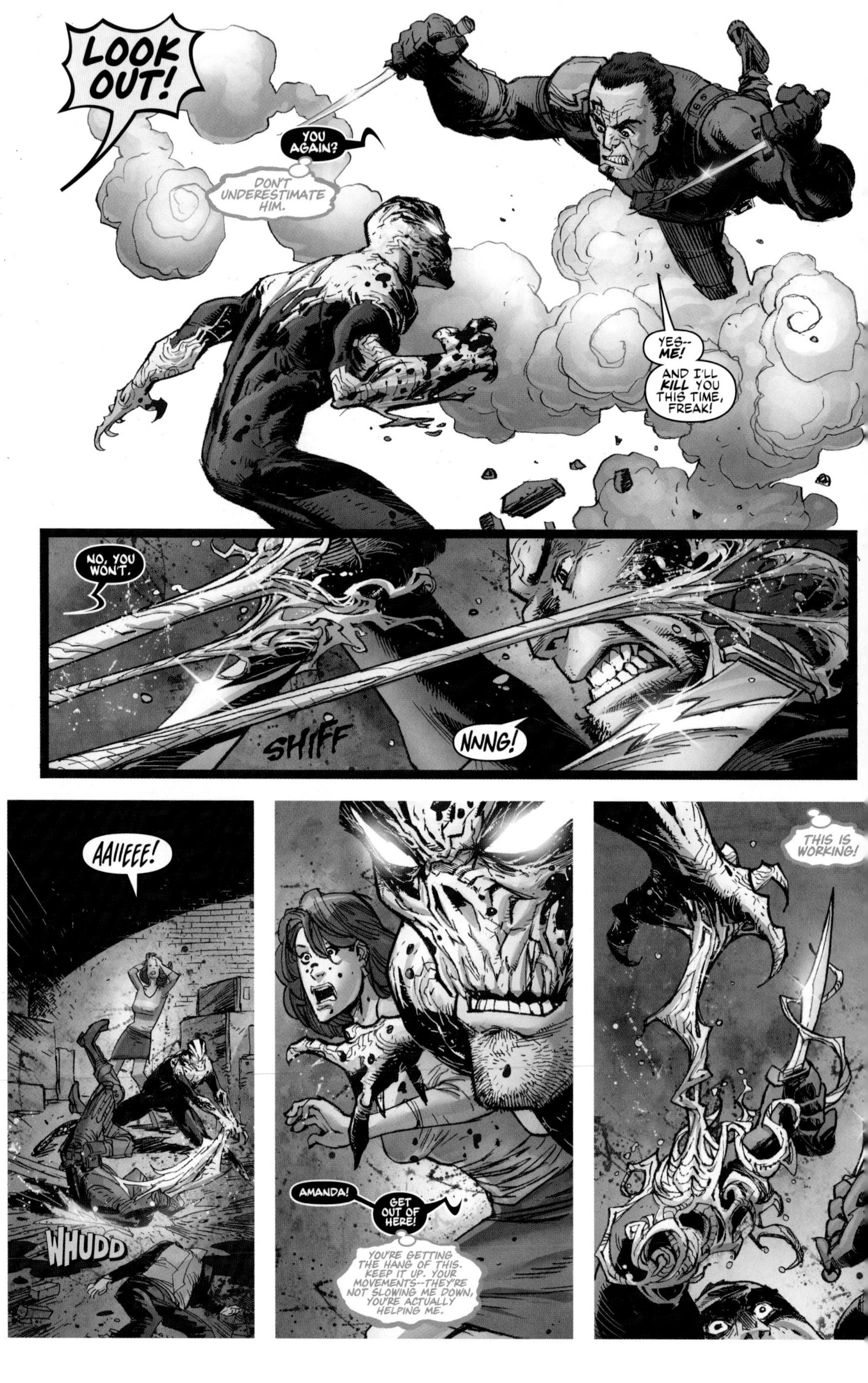
LOOK OUT!
YOU AGAIN?
DON'T UNDERESTIMATE HIM.
YES-- ME!
AND I'LL KILL YOU THIS TIME, FREAK!
NO, YOU WON'T.
SHIFF
NNNG!
AAIIEEE!
WHUDD
AMANDA!
GET OUT OF HERE!
YOU'RE GETTING THE HANG OF THIS. KEEP IT UP. YOUR MOVEMENTS--THEY'RE NOT SLOWING ME DOWN, YOU'RE ACTUALLY HELPING ME.
THIS IS WORKING!

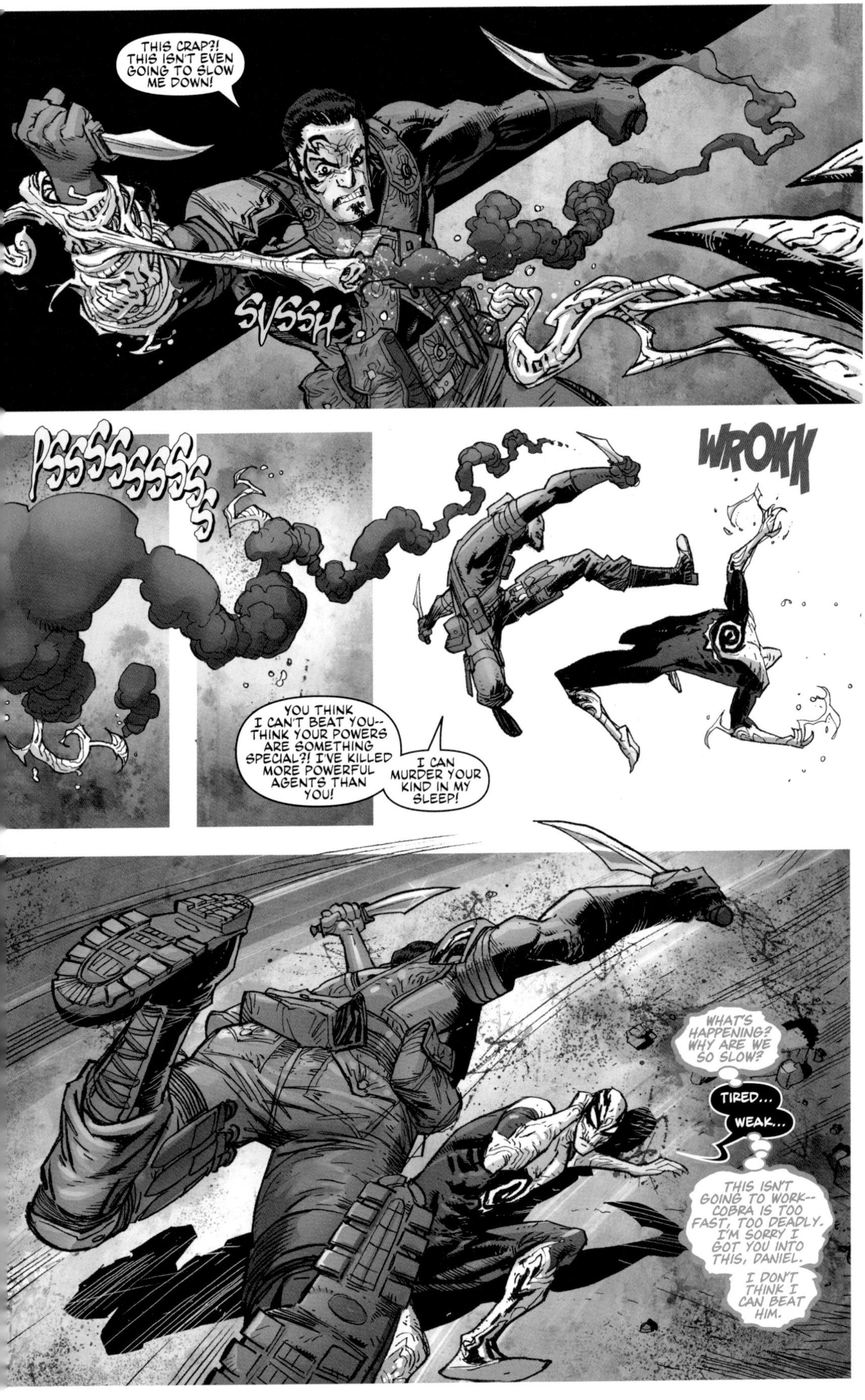
THIS CRAP?! THIS ISN'T EVEN GOING TO SLOW ME DOWN!
SVSSH
PSSSSSSSSSS
WROKK
YOU THINK I CAN'T BEAT YOU-- THINK YOUR POWERS ARE SOMETHING SPECIAL?! I'VE KILLED MORE POWERFUL AGENTS THAN YOU!
I CAN MURDER YOUR KIND IN MY SLEEP!
WHAT'S HAPPENING? WHY ARE WE SO SLOW?
TIRED...
WEAK...
THIS ISN'T GOING TO WORK-- COBRA IS TOO FAST, TOO DEADLY. I'M SORRY I GOT YOU INTO THIS, DANIEL.
I DON'T THINK I CAN BEAT HIM.

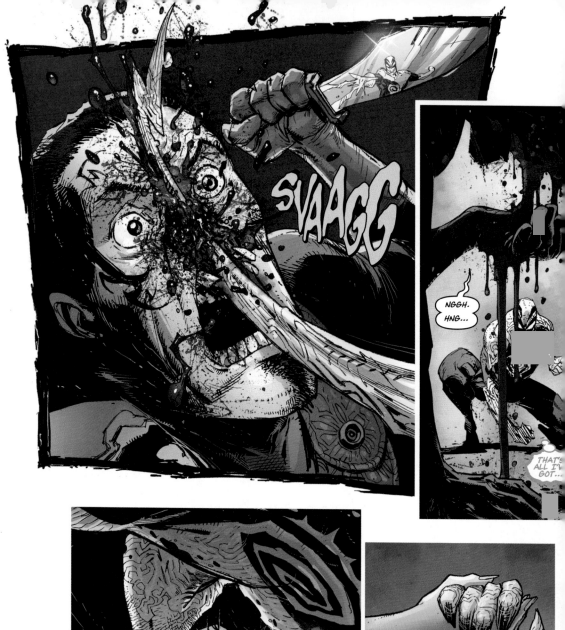

SVAAGG

NGGH. HNG...

THAT'S ALL I'V GOT...

IF HE TURNS AROUND...

CAN'T...

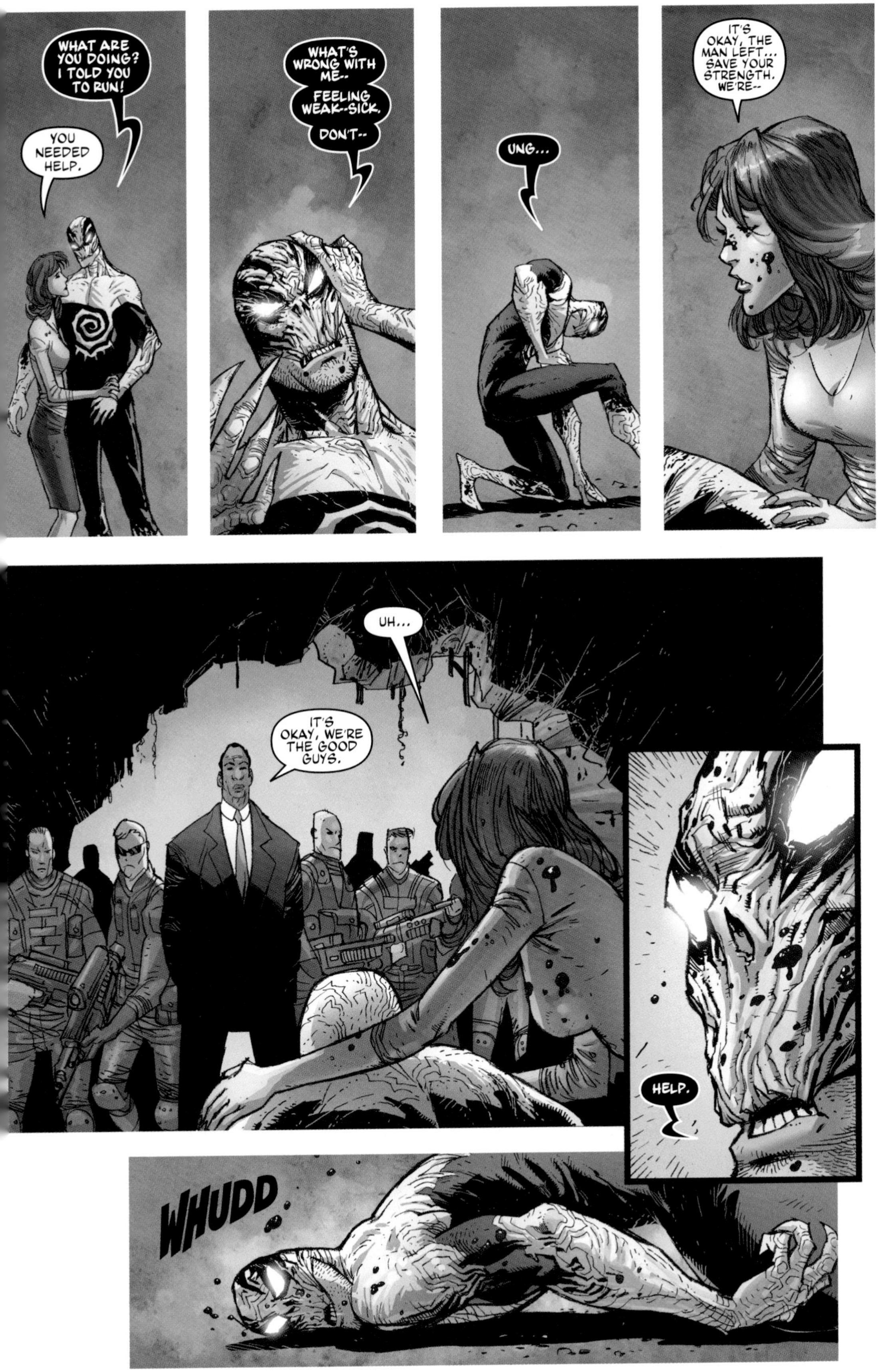

WHAT ARE YOU DOING? I TOLD YOU TO RUN!
YOU NEEDED HELP.
WHAT'S WRONG WITH ME--
FEELING WEAK--SICK.
DON'T--
UNG...
IT'S OKAY, THE MAN LEFT... SAVE YOUR STRENGTH. WE'RE--
UH...
IT'S OKAY, WE'RE THE GOOD GUYS.
HELP.
WHUDD

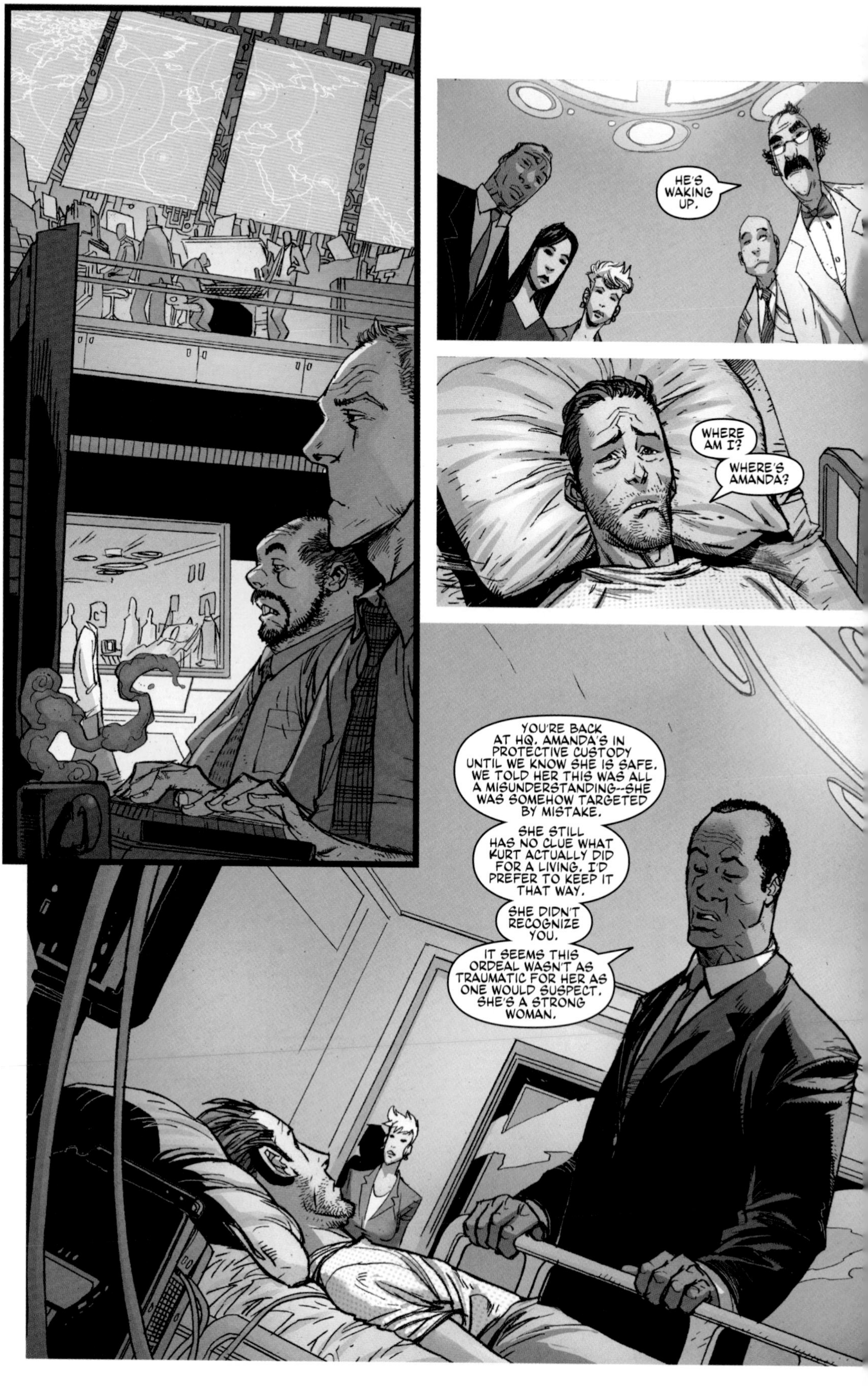
HE'S WAKING UP.
WHERE AM I?
WHERE'S AMANDA?
YOU'RE BACK AT HQ. AMANDA'S IN PROTECTIVE CUSTODY UNTIL WE KNOW SHE IS SAFE. WE TOLD HER THIS WAS ALL A MISUNDERSTANDING--SHE WAS SOMEHOW TARGETED BY MISTAKE.
SHE STILL HAS NO CLUE WHAT KURT ACTUALLY DID FOR A LIVING. I'D PREFER TO KEEP IT THAT WAY.
SHE DIDN'T RECOGNIZE YOU.
IT SEEMS THIS ORDEAL WASN'T AS TRAUMATIC FOR HER AS ONE WOULD SUSPECT. SHE'S A STRONG WOMAN.

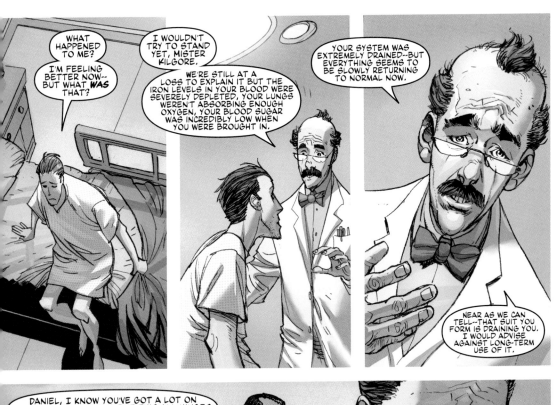

WHAT HAPPENED TO ME?

I'M FEELING BETTER NOW-- BUT WHAT *WAS* THAT?

I WOULDN'T TRY TO STAND YET, MISTER KILGORE.

WE'RE STILL AT A LOSS TO EXPLAIN IT BUT THE IRON LEVELS IN YOUR BLOOD WERE SEVERELY DEPLETED, YOUR LUNGS WEREN'T ABSORBING ENOUGH OXYGEN, YOUR BLOOD SUGAR WAS INCREDIBLY LOW WHEN YOU WERE BROUGHT IN.

YOUR SYSTEM WAS EXTREMELY DRAINED--BUT EVERYTHING SEEMS TO BE SLOWLY RETURNING TO NORMAL NOW.

NEAR AS WE CAN TELL--THAT SUIT YOU FORM IS DRAINING YOU. I WOULD ADVISE AGAINST LONG-TERM USE OF IT.

DANIEL, I KNOW YOU'VE GOT A LOT ON YOUR MIND RIGHT NOW--BUT THIS ALL HINGES ON THAT NOTEBOOK, SHILLINGER'S NOTES, RECORDS OF HIS EXPERIMENTS.

WE NEED IT, THEY'RE AFTER IT. NO ONE CONNECTED TO KURT IS GOING TO BE SAFE UNTIL WE LOCATE IT.

DO YOU KNOW ANYTHING?

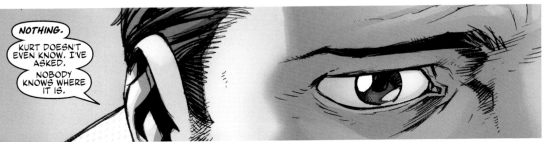

NOTHING.

KURT DOESN'T EVEN KNOW. I'VE ASKED.

NOBODY KNOWS WHERE IT IS.

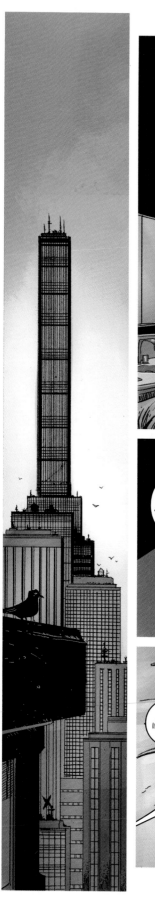

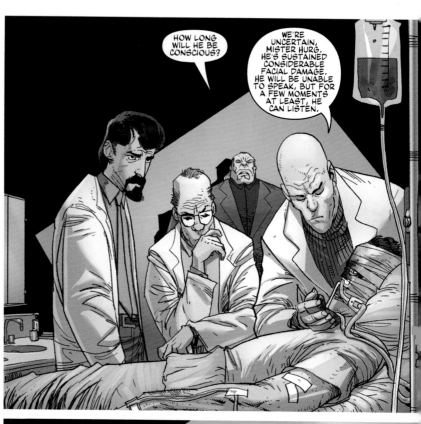

HOW LONG WILL HE BE CONSCIOUS?

WE'RE UNCERTAIN, MISTER HURG. HE'S SUSTAINED CONSIDERABLE FACIAL DAMAGE. HE WILL BE UNABLE TO SPEAK, BUT FOR A FEW MOMENTS AT LEAST, HE CAN LISTEN.

THAT WILL BE ENOUGH. I DO NOT APPRECIATE FAILURE, MISTER COBRA. I HOPE THAT YOU DO RECOGNIZE THAT AFTER YEARS OF LOYAL SERVICE, THESE LAST FEW DAYS YOU'VE FAILED ME TWICE.

I CAN'T HELP BUT FEEL I SHOULD HAVE LEFT YOU TO DIE.

NEVERTHELESS, HERE YOU ARE. I HAVE MADE A CONSIDERABLE INVESTMENT IN YOU, AND I PLAN TO RECOUP THAT INVESTMENT.

BUT DON'T CONSIDER THIS A SECOND CHANCE, MY FRIEND. MAKE NO MISTAKE, THIS IS YOUR LAST CHANCE.

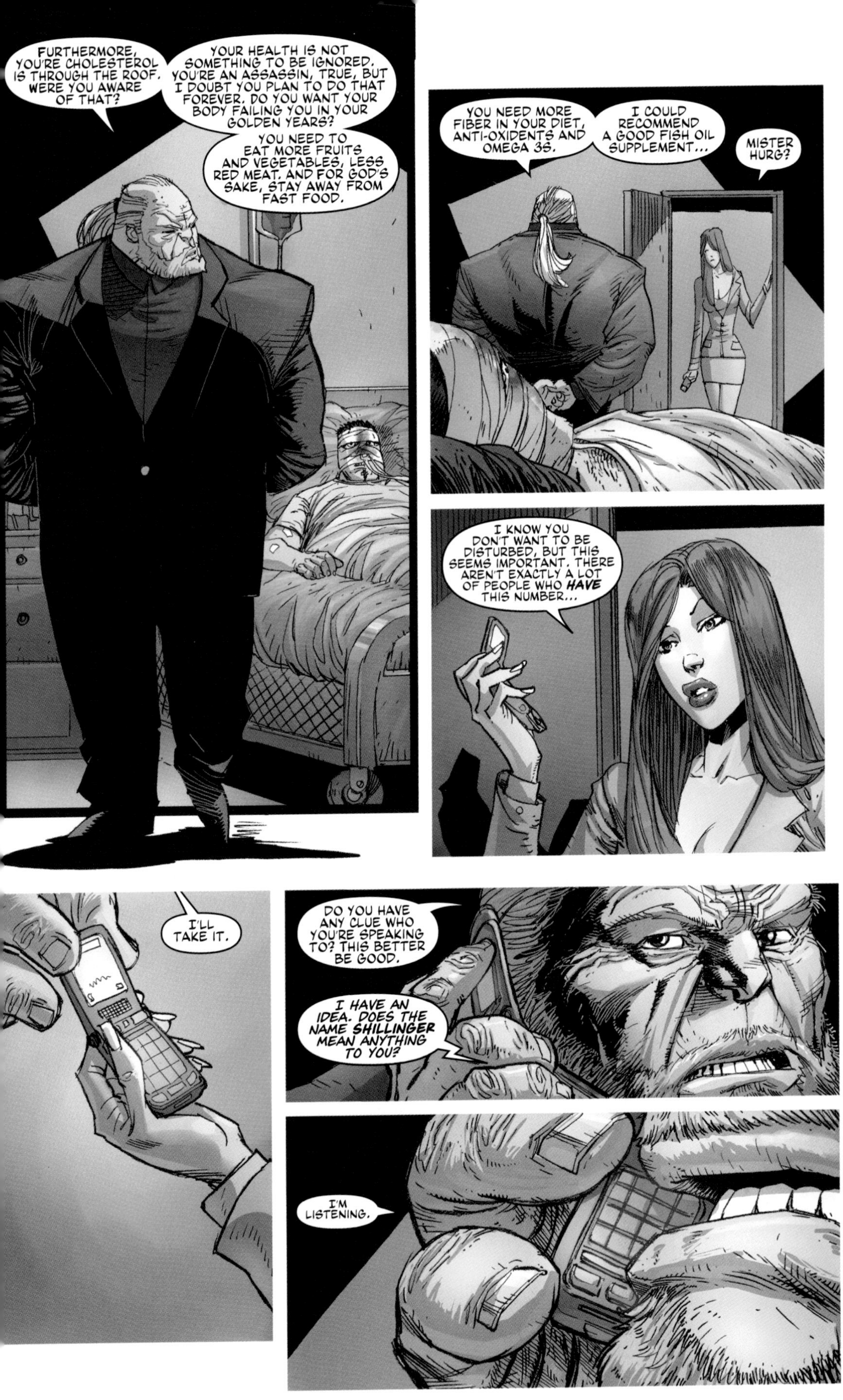
FURTHERMORE, YOU'RE CHOLESTEROL IS THROUGH THE ROOF. WERE YOU AWARE OF THAT?
YOUR HEALTH IS NOT SOMETHING TO BE IGNORED. YOU'RE AN ASSASSIN, TRUE, BUT I DOUBT YOU PLAN TO DO THAT FOREVER. DO YOU WANT YOUR BODY FAILING YOU IN YOUR GOLDEN YEARS?
YOU NEED TO EAT MORE FRUITS AND VEGETABLES, LESS RED MEAT. AND FOR GOD'S SAKE, STAY AWAY FROM FAST FOOD.
YOU NEED MORE FIBER IN YOUR DIET, ANTI-OXIDENTS AND OMEGA 3S.
I COULD RECOMMEND A GOOD FISH OIL SUPPLEMENT...
MISTER HURG?
I KNOW YOU DON'T WANT TO BE DISTURBED, BUT THIS SEEMS IMPORTANT. THERE AREN'T EXACTLY A LOT OF PEOPLE WHO HAVE THIS NUMBER...
I'LL TAKE IT.
DO YOU HAVE ANY CLUE WHO YOU'RE SPEAKING TO? THIS BETTER BE GOOD.
I HAVE AN IDEA. DOES THE NAME SHILLINGER MEAN ANYTHING TO YOU?
I'M LISTENING.

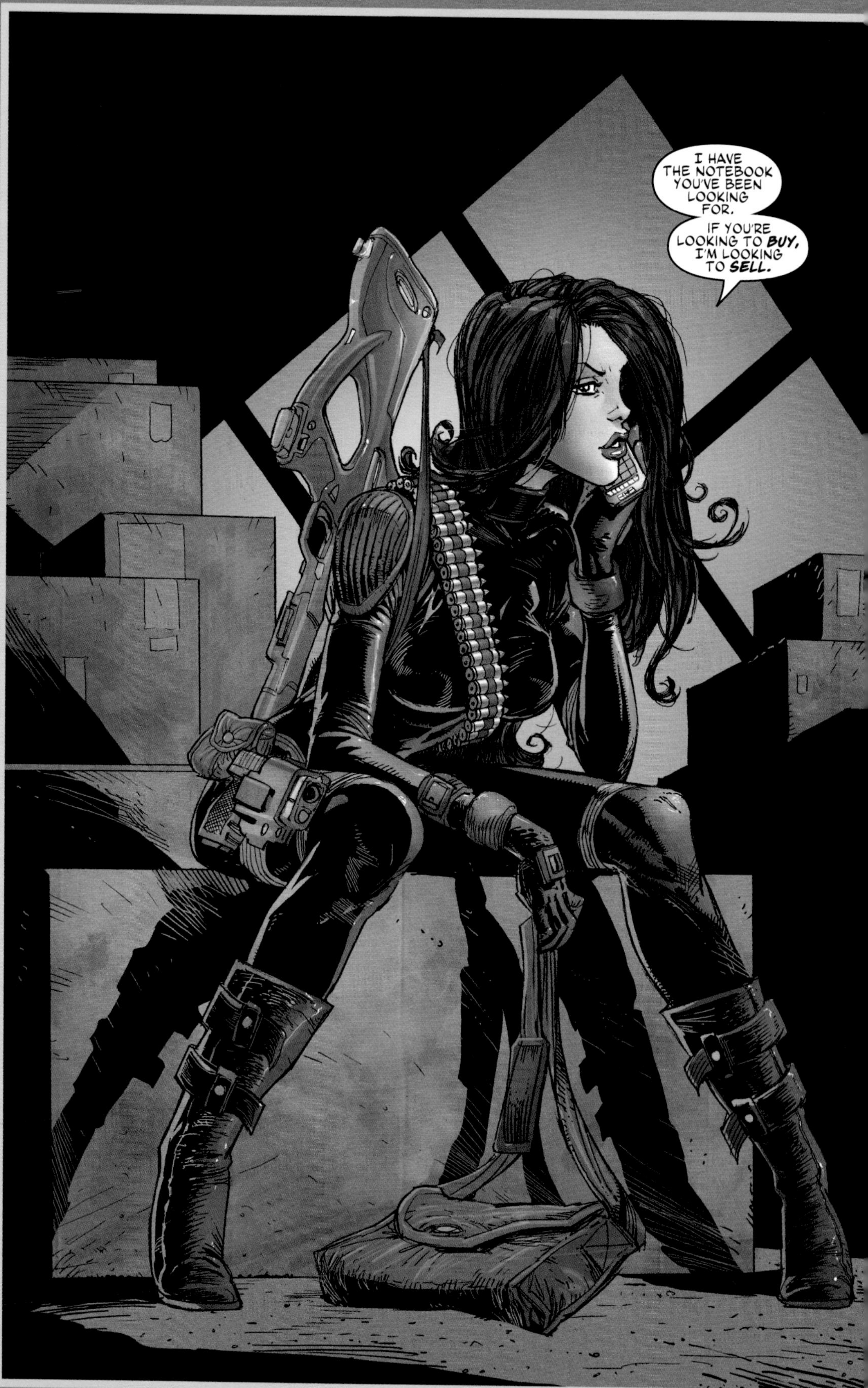
I HAVE THE NOTEBOOK YOU'VE BEEN LOOKING FOR.
IF YOU'RE LOOKING TO **BUY,** I'M LOOKING TO **SELL.**

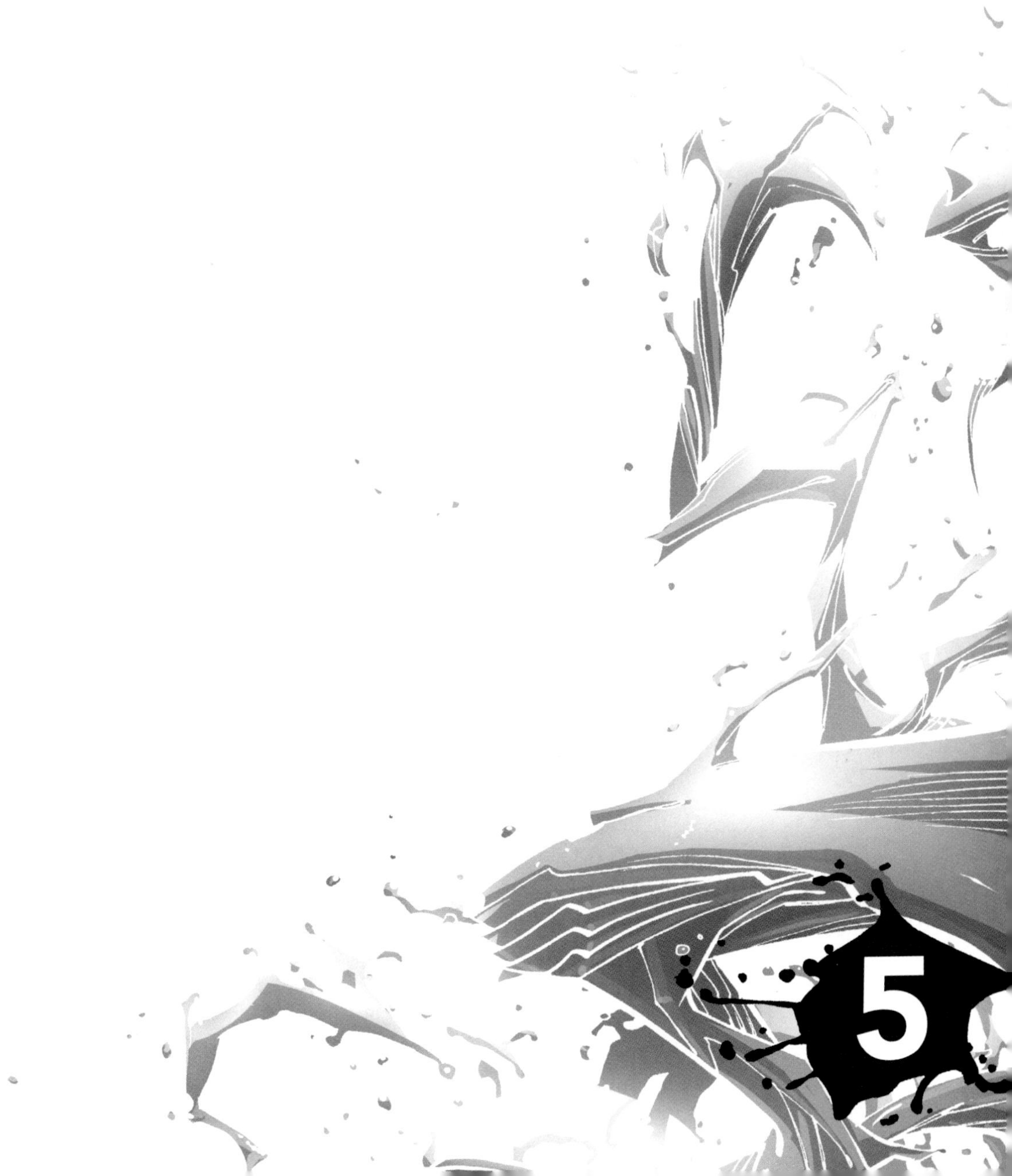
5

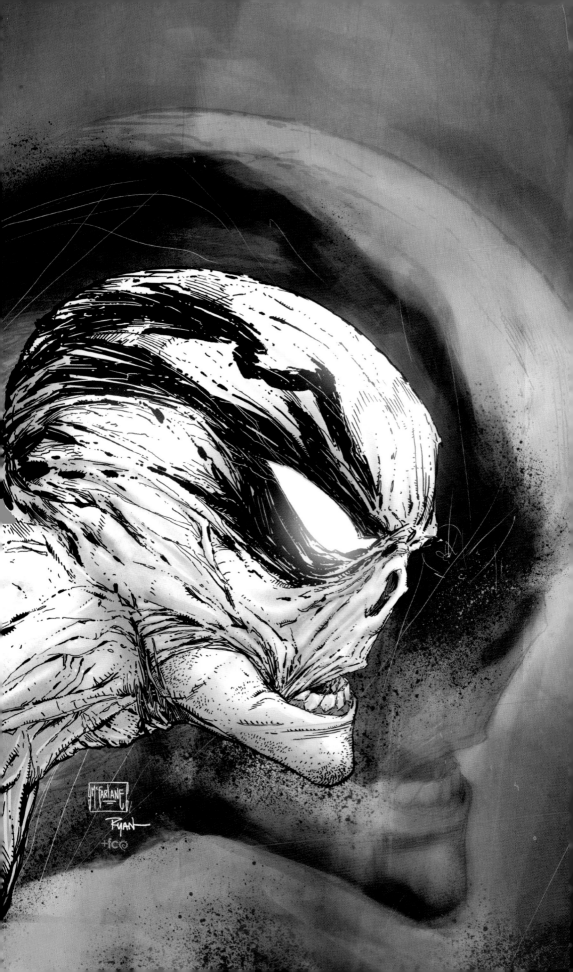

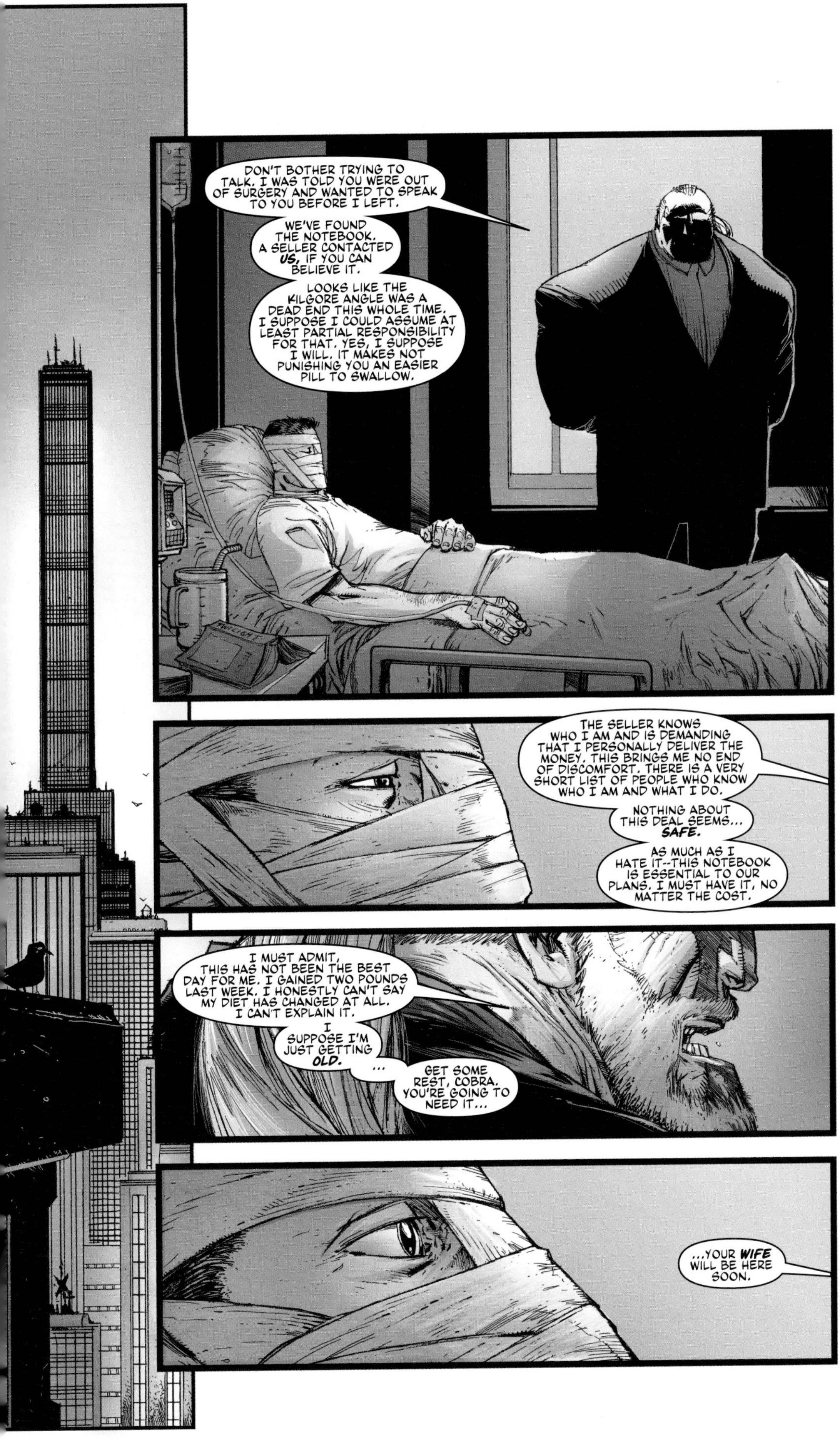
DON'T BOTHER TRYING TO TALK. I WAS TOLD YOU WERE OUT OF SURGERY AND WANTED TO SPEAK TO YOU BEFORE I LEFT.
WE'VE FOUND THE NOTEBOOK. A SELLER CONTACTED *US*, IF YOU CAN BELIEVE IT.
LOOKS LIKE THE KILGORE ANGLE WAS A DEAD END THIS WHOLE TIME. I SUPPOSE I COULD ASSUME AT LEAST PARTIAL RESPONSIBILITY FOR THAT. YES, I SUPPOSE I WILL. IT MAKES NOT PUNISHING YOU AN EASIER PILL TO SWALLOW.
TWILIGHT
THE SELLER KNOWS WHO I AM AND IS DEMANDING THAT I PERSONALLY DELIVER THE MONEY. THIS BRINGS ME NO END OF DISCOMFORT. THERE IS A VERY SHORT LIST OF PEOPLE WHO KNOW WHO I AM AND WHAT I DO.
NOTHING ABOUT THIS DEAL SEEMS... **SAFE.**
AS MUCH AS I HATE IT--THIS NOTEBOOK IS ESSENTIAL TO OUR PLANS. I MUST HAVE IT, NO MATTER THE COST.
I MUST ADMIT, THIS HAS NOT BEEN THE BEST DAY FOR ME. I GAINED TWO POUNDS LAST WEEK. I HONESTLY CAN'T SAY MY DIET HAS CHANGED AT ALL. I CAN'T EXPLAIN IT.
I SUPPOSE I'M JUST GETTING ***OLD.***
...
GET SOME REST, COBRA. YOU'RE GOING TO NEED IT...
...YOUR ***WIFE*** WILL BE HERE SOON.

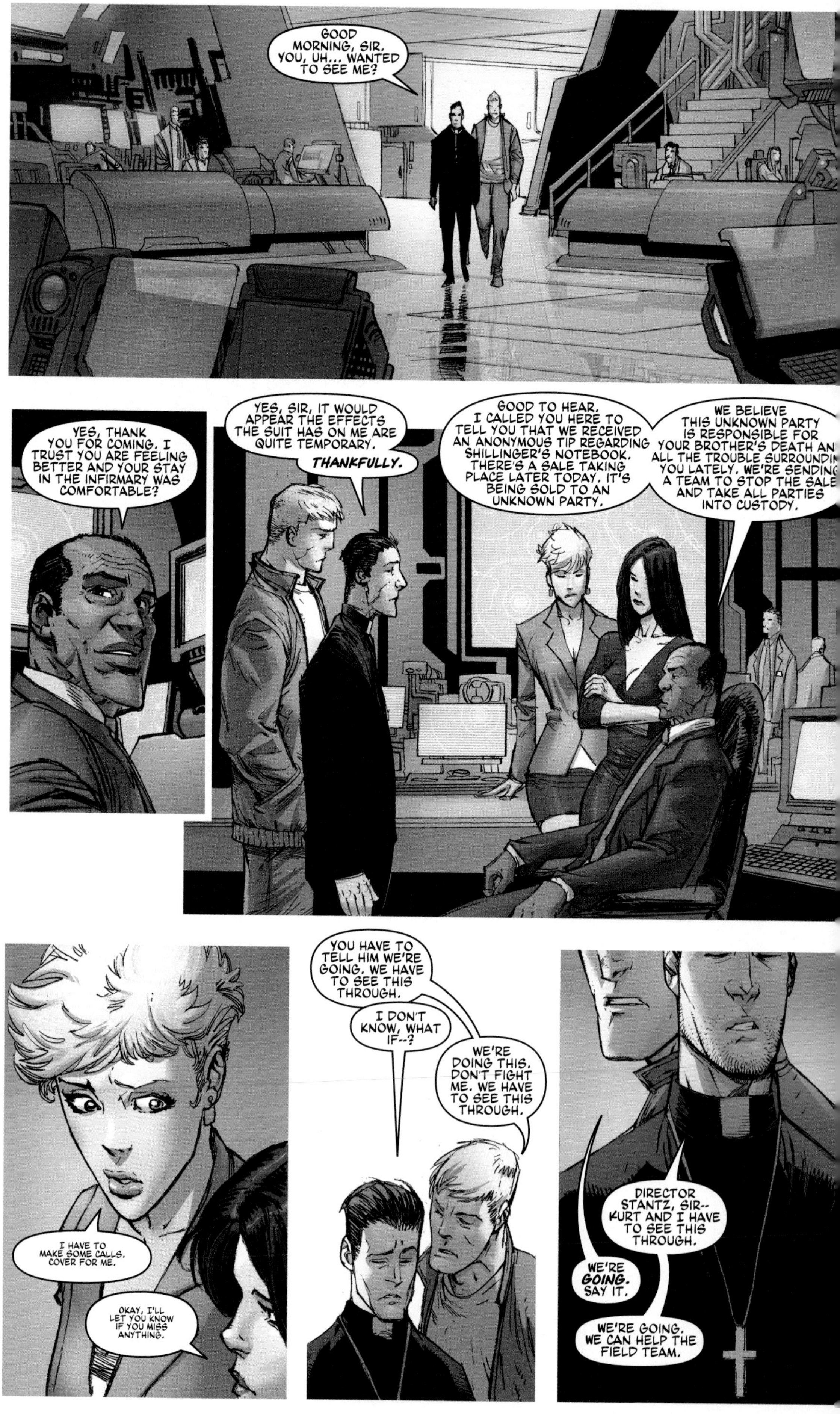

GOOD MORNING, SIR. YOU, UH... WANTED TO SEE ME?
YES, THANK YOU FOR COMING. I TRUST YOU ARE FEELING BETTER AND YOUR STAY IN THE INFIRMARY WAS COMFORTABLE?
YES, SIR, IT WOULD APPEAR THE EFFECTS THE SUIT HAS ON ME ARE QUITE TEMPORARY.
THANKFULLY.
GOOD TO HEAR. I CALLED YOU HERE TO TELL YOU THAT WE RECEIVED AN ANONYMOUS TIP REGARDING SHILLINGER'S NOTEBOOK. THERE'S A SALE TAKING PLACE LATER TODAY. IT'S BEING SOLD TO AN UNKNOWN PARTY.
WE BELIEVE THIS UNKNOWN PARTY IS RESPONSIBLE FOR YOUR BROTHER'S DEATH AN ALL THE TROUBLE SURROUNDI YOU LATELY. WE'RE SENDIN A TEAM TO STOP THE SALE AND TAKE ALL PARTIES INTO CUSTODY.
I HAVE TO MAKE SOME CALLS. COVER FOR ME.
OKAY, I'LL LET YOU KNOW IF YOU MISS ANYTHING.
YOU HAVE TO TELL HIM WE'RE GOING. WE HAVE TO SEE THIS THROUGH.
I DON'T KNOW, WHAT IF--?
WE'RE DOING THIS. DON'T FIGHT ME. WE HAVE TO SEE THIS THROUGH.
DIRECTOR STANTZ, SIR-- KURT AND I HAVE TO SEE THIS THROUGH.
WE'RE GOING. SAY IT.
WE'RE GOING. WE CAN HELP THE FIELD TEAM.

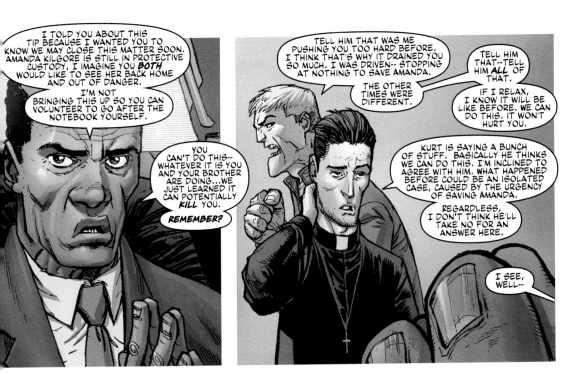

I TOLD YOU ABOUT THIS TIP BECAUSE I WANTED YOU TO KNOW WE MAY CLOSE THIS MATTER SOON. AMANDA KILGORE IS STILL IN PROTECTIVE CUSTODY, I IMAGINE YOU *BOTH* WOULD LIKE TO SEE HER BACK HOME AND OUT OF DANGER.

I'M NOT BRINGING THIS UP SO YOU CAN VOLUNTEER TO GO AFTER THE NOTEBOOK YOURSELF.

YOU CAN'T DO THIS-- WHATEVER IT IS YOU AND YOUR BROTHER ARE DOING...WE JUST LEARNED IT CAN POTENTIALLY *KILL* YOU.

REMEMBER?

TELL HIM THAT WAS ME PUSHING YOU TOO HARD BEFORE. I THINK THAT'S WHY IT DRAINED YOU SO MUCH. I WAS DRIVEN-- STOPPING AT NOTHING TO SAVE AMANDA.

THE OTHER TIMES WERE DIFFERENT.

TELL HIM THAT--TELL HIM *ALL* OF THAT.

IF I RELAX, I KNOW IT WILL BE LIKE BEFORE. WE CAN DO THIS. IT WON'T HURT YOU.

KURT IS SAYING A BUNCH OF STUFF. BASICALLY HE THINKS WE CAN DO THIS. I'M INCLINED TO AGREE WITH HIM. WHAT HAPPENED BEFORE COULD BE AN ISOLATED CASE, CAUSED BY THE URGENCY OF SAVING AMANDA.

REGARDLESS, I DON'T THINK HE'LL TAKE NO FOR AN ANSWER HERE.

I SEE, WELL--

I'M SORRY TO INTERRUPT, SIR. WE'VE COMPLETED THE VOICE ANALYSIS AND CONFIRMED THAT THE PERSON WHO CALLED IN THE TIP IS MIRAGE.

OH YEAH! SHE'S STILL ON OUR SIDE! I KNEW IT!

GOOD WORK MIKE...

...AND SCOTT.

SHE'S GOING THROUGH WITH IT...

WHAT?

DANIEL, I TAKE NO RESPONSIBILITY IN WHATEVER HAPPENS TO YOU IF YOU GO OUT IN THE FIELD, BUT WE DON'T HAVE TIME TO FIGHT YOU AND KURT ON THIS.

DO WHAT YOU FEEL IS NECESSARY.

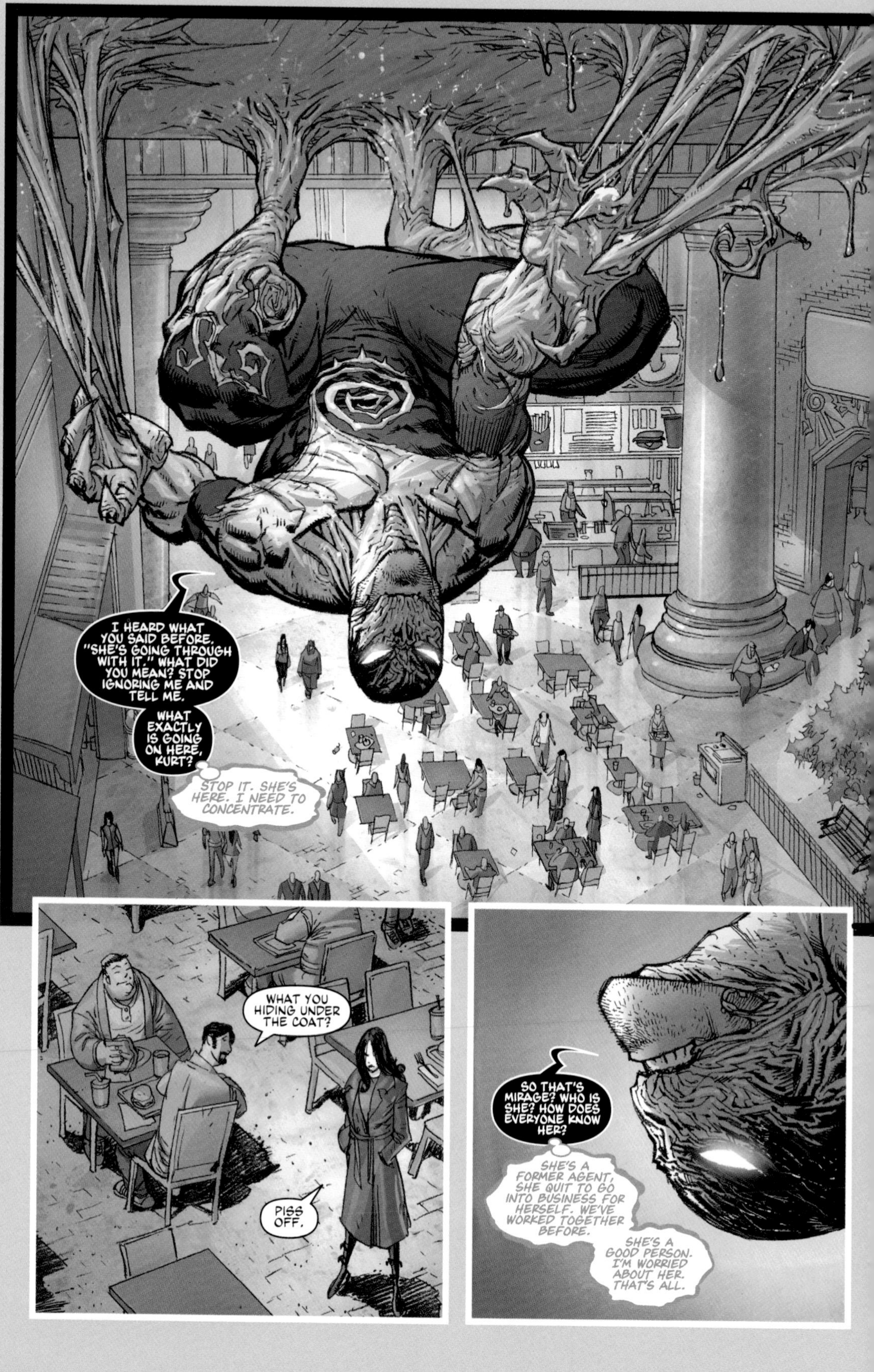
I HEARD WHAT YOU SAID BEFORE. "SHE'S GOING THROUGH WITH IT." WHAT DID YOU MEAN? STOP IGNORING ME AND TELL ME.
WHAT EXACTLY IS GOING ON HERE, KURT?
STOP IT. SHE'S HERE. I NEED TO CONCENTRATE.
WHAT YOU HIDING UNDER THE COAT?
PISS OFF.
SO THAT'S MIRAGE? WHO IS SHE? HOW DOES EVERYONE KNOW HER?
SHE'S A FORMER AGENT, SHE QUIT TO GO INTO BUSINESS FOR HERSELF. WE'VE WORKED TOGETHER BEFORE.
SHE'S A GOOD PERSON. I'M WORRIED ABOUT HER. THAT'S ALL.

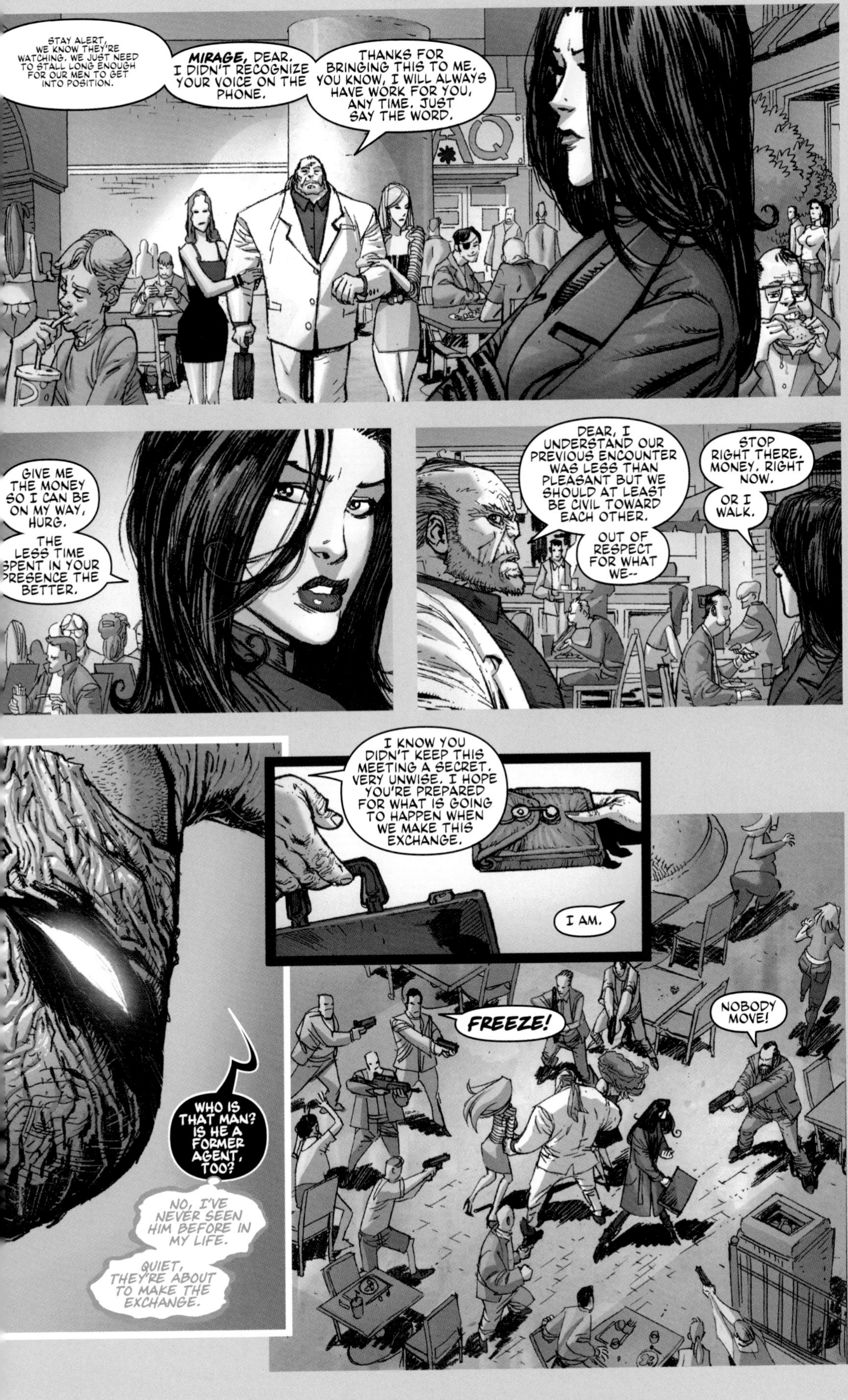
STAY ALERT, WE KNOW THEY'RE WATCHING. WE JUST NEED TO STALL LONG ENOUGH FOR OUR MEN TO GET INTO POSITION.
MIRAGE, DEAR. I DIDN'T RECOGNIZE YOUR VOICE ON THE PHONE.
THANKS FOR BRINGING THIS TO ME. YOU KNOW, I WILL ALWAYS HAVE WORK FOR YOU, ANY TIME. JUST SAY THE WORD.
GIVE ME THE MONEY SO I CAN BE ON MY WAY, HURG.
THE LESS TIME SPENT IN YOUR PRESENCE THE BETTER.
DEAR, I UNDERSTAND OUR PREVIOUS ENCOUNTER WAS LESS THAN PLEASANT BUT WE SHOULD AT LEAST BE CIVIL TOWARD EACH OTHER.
OUT OF RESPECT FOR WHAT WE--
STOP RIGHT THERE. MONEY. RIGHT NOW.
OR I WALK.
I KNOW YOU DIDN'T KEEP THIS MEETING A SECRET. VERY UNWISE. I HOPE YOU'RE PREPARED FOR WHAT IS GOING TO HAPPEN WHEN WE MAKE THIS EXCHANGE.
I AM.
WHO IS THAT MAN? IS HE A FORMER AGENT, TOO?
NO, I'VE NEVER SEEN HIM BEFORE IN MY LIFE.
QUIET, THEY'RE ABOUT TO MAKE THE EXCHANGE.
FREEZE!
NOBODY MOVE!

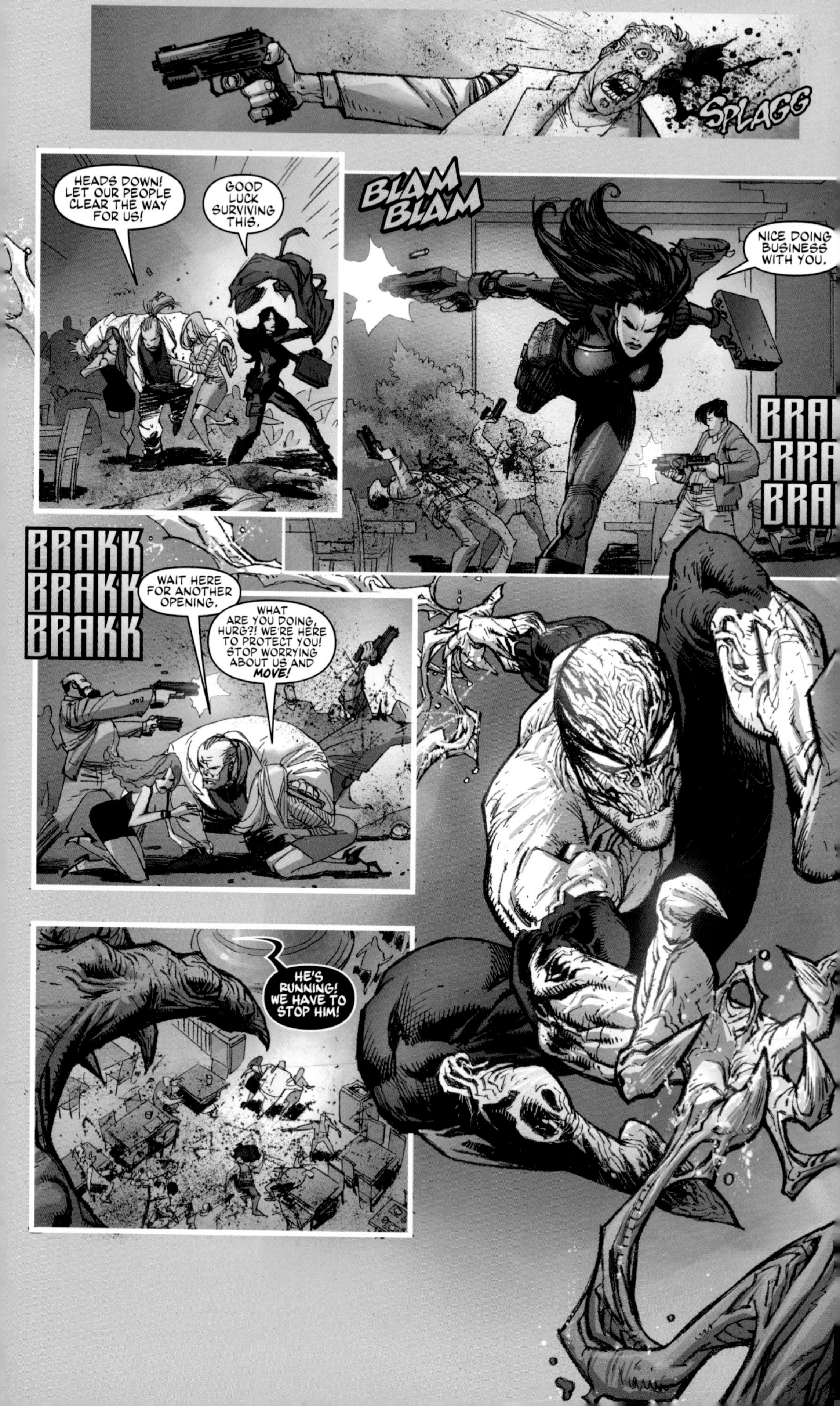
SPLAGG
HEADS DOWN! LET OUR PEOPLE CLEAR THE WAY FOR US!
GOOD LUCK SURVIVING THIS.
BLAM BLAM
NICE DOING BUSINESS WITH YOU.
BRAKK BRAKK BRAKK
WAIT HERE FOR ANOTHER OPENING.
WHAT ARE YOU DOING, HURG?! WE'RE HERE TO PROTECT YOU! STOP WORRYING ABOUT US AND MOVE!
HE'S RUNNING! WE HAVE TO STOP HIM!

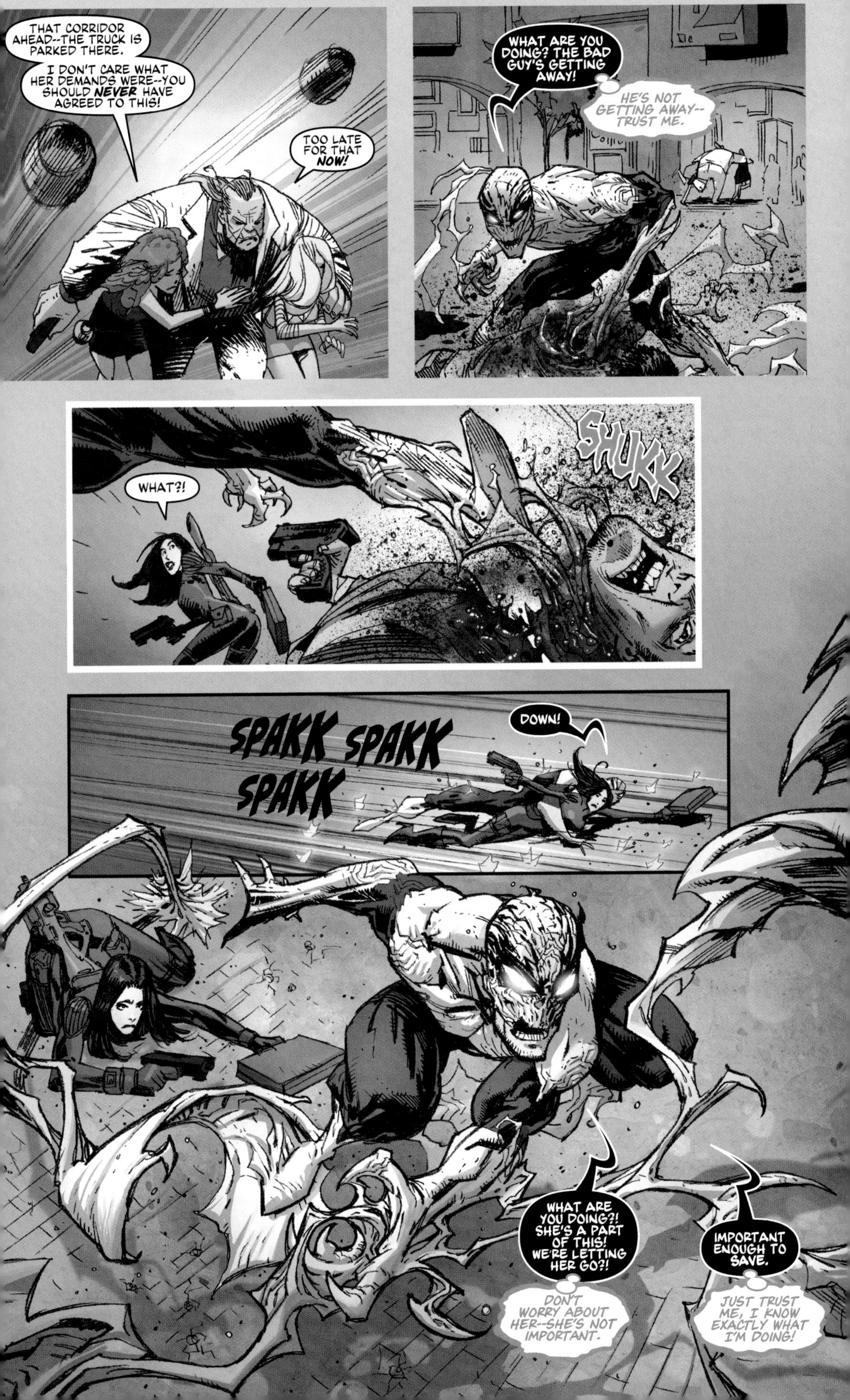

THAT CORRIDOR AHEAD--THE TRUCK IS PARKED THERE.
I DON'T CARE WHAT HER DEMANDS WERE--YOU SHOULD NEVER HAVE AGREED TO THIS!
TOO LATE FOR THAT NOW!
WHAT ARE YOU DOING? THE BAD GUY'S GETTING AWAY!
HE'S NOT GETTING AWAY-- TRUST ME.
WHAT?!
SHUKK
SPAKK SPAKK SPAKK
DOWN!
WHAT ARE YOU DOING?! SHE'S A PART OF THIS! WE'RE LETTING HER GO?!
DON'T WORRY ABOUT HER--SHE'S NOT IMPORTANT.
IMPORTANT ENOUGH TO SAVE.
JUST TRUST ME, I KNOW EXACTLY WHAT I'M DOING!

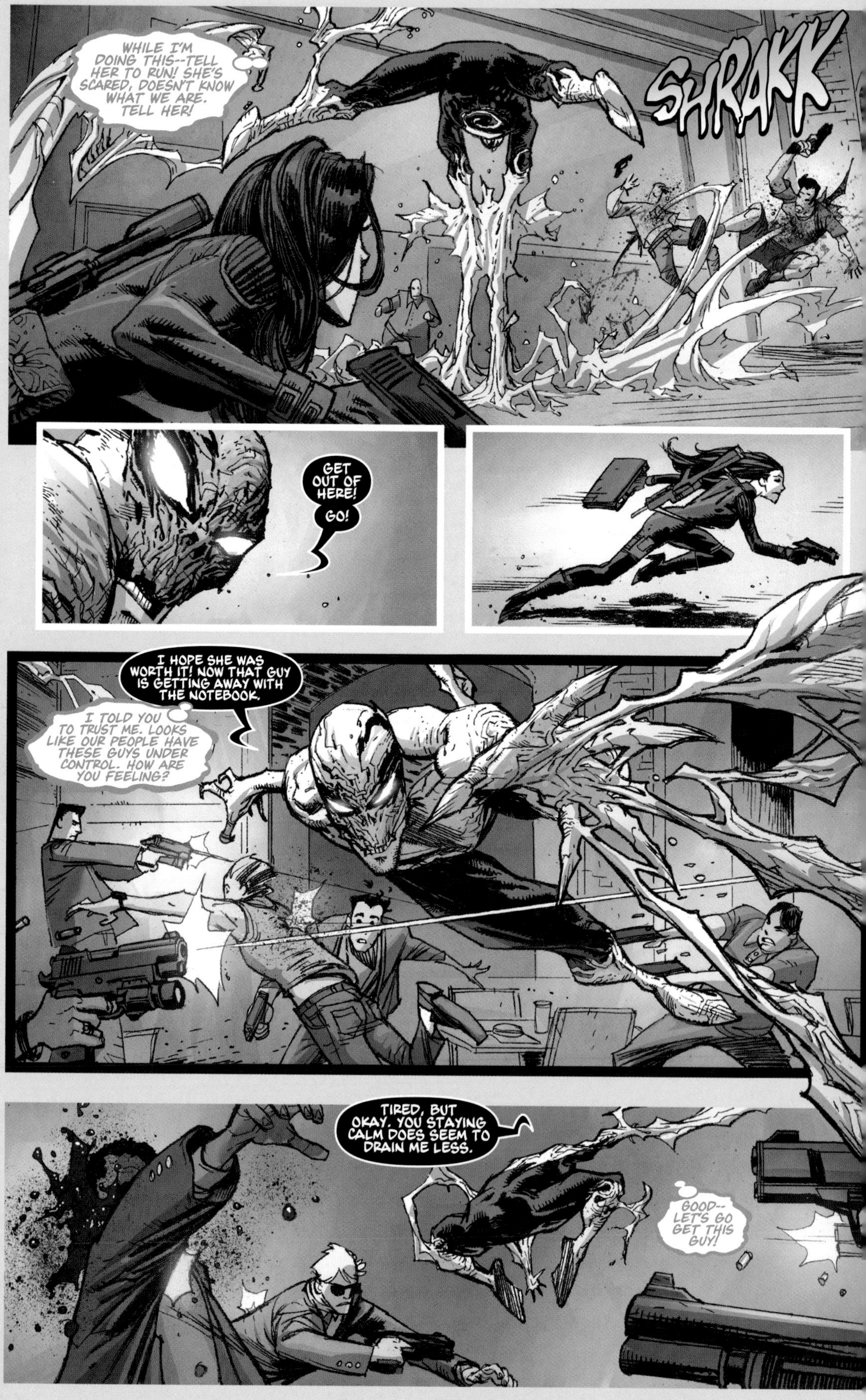
WHILE I'M DOING THIS--TELL HER TO RUN! SHE'S SCARED, DOESN'T KNOW WHAT WE ARE. TELL HER!
SHRAKK
GET OUT OF HERE!
GO!
I HOPE SHE WAS WORTH IT! NOW THAT GUY IS GETTING AWAY WITH THE NOTEBOOK.
I TOLD YOU TO TRUST ME. LOOKS LIKE OUR PEOPLE HAVE THESE GUYS UNDER CONTROL. HOW ARE YOU FEELING?
TIRED, BUT OKAY. YOU STAYING CALM DOES SEEM TO DRAIN ME LESS.
GOOD-- LET'S GO GET THIS GUY!

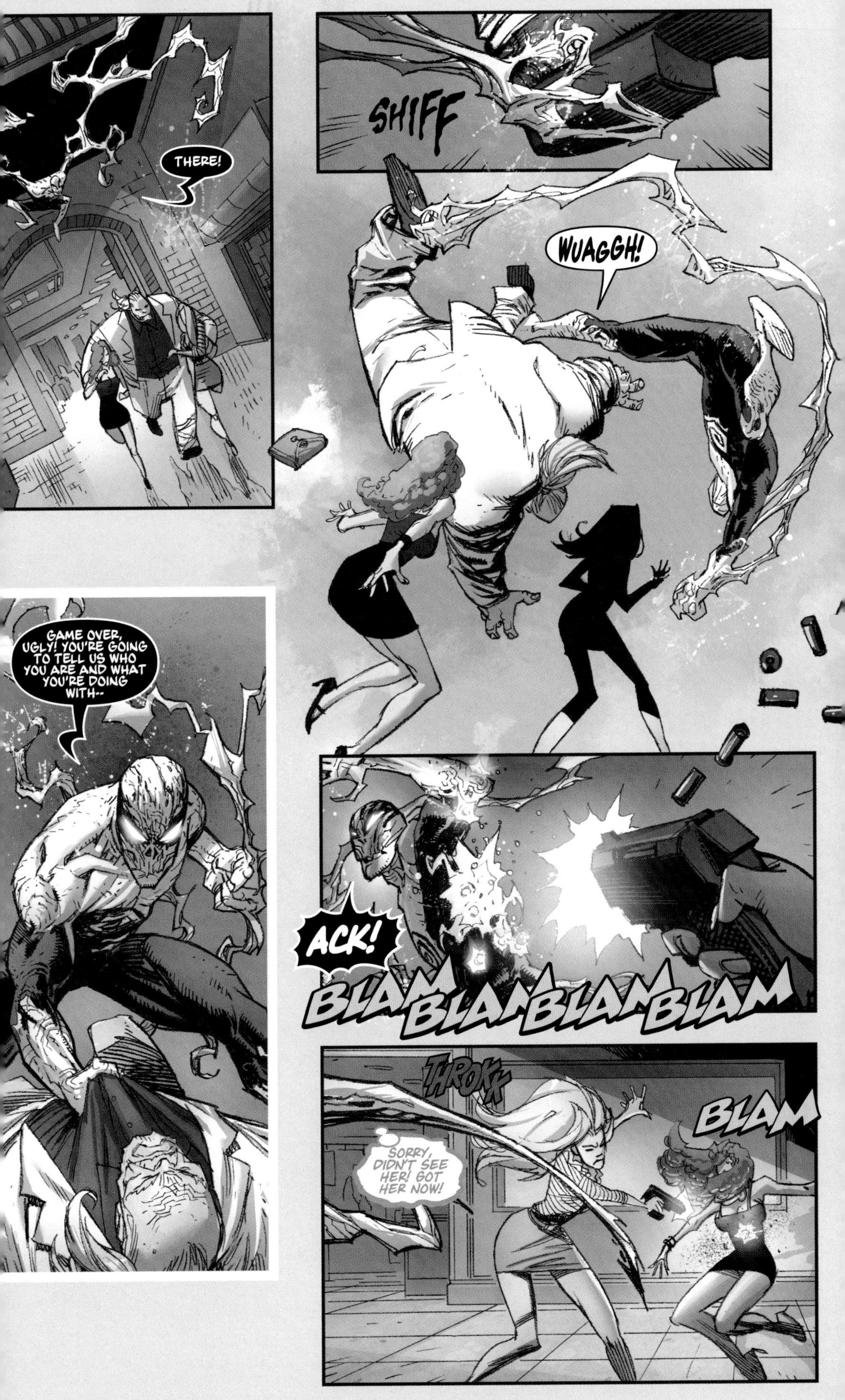
THERE!
SHIFF
WUAGGH!
GAME OVER, UGLY! YOU'RE GOING TO TELL US WHO YOU ARE AND WHAT YOU'RE DOING WITH--
ACK!
BLAM BLAM BLAM BLAM
THROKK
BLAM
SORRY, DIDN'T SEE HER! GOT HER NOW!

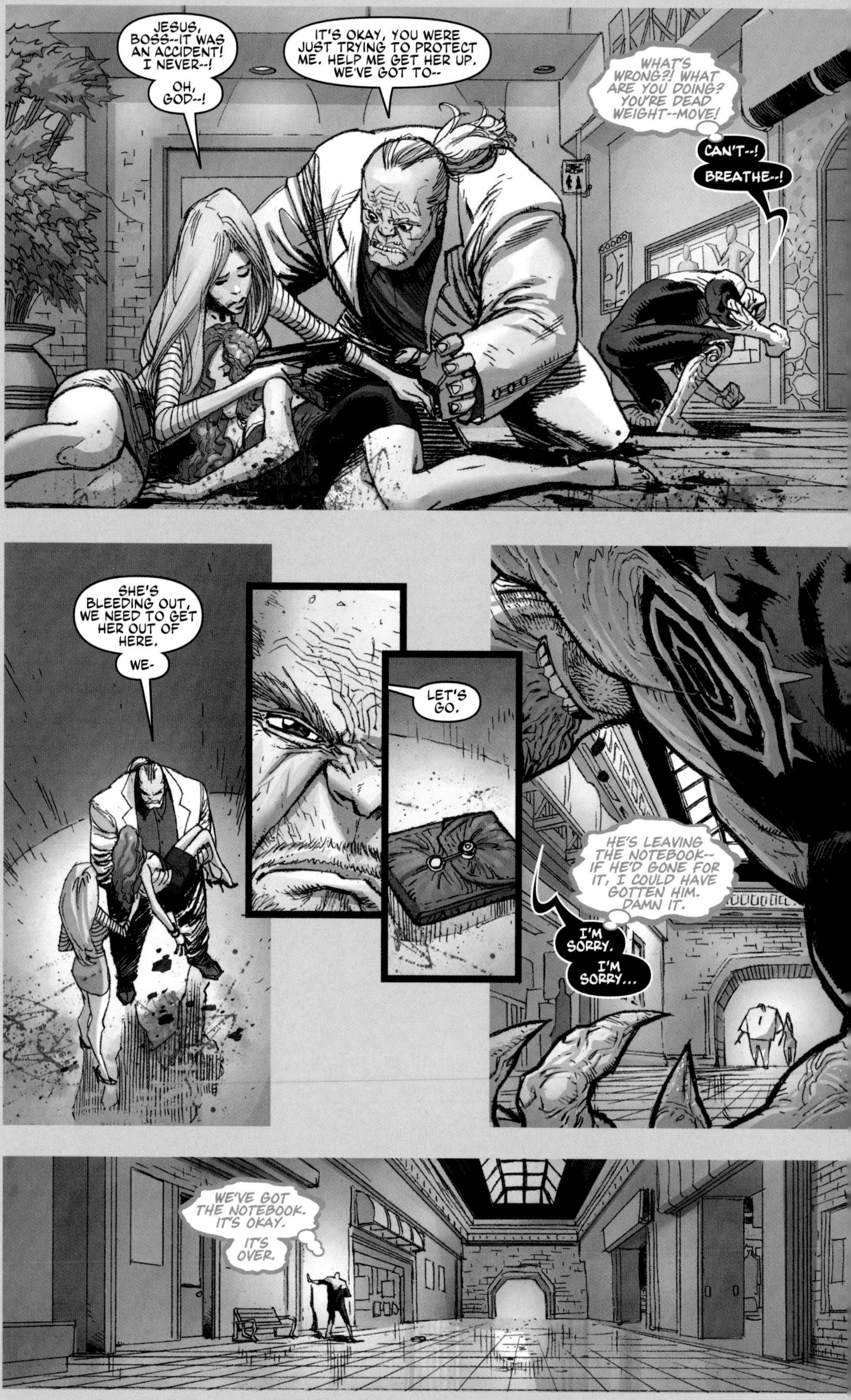
JESUS, BOSS--IT WAS AN ACCIDENT! I NEVER--!
OH, GOD--!
IT'S OKAY, YOU WERE JUST TRYING TO PROTECT ME. HELP ME GET HER UP. WE'VE GOT TO--
WHAT'S WRONG?! WHAT ARE YOU DOING? YOU'RE DEAD WEIGHT--MOVE!
CAN'T--!
BREATHE--!
SHE'S BLEEDING OUT, WE NEED TO GET HER OUT OF HERE.
WE-
LET'S GO.
HE'S LEAVING THE NOTEBOOK--IF HE'D GONE FOR IT, I COULD HAVE GOTTEN HIM. DAMN IT.
I'M SORRY.
I'M SORRY...
WE'VE GOT THE NOTEBOOK. IT'S OKAY.
IT'S OVER.

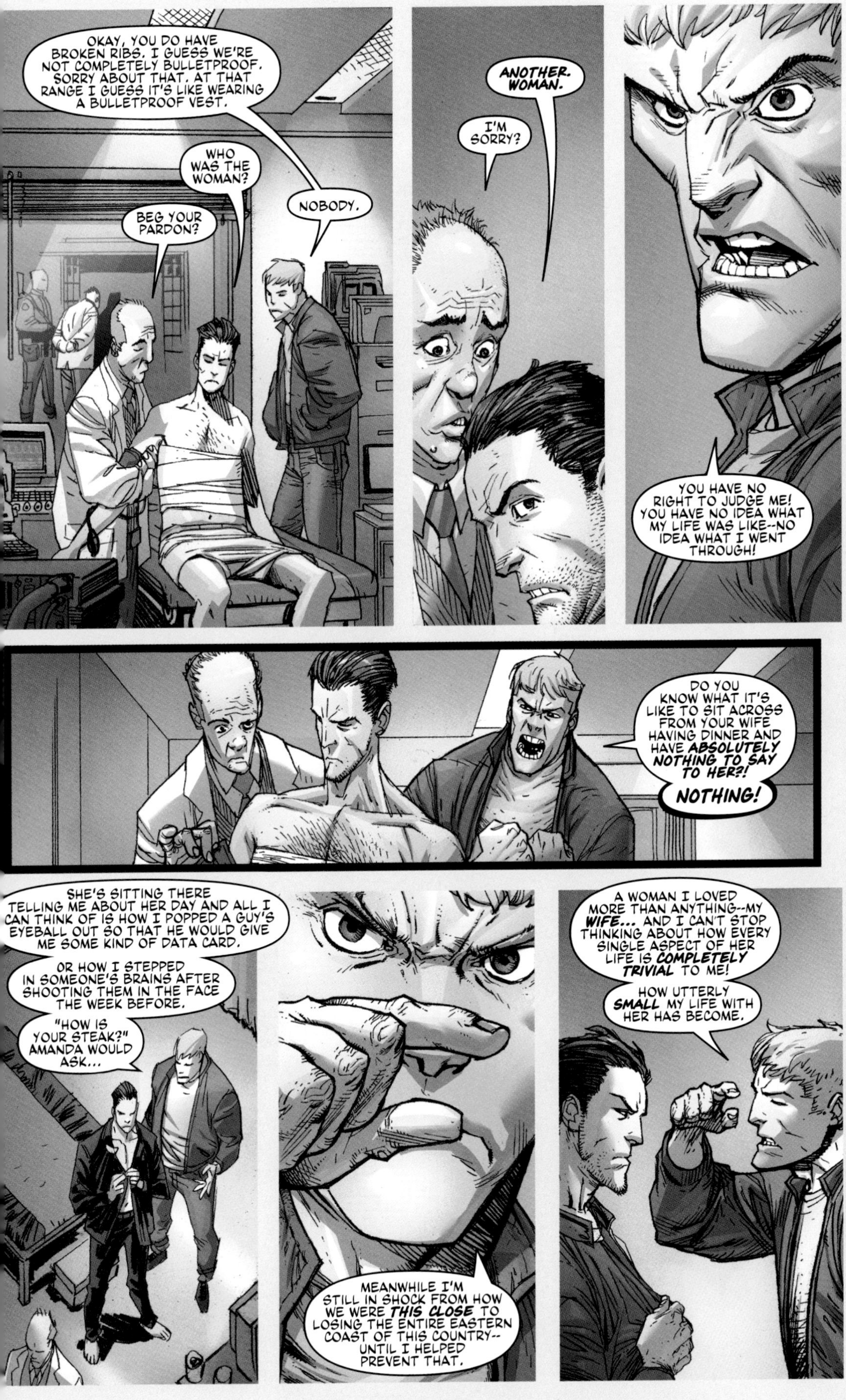
OKAY, YOU DO HAVE BROKEN RIBS. I GUESS WE'RE NOT COMPLETELY BULLETPROOF. SORRY ABOUT THAT. AT THAT RANGE I GUESS IT'S LIKE WEARING A BULLETPROOF VEST.
WHO WAS THE WOMAN?
BEG YOUR PARDON?
NOBODY.
ANOTHER. WOMAN.
I'M SORRY?
YOU HAVE NO RIGHT TO JUDGE ME! YOU HAVE NO IDEA WHAT MY LIFE WAS LIKE--NO IDEA WHAT I WENT THROUGH!
DO YOU KNOW WHAT IT'S LIKE TO SIT ACROSS FROM YOUR WIFE HAVING DINNER AND HAVE ABSOLUTELY NOTHING TO SAY TO HER?!
NOTHING!
SHE'S SITTING THERE TELLING ME ABOUT HER DAY AND ALL I CAN THINK OF IS HOW I POPPED A GUY'S EYEBALL OUT SO THAT HE WOULD GIVE ME SOME KIND OF DATA CARD.
OR HOW I STEPPED IN SOMEONE'S BRAINS AFTER SHOOTING THEM IN THE FACE THE WEEK BEFORE.
"HOW IS YOUR STEAK?" AMANDA WOULD ASK...
MEANWHILE I'M STILL IN SHOCK FROM HOW WE WERE THIS CLOSE TO LOSING THE ENTIRE EASTERN COAST OF THIS COUNTRY-- UNTIL I HELPED PREVENT THAT.
A WOMAN I LOVED MORE THAN ANYTHING--MY WIFE... AND I CAN'T STOP THINKING ABOUT HOW EVERY SINGLE ASPECT OF HER LIFE IS COMPLETELY TRIVIAL TO ME!
HOW UTTERLY SMALL MY LIFE WITH HER HAS BECOME.

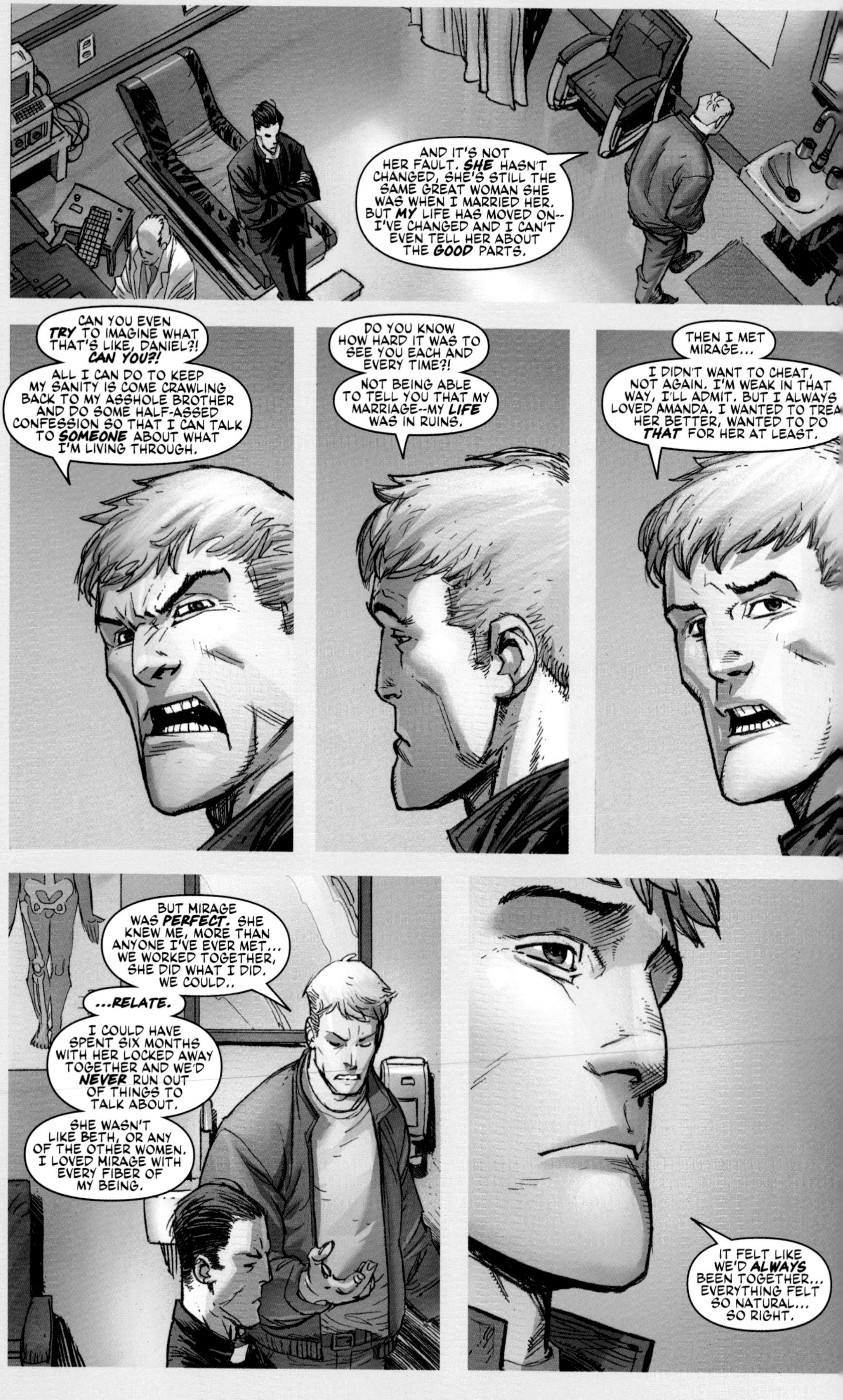
AND IT'S NOT HER FAULT. SHE HASN'T CHANGED, SHE'S STILL THE SAME GREAT WOMAN SHE WAS WHEN I MARRIED HER. BUT MY LIFE HAS MOVED ON-- I'VE CHANGED AND I CAN'T EVEN TELL HER ABOUT THE GOOD PARTS.
CAN YOU EVEN TRY TO IMAGINE WHAT THAT'S LIKE, DANIEL?! CAN YOU?!
ALL I CAN DO TO KEEP MY SANITY IS COME CRAWLING BACK TO MY ASSHOLE BROTHER AND DO SOME HALF-ASSED CONFESSION SO THAT I CAN TALK TO SOMEONE ABOUT WHAT I'M LIVING THROUGH.
DO YOU KNOW HOW HARD IT WAS TO SEE YOU EACH AND EVERY TIME?!
NOT BEING ABLE TO TELL YOU THAT MY MARRIAGE--MY LIFE WAS IN RUINS.
THEN I MET MIRAGE...
I DIDN'T WANT TO CHEAT, NOT AGAIN. I'M WEAK IN THAT WAY, I'LL ADMIT. BUT I ALWAYS LOVED AMANDA. I WANTED TO TREA HER BETTER, WANTED TO DO THAT FOR HER AT LEAST.
BUT MIRAGE WAS PERFECT. SHE KNEW ME, MORE THAN ANYONE I'VE EVER MET... WE WORKED TOGETHER, SHE DID WHAT I DID. WE COULD..
...RELATE.
I COULD HAVE SPENT SIX MONTHS WITH HER LOCKED AWAY TOGETHER AND WE'D NEVER RUN OUT OF THINGS TO TALK ABOUT.
SHE WASN'T LIKE BETH, OR ANY OF THE OTHER WOMEN. I LOVED MIRAGE WITH EVERY FIBER OF MY BEING.
IT FELT LIKE WE'D ALWAYS BEEN TOGETHER... EVERYTHING FELT SO NATURAL... SO RIGHT.

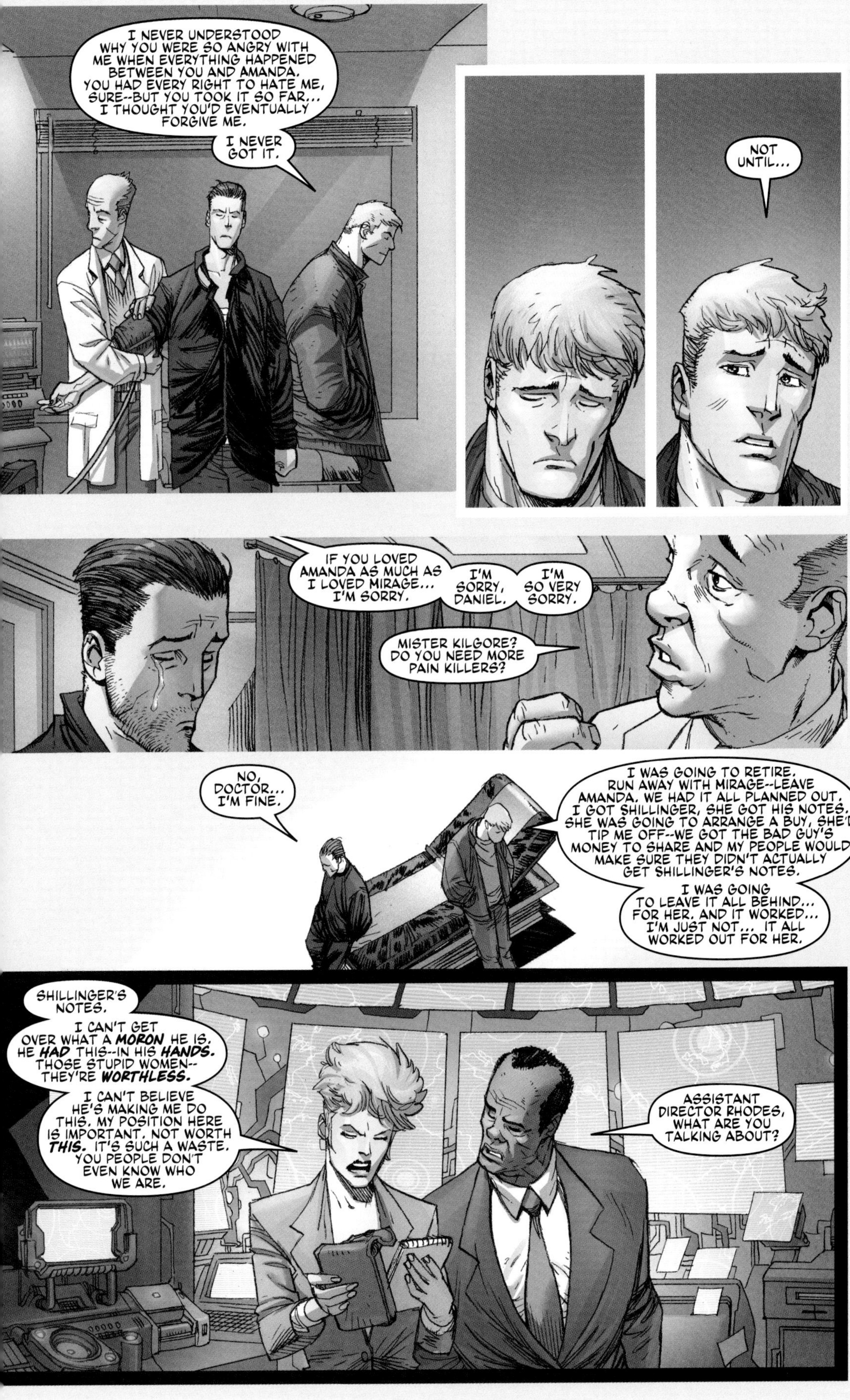
I NEVER UNDERSTOOD WHY YOU WERE SO ANGRY WITH ME WHEN EVERYTHING HAPPENED BETWEEN YOU AND AMANDA. YOU HAD EVERY RIGHT TO HATE ME, SURE--BUT YOU TOOK IT SO FAR... I THOUGHT YOU'D EVENTUALLY FORGIVE ME.
I NEVER GOT IT.
NOT UNTIL...
IF YOU LOVED AMANDA AS MUCH AS I LOVED MIRAGE... I'M SORRY.
I'M SORRY, DANIEL.
I'M SO VERY SORRY.
MISTER KILGORE? DO YOU NEED MORE PAIN KILLERS?
NO, DOCTOR... I'M FINE.
I WAS GOING TO RETIRE. RUN AWAY WITH MIRAGE--LEAVE AMANDA. WE HAD IT ALL PLANNED OUT. I GOT SHILLINGER, SHE GOT HIS NOTES. SHE WAS GOING TO ARRANGE A BUY, SHE'D TIP ME OFF--WE GOT THE BAD GUY'S MONEY TO SHARE AND MY PEOPLE WOULD MAKE SURE THEY DIDN'T ACTUALLY GET SHILLINGER'S NOTES.
I WAS GOING TO LEAVE IT ALL BEHIND... FOR HER. AND IT WORKED... I'M JUST NOT... IT ALL WORKED OUT FOR HER.
SHILLINGER'S NOTES.
I CAN'T GET OVER WHAT A MORON HE IS. HE HAD THIS--IN HIS HANDS. THOSE STUPID WOMEN-- THEY'RE WORTHLESS.
I CAN'T BELIEVE HE'S MAKING ME DO THIS. MY POSITION HERE IS IMPORTANT. NOT WORTH THIS. IT'S SUCH A WASTE. YOU PEOPLE DON'T EVEN KNOW WHO WE ARE.
ASSISTANT DIRECTOR RHODES, WHAT ARE YOU TALKING ABOUT?

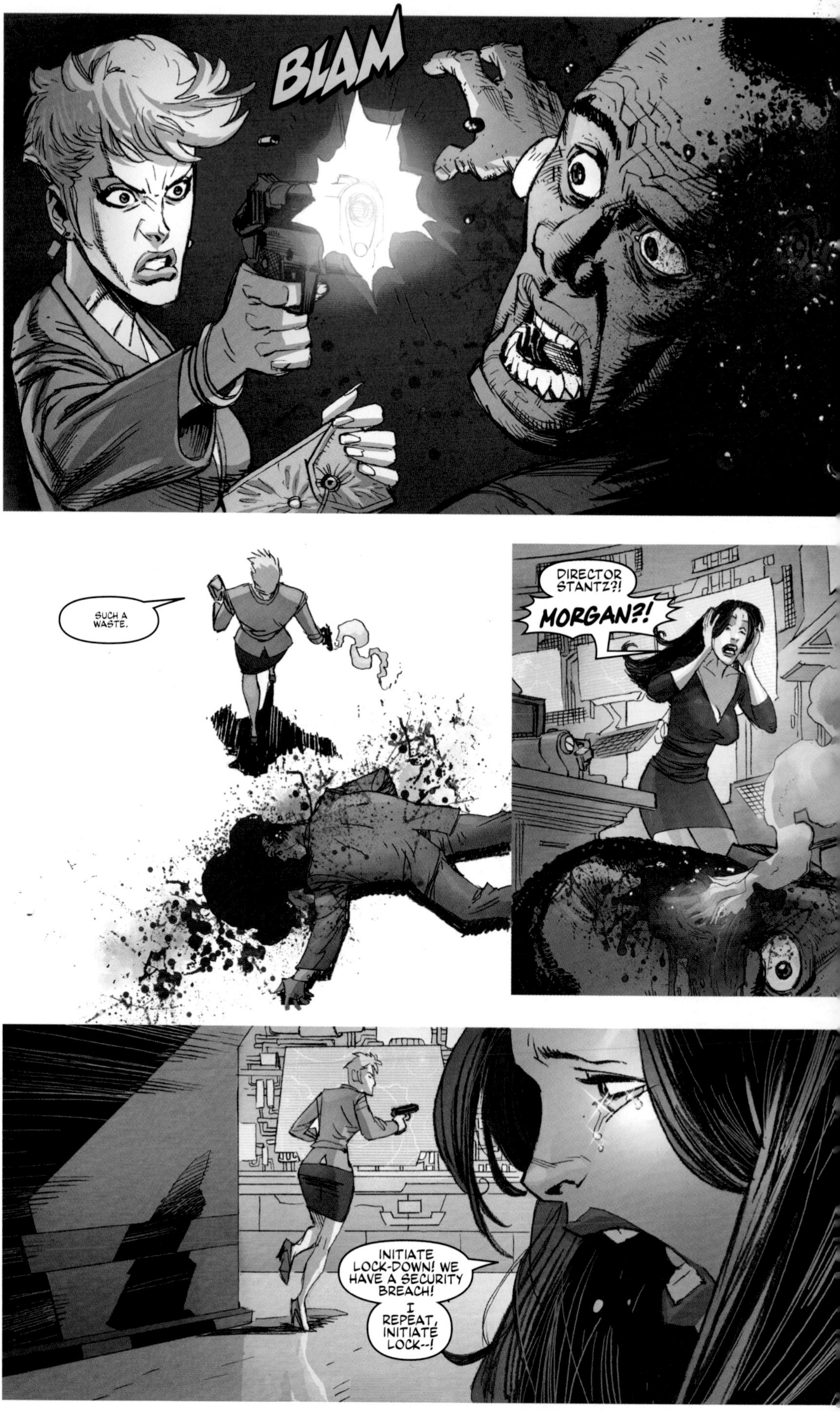
BLAM
SUCH A WASTE.
DIRECTOR STANTZ?!
MORGAN?!
INITIATE LOCK-DOWN! WE HAVE A SECURITY BREACH!
I REPEAT, INITIATE LOCK--!

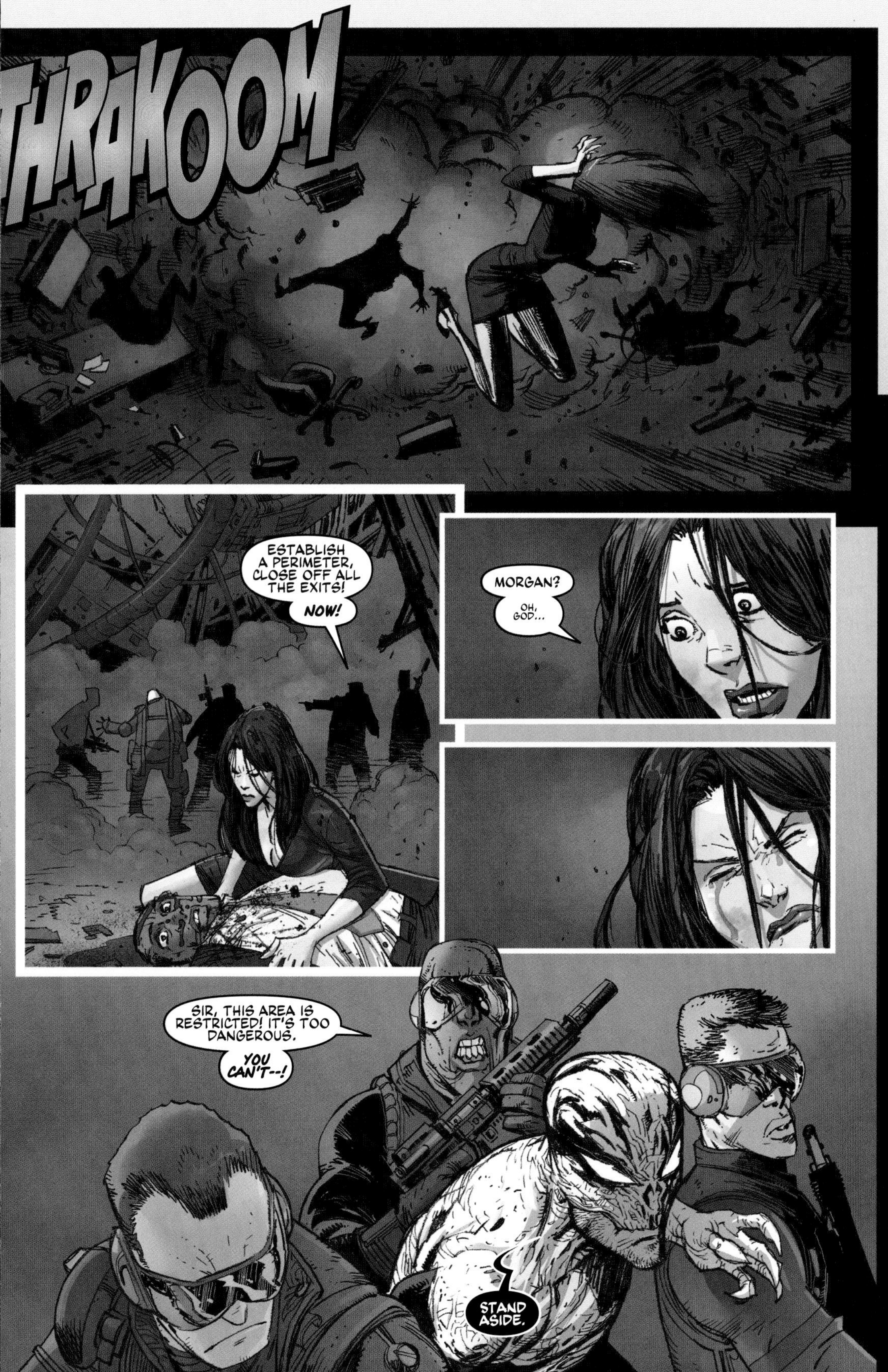
THRAKOOM
ESTABLISH A PERIMETER, CLOSE OFF ALL THE EXITS!
NOW!
MORGAN?
OH, GOD...
SIR, THIS AREA IS RESTRICTED! IT'S TOO DANGEROUS.
YOU CAN'T--!
STAND ASIDE.

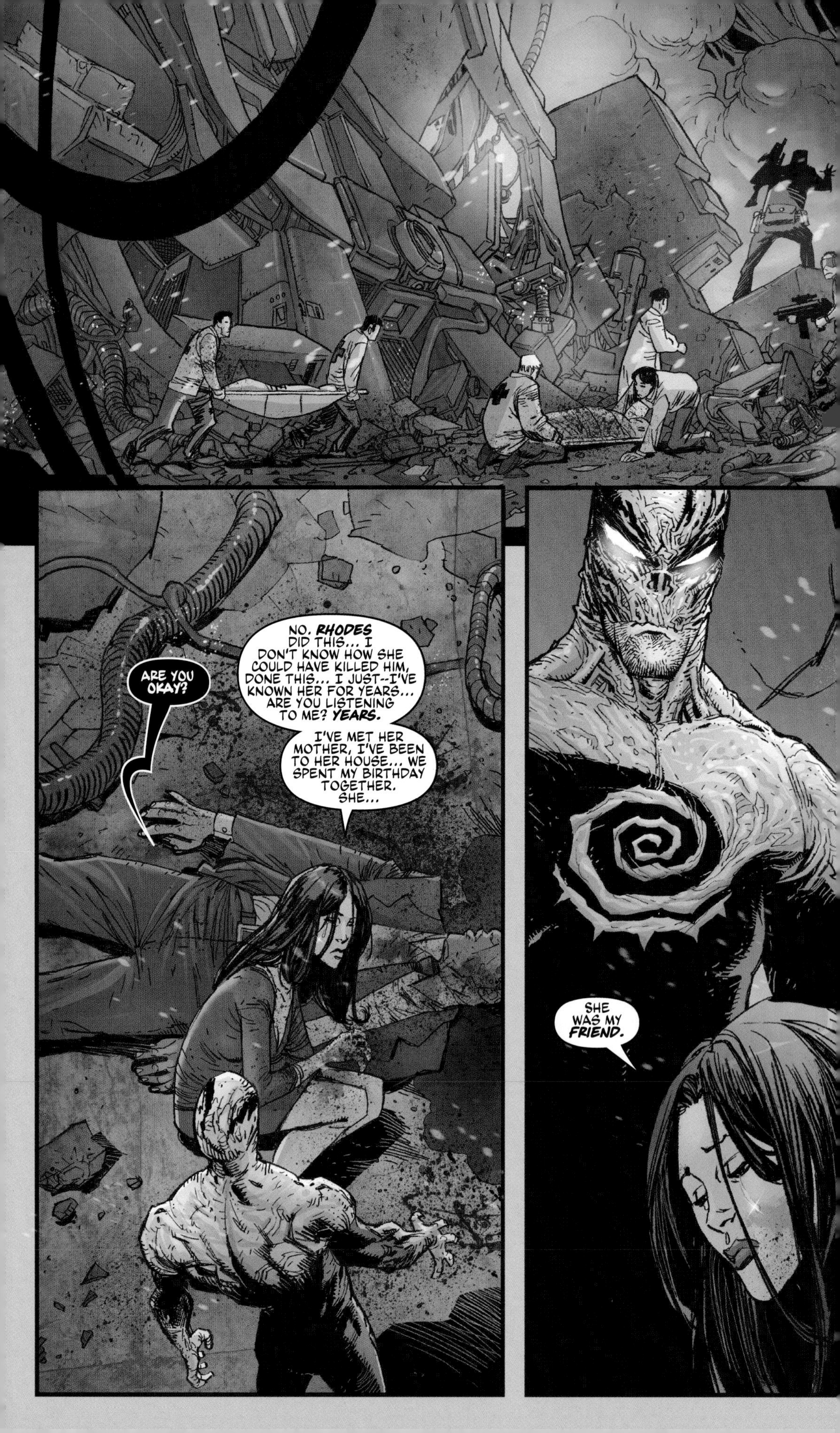
ARE YOU OKAY?
NO. *RHODES* DID THIS... I DON'T KNOW HOW SHE COULD HAVE KILLED HIM, DONE THIS... I JUST--I'VE KNOWN HER FOR YEARS... ARE YOU LISTENING TO ME? *YEARS.*
I'VE MET HER MOTHER, I'VE BEEN TO HER HOUSE... WE SPENT MY BIRTHDAY TOGETHER. SHE...
SHE WAS MY *FRIEND.*

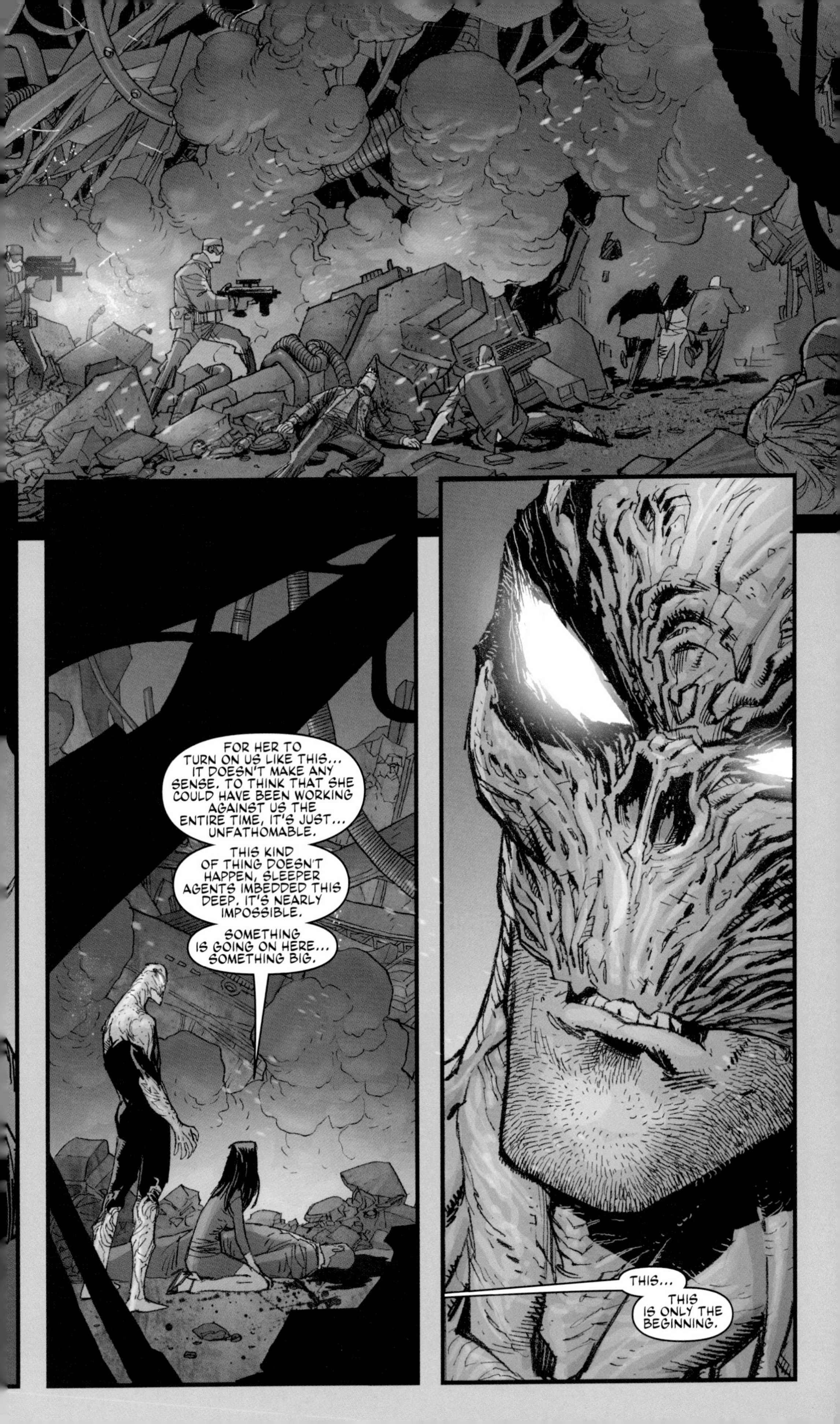
FOR HER TO TURN ON US LIKE THIS... IT DOESN'T MAKE ANY SENSE. TO THINK THAT SHE COULD HAVE BEEN WORKING AGAINST US THE ENTIRE TIME, IT'S JUST... UNFATHOMABLE.
THIS KIND OF THING DOESN'T HAPPEN, SLEEPER AGENTS IMBEDDED THIS DEEP. IT'S NEARLY IMPOSSIBLE.
SOMETHING IS GOING ON HERE... SOMETHING BIG.
THIS...
THIS IS ONLY THE BEGINNING.

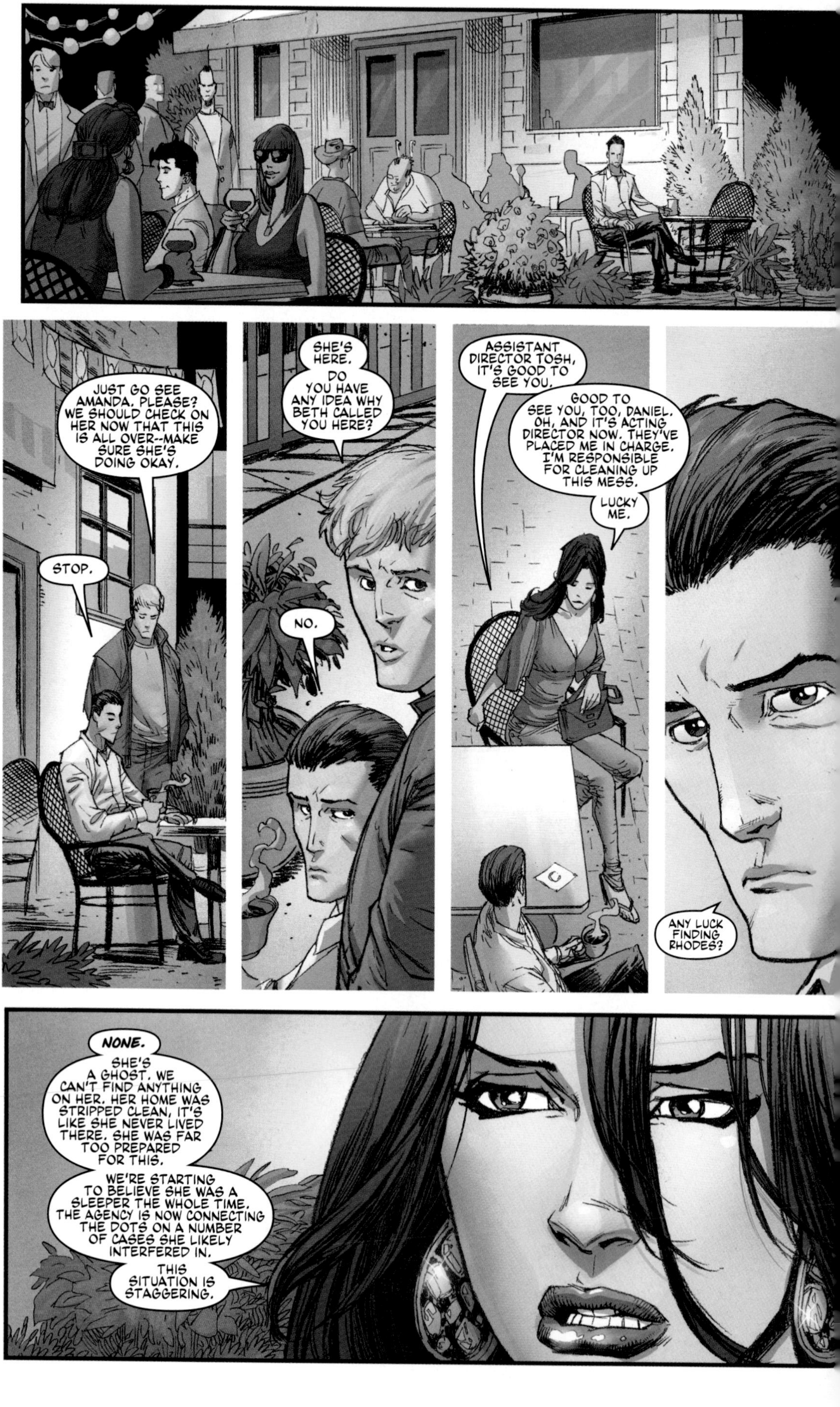
JUST GO SEE AMANDA, PLEASE? WE SHOULD CHECK ON HER NOW THAT THIS IS ALL OVER--MAKE SURE SHE'S DOING OKAY.
STOP.
SHE'S HERE.
DO YOU HAVE ANY IDEA WHY BETH CALLED YOU HERE?
NO.
ASSISTANT DIRECTOR TOSH, IT'S GOOD TO SEE YOU.
GOOD TO SEE YOU, TOO, DANIEL. OH, AND IT'S ACTING DIRECTOR NOW. THEY'VE PLACED ME IN CHARGE. I'M RESPONSIBLE FOR CLEANING UP THIS MESS.
LUCKY ME.
ANY LUCK FINDING RHODES?
NONE.
SHE'S A GHOST. WE CAN'T FIND ANYTHING ON HER. HER HOME WAS STRIPPED CLEAN, IT'S LIKE SHE NEVER LIVED THERE. SHE WAS FAR TOO PREPARED FOR THIS.
WE'RE STARTING TO BELIEVE SHE WAS A SLEEPER THE WHOLE TIME. THE AGENCY IS NOW CONNECTING THE DOTS ON A NUMBER OF CASES SHE LIKELY INTERFERED IN.
THIS SITUATION IS STAGGERING.

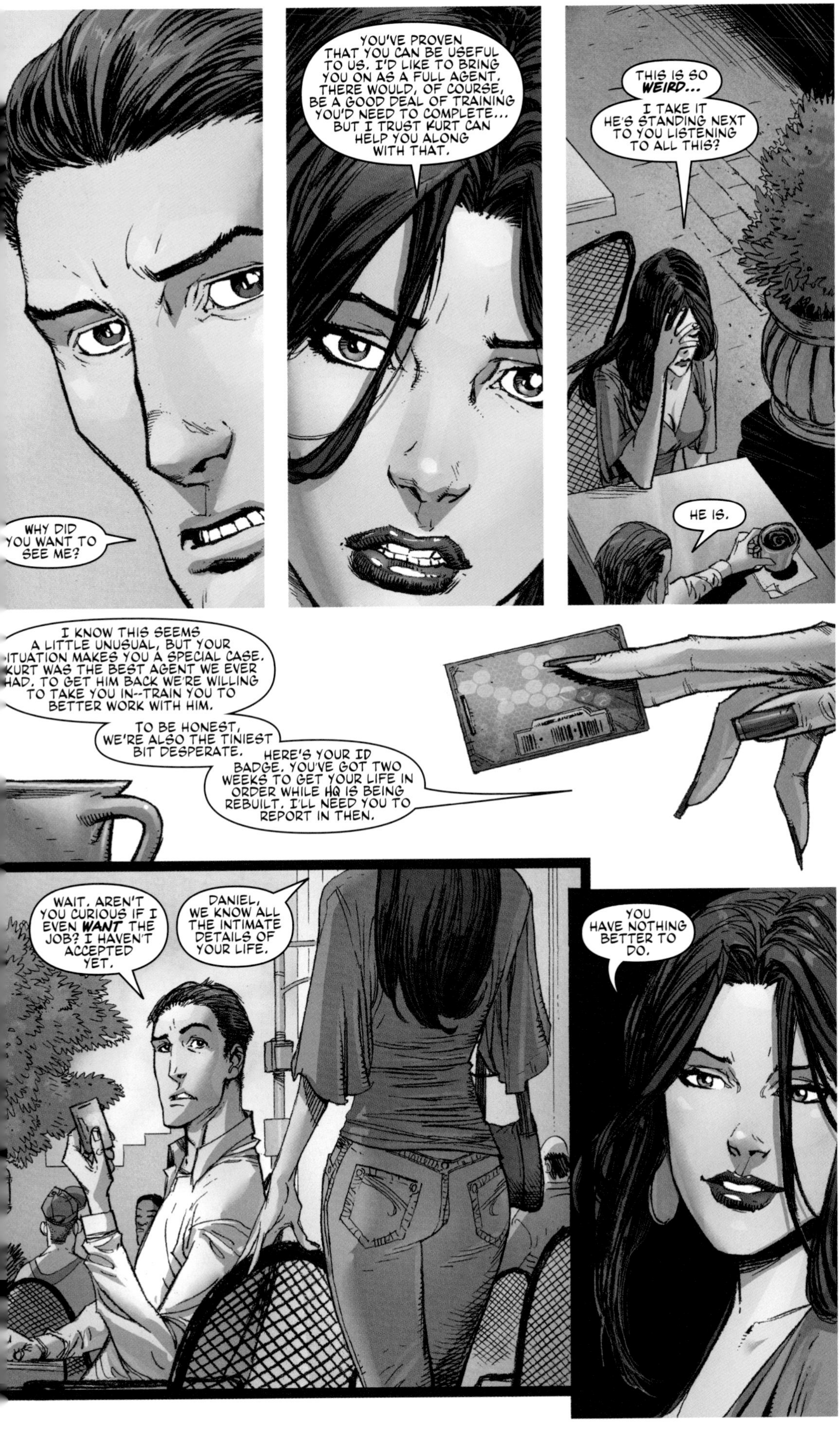
WHY DID YOU WANT TO SEE ME?
YOU'VE PROVEN THAT YOU CAN BE USEFUL TO US. I'D LIKE TO BRING YOU ON AS A FULL AGENT. THERE WOULD, OF COURSE, BE A GOOD DEAL OF TRAINING YOU'D NEED TO COMPLETE... BUT I TRUST KURT CAN HELP YOU ALONG WITH THAT.
THIS IS SO WEIRD...
I TAKE IT HE'S STANDING NEXT TO YOU LISTENING TO ALL THIS?
HE IS.
I KNOW THIS SEEMS A LITTLE UNUSUAL, BUT YOUR SITUATION MAKES YOU A SPECIAL CASE. KURT WAS THE BEST AGENT WE EVER HAD. TO GET HIM BACK WE'RE WILLING TO TAKE YOU IN--TRAIN YOU TO BETTER WORK WITH HIM.
TO BE HONEST, WE'RE ALSO THE TINIEST BIT DESPERATE.
HERE'S YOUR ID BADGE. YOU'VE GOT TWO WEEKS TO GET YOUR LIFE IN ORDER WHILE HQ IS BEING REBUILT. I'LL NEED YOU TO REPORT IN THEN.
WAIT. AREN'T YOU CURIOUS IF I EVEN WANT THE JOB? I HAVEN'T ACCEPTED YET.
DANIEL, WE KNOW ALL THE INTIMATE DETAILS OF YOUR LIFE.
YOU HAVE NOTHING BETTER TO DO.

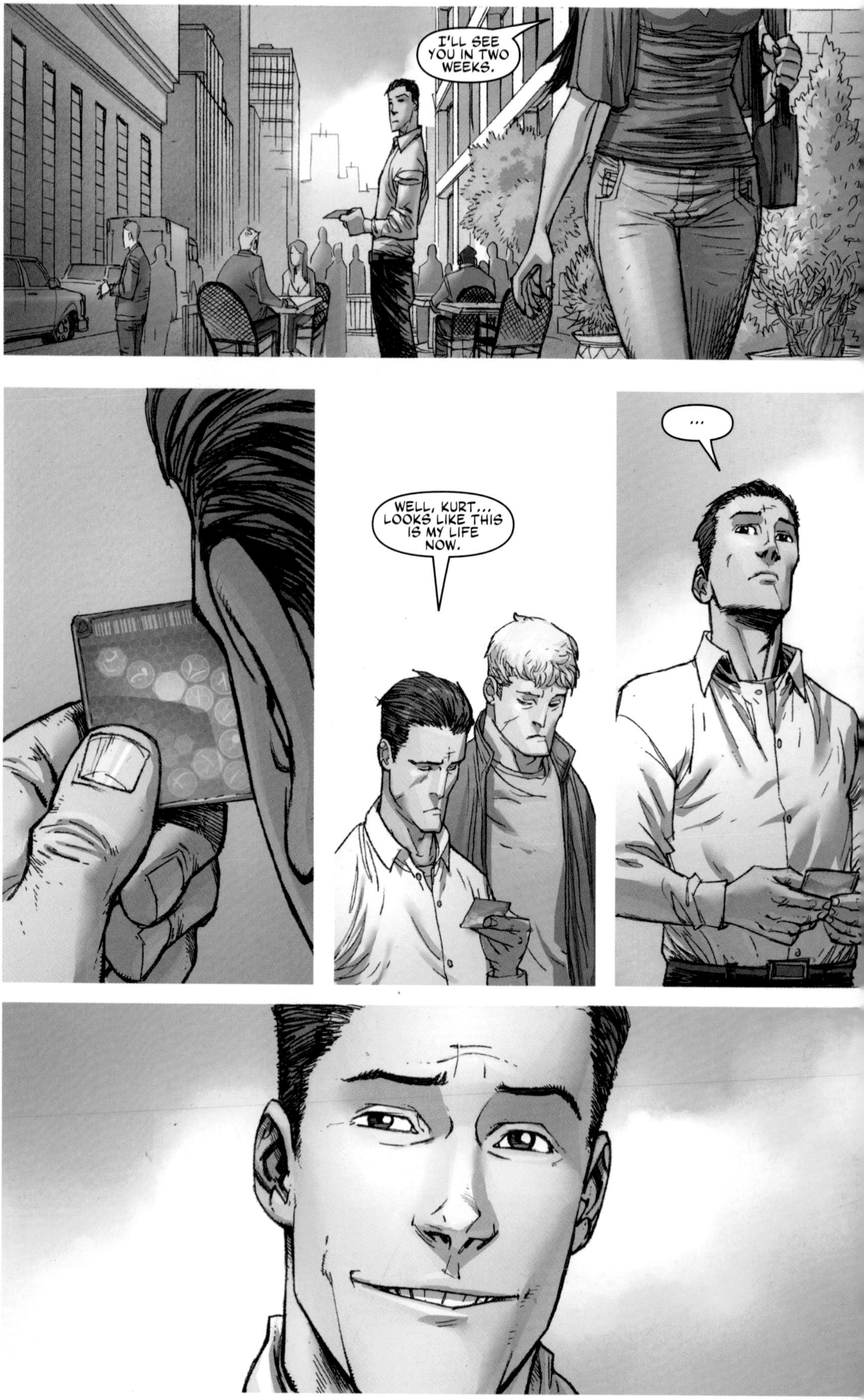
I'LL SEE YOU IN TWO WEEKS.
WELL, KURT... LOOKS LIKE THIS IS MY LIFE NOW.
...